# Intrusion Detection

# Network Security
# Beyond the Firewall

## Terry Escamilla

Wiley Computer Publishing

John Wiley & Sons, Inc.
New York ◆ Chichester ◆ Weinheim ◆ Brisbane ◆ Singapore ◆ Toronto

Publisher: Robert Ipsen
Editor: Carol Long
Assistant Editor: Pam Sobotka
Managing Editor: Brian Snapp
Electronic Products, Associate Editor: Mike Sosa
Text Design & Composition: D&G Limited, LLC

Designations used by companies to distinguish their products are often claimed as trademarks. In all instances where John Wiley & Sons, Inc., is aware of a claim, the product names appear in initial capital or all capital letters. Readers, however, should contact the appropriate companies for more complete information regarding trademarks and registration.

This book is printed on acid-free paper. ⊗

Published by John Wiley & Sons, Inc.

Published simultaneously in Canada.

This publication is designed to provide accurate and authoritative information in regard to the subject matter covered. It is sold with the understanding that the publisher is not engaged in professional services. If professional advice or other expert assistance is required, the services of a competent professional person should be sought.

*Library of Congress Cataloging-in-Publication Data:*

Escamilla, Terry, 1956–
    Instruction detection : network security beyond the firewall / Terry
Escamilla.
        p.   cm.
    Includes index.
    ISBN 0-471-29000-9 (alk. paper)
    1. Computer networks--Security measures.    2. Computer security.
I. Title,.
TK5105.59.E83 1998
C05.8--dc21                                          98-33703
                                                       CIP

Printed in the United States of America.
10 9 8 7 6 5 4 3 2 1

# Contents

# Preface

The crew at John Wiley & Sons first asked me to consider writing a book on computer security in the summer of 1997. After a few meetings with Carol Long, I was convinced of the need for a book that offered a glimpse at the fascinating area of intrusion detection. During the last several months, the flow of the book was revised many times, mostly to reflect the changing landscape of the computer security industry.

I was working for Haystack Labs in Austin, Texas when Carol and Pam Sobotka approved the first outline. My original intent was to catalogue the many ways in which systems were hacked in an effort to set a baseline upon which other books could rely. However, I also saw the value of providing an overview of intrusion detection while comparing it to other computer security approaches. Many times I had worked with customers who asked questions such as, "How does intrusion detection differ from a firewall?" or "I already use encryption. Isn't that enough?" I decided that writing a book would be better than repeating myself for the next several months while working with business partners or customers.

Several sections of the book were written in the fall of 1997, only to be revised in 1998 to include recent changes in product positioning. The experience has been analogous to trying to paint a ship while it is rocking in active seas. It has certainly been exciting.

About three quarters of the way through the writing of this book, Haystack was acquired by Trusted Information Systems. In the security industry, we had been forecasting mergers and acquisitions, but like the Web, no one expected the speed with which events unfolded. TIS was soon part of Network Associates, and many other mergers and acquisitions occurred as the major security vendors maneuvered to field better solutions. Although the environment was appealing, I decided to return to my former employee, IBM, and focus on practical applications of security.

As with any endeavor, there are the unavoidable tradeoffs. After several discussions with the Wiley team, we decided on a practical, high-level book rather than an in-depth treatment of intrusion detection. Our goal is thus to differentiate intrusion detection from other forms of computer security and to show how each product category adds value. Over time, offerings from vendors will certainly overlap more, perhaps calling for a second edition. We did not cover products in great detail either. The overall theory is more important than the minutiae of products, which changes several times a year. We also wanted to avoid a product shopping comparison. These reports are best left to the trade press and to your own laboratories. Products described in the book were chosen because they are representative. Inclusion of a product does not imply superiority in the marketplace.

I have made every effort not to judge hackers and crackers either. Many security holes are announced by people who want to plug leaks, not by people who want to exploit them. The assumption is that you want to protect information assets, and therefore, you need to understand how systems are compromised, defended, and monitored. My approach is practical and objective. Ethical arguments and legal discussions are best left to the experts in those fields.

Unfortunately, ample room was not available for coverage of intrusion detection research. Although this field is of great interest to me, I did not feel that justice could be done in a single chapter or appendix. A complete book detailing historical and current intrusion detection research would be more appropriate. The interested reader can find original papers and pointers at Web sites managed by SRI, LLNL, COAST, and U.C. Davis.

My hat also is tipped to the security professionals and researchers outside of the United States. Many excellent projects and products originate in other geographies, but these were omitted because of my lack of experience with them. Hopefully, you will investigate these alternatives on your own.

I would like to emphasize that this book and its contents are not endorsed by IBM in any way. The project was conceived and written mostly while I was at Haystack and TIS. I have tried to be impartial in my presentation of important topics, although one's opinions certainly have a way of creeping into the text.

You might want to know that a portion of the royalties from this book are being donated to charity. The idea came to me when I had the honor of participating in a panel with Peter Neumann at a firewall conference. Dr. Neumann donated his honorarium to a foundation of personal significance to him, and I was reminded that, as researchers and professionals, we are obliged to contribute to society in other ways.

The organization to which royalties are designated may change from year to year, but I have initially chosen the National Children's Advocacy Center (fly.hiwaay.net/~ncacadm/). Neither I nor any members of my family were ever victims of child abuse, but I view this as one of the pivotal problems in the world today. It should be comforting to know that others less fortunate will benefit when you add this book to your collection. A growing number of child abuse cases originate on the Internet today. Often, children are electronically "stalked" through e-mail and chat rooms. Some security tools provide protection today.

URL blockers, Web site ratings, and scanners that look for unacceptable phrases in packets can help reduce the risk to children. Although not addressed in this book, these security offerings for the Internet are an important part of the evolving product landscape. The usual disclaimers apply. Any errors in the book are unintentional. Mistakes are mine alone. The appearance of vendor and product names in this book does not indicate their endorsement or approval of the material. Your mileage may vary with the solutions described.

—Terry D. Escamilla, Ph.D.
June, 1998
Boulder, Colorado

# Acknowledgments

*For my family — the people I can always count on to be there.*

My friends and professional colleagues at Haystack Labs during 1996–97 were an endless source of ideas and humor. Steve Snapp, Scott Chapman, Crosby Marks, Tom Bernhard, Marta Z., Bill Leddy, Bill Kainer, Virgil Itliong, Rich Letsinger, and Boomer all deserve my warmest thanks. Fred Pinkett, Steve Artick, and Jim Geary provided guidance and insight about the broader computer security industry, and Steve proved to be a valuable career counselor as well. Charisse Castagnoli has delivered an endless stream of new information, practical experience, and friendship. She deserves a very special thanks. Steve Smaha and Jessica Winslow were always encouraging and insightful when I worked with them, and, of course, Steve's historical perspective on intrusion detection was invaluable.

A number of people influenced the book without knowing it. These professionals were kind enough to humor my ideas and to explore computer security with me in conversations. Thanks are thus also extended to Eli Singer, Dave Dalva, Lee Terrell, and Peter Crotty. Some of my new colleagues at IBM have been valuable because of their practical experiences and ideas about where network security is headed. John Simmons, Lance Walker, Grant Miller, Bob Pryor, Bill Althauser, Steve Burnham, and Michael Bauer have been especially helpful. I also am grateful to my manager, Alma Rosales, for being kind-hearted and understanding while the book was finished. Some people contributed graphics, comments, contacts, and other information when sorely needed. For their assistance, I wish to thank Marianne Rochelle, Paul Proctor, and David Drake.

Carol Long from Wiley used her knowledge of the security marketplace to keep the book focused appropriately. Carol also deserves credit for choosing the theme of the book and for recognizing the need for an overview of intrusion detection on the bookshelves. She was dependable for providing a solid perspective on the marketplace, for delightful conversation, and for saying the right things to keep me moving.

I cannot find enough words to thank Pam Sobotka (also from Wiley). Pam fulfilled many roles—motivator, scheduler, editor, reviewer, sounding board, and too many others to completely list. I could always count on a friendly voice of encouragement on the other end of the phone anytime Pam would call.

My parents, brothers, and sisters taught me many lessons about life, including the importance of being dedicated. Although they understandably had only a passing interest in intrusion detection, they regularly supplied enthusiasm and a kind reminder that some day the writing would be complete. I can scarcely begin to thank them for all the treasures they have given me.

Finally, my deepest thanks are reserved for my wife, Becky, and my two children, Brent and Meghann. They have tolerated the long writing sessions into the early hours of the morning, the scattered books and papers in the house, the seemingly endless business trips, and a fair dose of other inconveniences while I completed this book. Without their love and support, this task surely would have been impossible.

# Introduction

This book was written to help you understand how *intrusion detection systems* (IDSs) fit into your arsenal of security products. By the time you finish reading this book, you will have a clear understanding of how intrusion detection security products differ from one another, where they overlap, and how they help to provide comprehensive protection at your site.

## Overview of the Book and Intrusion Detection

The main focus of the book is intrusion detection. However, to understand why intrusion detection is important, you need to know quite a bit of background material.

Even if you want to grab public domain source code and customize a suite of tools, you will want to read further. The problems and solutions presented throughout apply equally to both commercial and free tools. You definitely need to understand the advantages and limitations of public domain tools as well. When you read a section describing some commercial software in detail, take notes and use them to complete a similar style of analysis when considering software that you can get freely from the Internet. By the way, many commercial products originated as software you could freely download, such as the TIS Firewall Toolkit.

You do not need to buy any products to benefit from the material in this book. The chapters do not require that you complete any exercises on a particular computer or with a specific software program. However, you certainly will learn more if you have the opportunity to try out some of the products. Most vendors offer evaluation copies of products or will ship you a full-featured version that is limited by a software key.

## Who Should Read This Book

You might be pondering whether you need intrusion detection. Another question you have is whether to put together some freely available tools or buy commercial products. Several other books adequately cover the range of public domain tools that are useful and perform some subset of intrusion detection tasks. In Part 2 of this book, "Intrusion Detection: Beyond Traditional Security," the focus is commercial rather than free tools. This should complement any other books already lining your shelves.

If you are a site security officer, you will definitely want to read this book to see how IDSs relate to other security products. You also will want to see what an IDS can detect and what it cannot. If you plan to support your site security policies with an IDS, you *must* know its strengths and weaknesses.

The material in the book is broad enough for any computer literate person to finish. For those who like more in-depth treatments, a few topics are covered in detail. Therefore, if you're a CIO or someone who is just interested in computer security, you'll definitely benefit from reading the book. Should you be interested in building your own IDS, plenty of information is presented to get you started.

One thing you will not find in this book is a description of ways to hack into systems. Nor are all of the known attacks described in detail. This information is easily available to those who know how to get it. This type of discussion also would require a separate book to adequately describe the common hacks in detail. Easily more than a hundred known hacks exist, and new discoveries are made every day.

## How the Book Is Organized

The book is divided into three main parts. Part 1, "Before Intrusion Detection: Traditional Computer Security," provides background and justification for why intrusion detection is important. Part 2, "Intrusion Detection: Beyond Traditional Security," dives into intrusion detection and shows you how it adds value. Part 3, "Rounding Out Your Environment," recommends actions for responding to intrusions and suggests how you can pull together all of your new knowledge for building a complete security solution.

To get the most out of the book, read the chapters in sequence. However, if you consider yourself to be beyond the novice level, feel free to jump around after glancing through Chapter 1, "Intrusion Detection and the Classic Security Model." If you find yourself looking for more breadth or depth, check out the references and Web sites in the Appendix, "Hot Links for Information." You are not expected to be a security expert before you read this book nor by the time you finish it.

Part 1, "Before Intrusion Detection: Traditional Computer Security," begins with an overview of classical computer security in Chapter 1. A primer is given on the important aspects of computer security by constructing a security model. If you learn to think about what the basic model should be doing, you will develop skills for asking deep, critical questions about security products. An understanding of the basic model clarifies which computer security problems are addressed by different products.

In Chapter 2, "The Role of Identification and Authentication in Your Environment," you will take a close look at identification and authentication (I&A). The first step in interacting with a computer is identification and authentication of the user. Because I&A establishes who you are on the system, it has important consequences for intrusion detection. One goal of a hacker is to gain access to the system by exploiting the I&A process. In Chapter 2, you will see how I&A can be attacked, what you can do to improve I&A, and why an IDS is needed even if you have strong authentication.

Chapter 3, "The Role of Access Control in Your Environment," moves to the next logical step—access control. When you have completed the I&A process, you will be limited by what you can do according to the access control policies defined in the system you are using. In this chapter, you will learn how access control is handled by the underlying operating system and how to improve upon access control with other tools. You'll also see how intrusion detection is needed beyond access control, even if you add other access control products in your network.

The role of the firewall is explored in Chapter 4, "Traditional Network Security Approaches," as are other aspects of network security. When you finish Chapter 4, you will know exactly what services a firewall provides beyond I&A and access control. You also will see why intrusion detection is needed even if you have a firewall. By the way, if your site is connected to the Internet, and you have not yet installed a firewall (or at least a screening router), stop reading and install one.

When you understand the role of these three traditional security areas—I&A, access control, and firewalls—Part 2, "Intrusion Detection: Beyond Traditional Security," will take you through the intrusion detection landscape. In Chapter 5, "Intrusion Detection and Why You Need It," you will find an introduction to the three main categories of IDSs. There, you'll also find a brief overview of scanners, system-level IDSs, and network IDSs. You should know that even though there is tremendous interest in detecting people who try to break into systems from the outside, the FBI and other sources regularly report that 80 percent or more of losses due to computer crime are attributed to employees on the inside. Intrusion detection products try to catch both insiders and outsiders.

Chapter 6, "Detecting Intruders on Your System Is Fun and Easy," takes a closer look at how IDSs actually find out about hack attacks. You will see that it is not always easy to detect a hacker. It's even harder to uncover *everything* a hacker is doing if the attack covers a large network. Although scanners, system IDSs, and network IDSs overlap slightly, you see early on that each one fulfills an important role based on the types of hacks they detect.

Chapter 7, "Vulnerability Scanners," discusses intrusion detection scanner tools in detail. The emphasis is more on what a scanner can and cannot detect, as opposed to surveying all of the commercially available scanner tools on the market. A good discussion of some tools is provided, but you should consult the vendors mentioned for more current information. Intrusion detection tools change regularly, so it is better to know what questions to ask about a tool than it is to compare individual scanners as they exist today.

System-level IDSs are the subject of Chapter 8, "UNIX System-Level IDSs." As you will see, several hacks can be detected only by monitoring each system at your site. A number of tradeoffs are discussed. Specific UNIX hacks are described so that you can understand how a system-level IDS catches intruders. Naturally, there is mention of weaknesses and why you need to use scanners and network IDSs in addition to system monitors. Some of the earliest research in intrusion detection is centered on system-level tools.

Chapter 9, "Sniffing for Intruders," rounds out the IDS categories by describing the capabilities of network IDSs. Generally, these tools work by intelligently sniffing network packets. As with the other two IDS types, network sniffing can catch some attacks but misses others. By the time you finish Chapter 9, you will have a very good knowledge base on intrusion detection. You will be able to clearly describe how an IDS complements traditional security products that improve I&A, access control, or network security.

The subject of NT intrusion detection is given special consideration in Chapter 10, "Intrusion Detection for NT." As you will see, NT has been the chief target of a number of hackers. Although the source code for NT is not freely available (as is UNIX), a new hack against NT is discovered frequently. NT hacks and IDSs that detect them are combined in this chapter. Chapter 10 completes the survey of intrusion detection, but you still have more to consider.

Part 3, "Rounding Out Your Environment," closes the book with two important topics. Chapter 11, "You've Been Hit!" collects recommendations from a variety of sources and provides guidelines for handling security incidents. You'll see that the familiar suggestion to *be prepared* is especially important for incident response teams. If you are at risk for intrusions, you should roll out the suggestions in Chapter 11 as soon as possible.

Chapter 12, "Intrusion Detection: Not the Last Chapter When It Comes to Security," recaps the path you took to understanding intrusion detection. You will review the threats, vulnerabilities, and solutions covered in the classical computer security. Key points about the three main IDS categories are refreshed for you as well. The chapter then provides some suggestions on how you can deploy several complementary security products at your site. Closing remarks speculate about where intrusion detection might be in the near future.

Finally, useful Web links are provided in the Appendix, "Hot Links for Information."

## The Reality of Tradeoffs

Two important points are worth mentioning before moving forward.

First, successful software vendors are driven to make tradeoffs based on market demands. Because you are in business, too, you know that market demands seldom bear any resemblance to common sense. Numerous stories exist about companies that invent the best possible widget and then fail to create a market or unseat an already entrenched competitor in an emerging market. Companies add function to products for different reasons—competition, time to market, lost opportunities, and cost are a few. If you do not like what an IDS does today, find out the vendor's future plans. You may be forced to make one set of tradeoffs today but will see your needs met when a new version of the product is announced.

Second, you, too, will be required to make tradeoffs when implementing your site security. To begin with, your own resources are bounded. A frequently cited claim in cryptography is that given enough money and time, any cryptographic solution can be broken. Therefore, you start by holding the short end of the stick. You cannot build the ideal security environment because you have neither infinite time nor unlimited money. Tradeoffs are unavoidable.

People and companies buy a product for a variety of reasons—because their best friends recommended it, because it was cheap, because they liked the advertisements, because their boss recommended it, because their competitor uses it, because the service is good, or perhaps because it's the only one that supports the Japanese language. The best-selling IDS may not have the richest function, may not have the best quality, or may not be the easiest to use. It might be the best-selling product because it's endorsed by an authority widely respected or widely feared by the majority of computer users. You may be forced to adopt a product in your industry because some influential standards body issued a decree, even if 90 percent of the rest of the world is using a different product.

You have little control over some tradeoffs because they are handed to you from above. Other tradeoffs you have the freedom to influence. Your company might be using a product because you share a member of the Board of Directors between your two companies. You might prefer to use a different security product, but your hands are tied. This is a common market reality. What can you do about this situation, and how will this book help?

You should know *precisely* what a product can and cannot do. This book is designed to make you think critically about how a product works, what features it provides, and why you might need it. A computer network without security is a risky venture. *A false sense of security based upon the wrong products or upon incorrectly configured products is worse.* In the first case, at least people know the environment is not safe, and they will proceed with caution. In the latter situation, people think the network is safe when it really is not. They will be more careless, possibly sending confidential mail to another site because *they are under the impression* that the network traffic is secure.

Sometimes tradeoffs are not in the products, but in your configurations. These tradeoffs can involve variables that are inversely related. For example, if you want all user passwords stored in a central server, you definitely will make tradeoffs in network latency and network traffic. At 8 A.M. when 10,000 employees log in across the site, you can expect network delays and a spike in network traffic. On the other hand, all of your passwords will be stored in one or more authentication servers that can be physically secured. You will have reduced the threat of password theft but sacrificed some network performance. Despite the fact that you've improved security, at some cost in network performance, threats to your environment still exist. You still need to worry about social engineering, weak user passwords, flaws that might leave the passwords in local cache areas on your network clients, and other problems. Tradeoffs are unavoidable in computer technology. Only by being informed can you expect to make the right ones.

All of the products mentioned in this book are quality solutions that go a long way towards solving your problems. Indeed, all of the vendors deserve praise for stepping up to the challenges of computer security. Like the decisions you face, these vendors also make tradeoffs between a daunting set of variables. Educate yourself and use this knowledge to improve your understanding of the alternatives.

The focus of this book is intrusion detection. Like many topics, a rich history exists that tells why intrusion detection has become a market necessity. This book walks you through the background of classic security problems. It explains how classical security products address these problems and why intrusion detection is needed beyond I&A, access control, and network security products such as firewalls. Computer security is a fascinating field with many turns, bends, secrets, tricks, and plenty of strong opinions. You will see that intrusion detection contains all of these elements of computer security.

# PART 1

# BEFORE INTRUSION DETECTION: TRADITIONAL COMPUTER SECURITY

Most people think of computer security as trying to prevent things from going wrong. Even in recent history, which includes firewalls, this approach by itself has not been successful. In the first part of this book, you see how regularly deployed security products fit your needs and how they leave you looking for more. Knowing the strengths and weaknesses of different types of security products is key to seeing how intrusion detection can add value at your site. To accomplish this goal, you learn about the following:

- ◆ A standard security model that can be used to think critically about how products fit into your strategy
- ◆ The role of identification and authentication products and problems they do and do not solve
- ◆ Standard access control capabilities in operating systems and how you can improve upon your defenses
- ◆ How firewalls and other techniques can strengthen your network security and leave you looking for more
- ◆ Why you still need intrusion detection even if you add these other defenses

# Chapter 1

# Intrusion Detection and the Classic Security Model

Intrusion detection is a hot topic. In the last few months, several intrusion-detection companies have been gobbled up by larger security companies. All vendors want to make their security solutions different from their competitors, and adding an *intrusion detection system* (IDS) is one way to get ahead. But, why does anyone need an IDS? To really understand the answer, you have to get back to basics.

Computer security is a complex topic. To be precise about what you say, and what other people are saying as well, it's best to think in simple terms. Therefore, this chapter describes a basic *security model* that is at the heart of your environment. No matter how complicated your computers or networks might be, you can look at any subset and think about it in terms of *subjects*, *objects*, and *access control*.

## Back to Basics: The Classic Security Model

The universe is a complex beast, but it can also be reduced to a few simple nouns and verbs at the subatomic level, although you don't need to understand the universe at this level to drive to work. To deploy computer security solutions, you *do* need to think about the underlying details of each part of your environment in order to reduce the likelihood of security breaches. You should challenge yourself to understand components at your site and ask, "Hey, what's *really* happening under the covers here?" If someone approaches you and wants to deploy a new application, you should start with the same questions each time: Who are the subjects? What are the objects? How are accesses regulated? Who administers the security?

You'll want to ask plenty of other questions, which all stem from your understanding of a basic computer security model. In the first section of this chapter,

3

you find some generally accepted goals of computer security. When you know what to expect from computer security, the next task is to find a useful way of determining whether your expectations are being met. To accomplish this, you gradually construct the  security model beginning with simple abstract principles. The chapter closes with a classification scheme useful for understanding the relative roles of different products you might have at your site and how an IDS fits into the scheme.

Each site should have a well-defined *security policy* describing how information is to be handled. This same security policy might be enforced by a combination of different security models, because a security model is an abstraction that can be implemented in numerous ways. A product that implements a security model provides a vehicle which you can use to enforce a security policy. The same security model can support other security policies, too. Every product you use to enhance your site security could introduce its own security model. Many of the models interact when products are combined at a site. For example, a firewall and the operating system work together to provide a secure Internet connection for your company. Both the firewall and the operating system have different roles and responsibilities in delivering the total solution. The firewall depends upon the operating system to provide a safe environment in which the firewall's programs can run. If the operating system's kernel has been compromised, the firewall cannot be depended upon to fulfill its role. Because of interactions like this, you need to know what constitutes a basic security model and how you might evaluate one.

Briefly, a security model defines *entities* and the rules that govern how these entities interact or *reference* one another. You already are familiar with many different entities in your networks—users, groups, files, routers, workstations, printers, disk drives, application programs, clients, servers, and network adapters. These entities interact and reference each other in many different ways in computer networks. *Access control rules* constrain how entities reference and interact with each other. An access control rule you frequently encounter is one limiting which users are allowed to read a particular file on a computer. You probably can think of several other examples, which indicates that you already understand the concepts underlying security models.

Before exploring the basic security model, think about why security is needed in the first place. A security model, implemented by one or more products, should provide value for you, by attempting to satisfy three primary goals.

## Goals of Computer Security

To appreciate why intrusion-detection products are now being added to improve security, you need to know the goals that security products are trying to satisfy.

Because these goals are not being completely achieved with traditional products, enterprises are now deploying or investigating intrusion-detection solutions.

The acronym CIA is a clever, easily remembered string that represents three central goals in computer security:

**Confidentiality.** Protection of data so that it is not disclosed in an unauthorized fashion.

**Integrity.** Protection against unauthorized modifications to data.

**Availability.** Protection from unauthorized attempts to withhold information or computer resources.

When people are asked why they think computer security is important, their responses usually show concern for *confidentiality*. Most of us do not want our medical records made easily available to anyone curious enough to ask for them. Credit histories and other financial data hopefully are treated with confidence, too. Academic records, performance evaluations, and personnel files are other sources of information that we generally assume must be handled confidentially. Likewise, numerous manual procedures for the confidential care of banking transactions have been developed over hundreds of years. Therefore, a clear history of how to accomplish confidentiality has been established even if a computer is not in the loop.

*Integrity* of information is also of concern in everyday life. Unauthorized changes to your credit history represent a weakness in the capability of a system to maintain integrity of the data under its control. In network communications, if an adversary manages to alter the data packets before the destination is reached, the integrity of the information has been compromised. If you are browsing a Web site and a malicious person can gather information from your personal computer and then use this information to steal funds from your bank account, you have become a victim of both integrity and confidentiality violations.

Lack of data *availability* caused by security problems is a major concern. If the primary trading database for a securities brokerage firm is inaccessible, millions of dollars could be lost with every passing minute. If the database suddenly became unreachable because of a software bug, few people would be shocked. Neither would it be a surprise if the disk drives failed and crashed the database. However, if the database becomes unavailable as a result of industrial espionage, watch for front-page coverage in the newspapers! Despite this potential reaction, money more likely will be budgeted for redundant power supplies, redundant network adapters, redundant servers, and redundant disks but not allocated for the purchase of a security monitoring product.

How can we show that a security product provides confidentiality, integrity, and availability? Using techniques from theoretical computer science, we can formally define confidentiality and integrity within the context of a particular computer system. As a consequence, one can say that confidentiality and integrity are *computable*. This notion is very profound because it enables security researchers to know without doubt that a particular system enforces confidentiality and integrity (Brinkley and Schell, 1995). In commercial products, these formal methods are rarely used. However, it is comforting to know that, in principle, we can rigorously defend a product's claims about integrity and confidentiality.

Proving availability is more complicated. Statements regarding availability cannot be made with as much confidence as those for integrity and confidentiality. The main reason for this is that identifying all of the factors influencing availability in a particular computer system is almost impossible. That is, these influences cannot be exhaustively listed in mathematical expressions, and thus, a formal proof for availability is more elusive. Formal proofs and notations are not used in this book, but if you would like to learn more about formal models of computer security, many good references are available (Bell, 1990; LaPadula, 1990; Williams and Abrams, 1995), so check the references at the back of the book for these resources.

To summarize in computer security jargon, we can make statements about confidentiality and integrity with a high level of *assurance*, but we cannot make statements about the availability of a particular system with the same level of assurance. At least you can feel confident that products built to protect the confidentiality and integrity of your system can be provably secure assuming that the vendor has followed some sound design and development processes.

In computer security literature, you sometimes will find other goals of computer security including *authentication* and *nonrepudiation*. Authentication is the process of verifying the identity of someone or something, such as a when a user enters a password. Nonrepudiation is the process of proving that a message came from a particular sender and that the message could not have come from anyone else. As you see in this chapter, authentication is defined as a required supporting function of the basic security model, rather than as an explicit goal. Nonrepudiation might be needed at your site, but because it is not always required, nonrepudiation is omitted from the three primary goals listed previously.

Now that you know the security goals for your network, it's time to take a look at how the goals can be met—by implementing a security model.

## Learn to Ask Tough Questions

A security model is an abstraction used to define entities and how these entities are allowed to interact. A security model begins as a set of definitions on paper, but eventually the model is implemented in software, hardware, or both. Hopefully, the implementation is accurate and adheres to the model specification. If the implementation is flawed, the system will lack the capability to provide confidentiality, integrity, and availability.

A security model is found in every operating system. As part of the security model in most operating systems, access to each file can be limited in specific ways. In traditional UNIX systems, one rule controlling access might state that only Joe is allowed to read the file named JoeMail. The entities in this case are Joe and JoeMail, and both must be uniquely identifiable within the context of the operating system. Any ambiguity weakens the capability of the model to meet its three goals. The access control rule, or *authorization*, which is used to specify this particular part of the security policy consists of the triple *{Joe,JoeMail,read}*. Naturally, these few entities and this one rule represent only a fraction of the complete operating system security policy and underlying security model. Other operating system entities are files, processes, threads, queues, messages, processors, and the kernel itself.

Security products you deploy in your network also rely on a security model. You must know the purposes and scope of each security model in use at your site. To understand why, think about what happens when you add a database management system to an operating system. The operating system and the database manager have different notions of *user*. No requirement states that the names used to identify users in the operating system and users in the database manager should be identical. In fact, the user names could be derived from completely different alphabets or characters. Different entities are defined in these two products. The operating system works with entities such as files and directories, but the database manager introduces the notions of record, field, and schema. The scope or span of control exercised by the operating system and the database manager differ, too. The operating system controls whether a user is even allowed to install the database manager, but the database manager makes all of the decisions about which parts of each database a user can access.

The database manager and the operating system also participate in a *trust relationship*. The operating system provides device drivers that the database manager uses to write data to disk. If the device drivers are compromised by a hacker, the integrity of the database might be affected. The database manager trusts that the operating system has adequate controls in place to prevent this type of attack. A *trust boundary* occurs at the operating system's interface for calling the device driver. If a hacker can replace the device driver program on disk or if a hacker can intercept the database manager's request to use the device driver and temporarily substitute a bogus device driver, then security is not guaranteed.

The dependencies that security products and the operating system have on each other are often overlooked or taken for granted. Someone might assume that the database software integrity can be maintained by monitoring the executables and configuration files for tampering. If someone tries to replace one of the binaries making up the database manager itself, a warning could be signaled. However, this warning alone is not sufficient for a secure environment. Each piece of the environment must be secure. As noted, if components of the operating system can be replaced, the database manager can lose its integrity. The only way to understand how products interact is by looking at the security models they introduce.

Understanding the security model upon which a product is based will help in the following ways:

**You can precisely state the entities the product controls and describe how the entities interact.**   Thinking about a product in terms of its basic building blocks is the best way to find out whether the product meets its claims and for understanding how the product interacts with other products.

**You can evaluate the implementation of the product itself, not just how the product solves your original problem.**   You should question the security of the implementation itself. You need to know how entities in the product can be created, deleted, or modified to decide whether the product is trustworthy.

**You can recognize the product's scope.**   A product that improves login security at your site may not be designed to limit what a user does after access is gained. If you expect more protection from a product than it can reasonably provide, you will be disappointed.

**You should understand the product's trust boundaries.**   Identifying the boundaries of a product you use improves your awareness *because weaknesses often occur at the boundaries*. This statement is a basic principle in mechanical and civil engineering. The joints, interfaces, and connection points in an object tend to be the sources of structural problems. The same is true of software systems in general. When those systems are responsible for enforcing a security policy, boundary weaknesses can lead to exploits.

**You can recognize where trust relationships are established between products.**   When an improved login security program is installed at a site, a new trust relationship is created. Prior to the installation of this new security program, the operating system relied on its own software for login security. However, because this program was added, both the operating system and transitively any program running on this system must *trust* the new login program to do its job properly. Any weakness in the login security program or any weakness in the way it connects to the operating system will result in security problems that can ripple through many other software components.

Product boundaries are important because they present opportunities for attack. Interaction at a boundary involves passing information from one security model to another, where the information can be either data values or a task to perform. The login security product you might add interfaces with the operating system when it reports success or failure depending on the outcome of the login process. You might ask several questions about a product like this:

- Can a user with a normal account replace all or part of the login software?
- Is the handshake or protocol used between the operating system and the login program flawed?
- Can you capture a successful login interaction if performed over the network and then replay the captured network traffic later to spoof the system?
- How are user names and accounts accessed by the login program?
- Does the login program check the lengths of values keyed in by users?

In order to answer these questions, you must start with the basic building blocks and construct a security model.

## A Basic Computer Security Model

To show that a computer system can maintain confidentiality and integrity, an underlying security model is needed. At the lowest level of the model is an *entity* that is best thought of as a noun representing something of interest in your universe. Entities are further classified as either *subjects* or *objects*. Not surprisingly, this structure is similar to most spoken languages. Indeed, the next concept in the model is the verb *access*.

*Subjects access objects.* Upon this simple notion rests the foundation for all computer security products. When you purchase a security product, start by thinking of it in terms of these atomic definitions. What are the subjects? What are the objects? What kinds of access control can be specified between subjects and objects? You will have plenty of other questions to ask, but always start with these.

On different occasions, the same entity may be a subject or an object. A program is acting as a subject when it tries to read a file (the object in this case). When someone attempts to terminate that same process, the role switches to that of an object because the process is itself the target of an access request (termination) by yet another subject.

Where computers are concerned, the only types of access we need to define further are *read* and *write*. Remember the brief discussion regarding proofs of confidentiality and integrity? If you were performing a formal mathematical evaluation of a product, reducing all access statements to read and write would be required. Reading a security book at this low level would be about as interesting as watching wine age. Broadening the view is better because a variety of actions can be derived from read and write. These other actions might be creating an object, deleting an object, or renaming an object.

You use subjects, objects, and access rights to declare *what* can happen in a computer system. That is, they are used to specify the security policy you want to enforce. Now that you understand these basic definitions, the next topic of interest is *how* these relationships actually can be enforced.

## The Reference Monitor

The security *reference monitor* (Anderson, 1972) is the black box controlling what happens when subjects make references to objects or try to access them. A reference monitor is an abstract concept. Every operating system available today implements some type of reference monitor to enforce security. The purpose of the reference monitor is to control requests by subjects to access objects (see Figure 1.1). One good way to visualize this concept is to think of subjects on the left, the reference monitor in the middle, and objects on the right. The only path subjects can take to get to objects is through the reference monitor. In lay terms, the reference monitor acts as a *guard* for the objects.

The reference monitor consists of two main functions. First, the reference monitor provides *reference functions* that are used to evaluate access requests by subjects. Each time a subject wants to access an object, a reference function is computed and evaluated by the reference monitor. The reference monitor uses an *authorization database* to make decisions about whether to permit or deny requests it receives. When a request is forwarded to the reference monitor, it checks the authorization database to see whether the operation is permitted. A request in its most basic form is merely an attempt by a subject to access an object.

The authorization database conceptually contains entries or *authorizations* of the form {*subject, object, access mode*}. Recall from previous comments that only read and write access modes, or *rights*, need be considered. However, to have a meaningful discussion, other rights such as create and delete are permitted

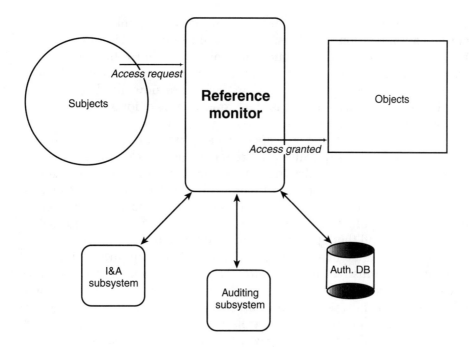

**Figure 1.1 The reference monitor regulates subjects accessing objects.**

throughout this book. The authorization database is not part of the reference monitor, but it is something upon which the reference monitor depends. It is interesting to note that in formal analysis, entries in the authorization database specify what is *not* permitted, rather than what is allowed. This may sound odd, but it makes the proofs much easier. When specifying a security policy for your site, you probably are more accustomed to stating who can access what and how. When access control rules or authorizations are described in this book, the more familiar form is used stating who can access what and how it can be accessed.

The reference monitor controls changes to the authorization database itself through the use of its second part—*authorization functions*. The authorization database is used to permit or deny accesses to objects. Because the process of changing an entry in the authorization database is also an access request, this process can be similarly regulated using the notions of subject, object, and access. The reference monitor not only controls how subjects access objects, it also controls changes to the individual access rules.

That's it. The reference monitor contains only two components—reference functions and authorization functions. True, building a secure computer system requires much more than just a reference monitor. The authorization database is one example of another component needed to ensure a secure system. Others will be added to the security model momentarily. For now, the key point to remember is that a reference monitor is an abstract engine enforcing access control using only two simple functions.

When you protect a file so that only specific users or groups can read the file, you are entering access control rules. The reference monitor is activated when you define the access control rules that conceptually exist in an authorization database. In reality, the access control rules probably are stored as permission bits or indicators with the file. When someone attempts to read the file, the reference monitor is activated again to evaluate the request. The reference monitor helps you define a policy, and then it helps you enforce the policy.

Plenty of example reference monitors exist outside of computer science. A teller at a bank performs reference-monitor functions by deciding whether to allow you (the subject) access to an account (the object). Possible actions include making a deposit, withdrawing a sum, or querying a balance. A manager or employee in the payroll department controls reference requests by responding to an employee who calls for personal payroll information. The payroll manager alone, though, controls authorization change requests. This control occurs when a new payroll employee is given limited power to look up information for regular employees but not for executives. Naturally, the right to change the authorization database is a powerful right in itself.

## What Makes a Good Reference Monitor

A reference monitor should meet three requirements (Anderson, 1972). First, you must be able to isolate the reference monitor; it should be resistant to tampering. Next, the reference monitor must be complete in that it is invoked for every reference to an object by a subject. If a subject is allowed to access an object without going through the reference monitor, say good-bye to CIA. Finally, you must have some way to verify the reference monitor. In practice, this verification is done in many ways. You might trust the vendor's reputation; you might have access to the source code; or the product may have been used for years without problems. Look for compact and simple implementations. If the reference monitor is a few hundred lines of code, you might feel more comfortable that the vendor was able to adequately test the implementation.

The reference monitor is an abstraction that must be programmed into a product to help enforce security. You can think of the reference monitor as a high-level design. The actual implementation of the reference monitor is called the *security kernel*.

## The Security Kernel

The security kernel is the real-world implementation of the abstract reference monitor defined in the preceding section. In most systems, the security kernel includes hardware, firmware, and software that work together to control access in the system. The main design goal of a security kernel is simplicity. Ideally, the security kernel design can be written in such precise terms that you can perform mathematical proofs which conclusively show it works as designed. This naturally represents a very high level of assurance. In practice, few vendors go through this much trouble, and, for only a few, such formal mathematical undertakings have been successful (Schell and Brinkley, 1995).

You probably will not find mathematical proofs in the documentation accompanying commercial products. There is a continuum with poor software quality on the low end and provably secure systems on the high end. Decide what you can live with when looking for a product. Ask the vendor whether it is possible to discuss the security kernel design with you. Make inquiries about the degree of testing that the security kernel undergoes. If the security kernel includes software only, you need to verify fewer components. When the security kernel consists of hardware, firmware, and software, the resulting implementation naturally will be more complex. Workstations or servers running UNIX or NT naturally contain all three components in the security kernel.

Security kernels are found in a variety of products. Clearly, operating systems provide security kernels. Each commercial product you deploy also contains a security kernel. For example, did you know that firewalls also implement their own security kernels? When a firewall makes decisions about whether to permit or deny network traffic, it is consulting an authorization database commonly referred to as the firewall rule base. Like the reference monitor described, the firewall security kernel is also responsible for restricting who can change the rule base itself.

If you ask the vendor to explain the underlying security kernel, you are showing that you are an educated buyer. Seek clarification on the following three aspects of the product:

1. Is the reference monitor complete? In other words, is the reference monitor activated each time a subject accesses an object? Is every reference by a subject to an object passing through the reference monitor?
2. How is the reference monitor itself protected from unauthorized tampering? How is the authorization database protected?

3. Is the implementation of the reference monitor simple enough to verify with test cases? If the answer to this question is "No," decide what information you will accept as proof that the reference monitor works.

## Enhancing the Security Model Further

At this point, you must surely be asking how the reference monitor alone can adequately provide confidentiality and integrity. In fact, the reference monitor or security kernel trusts other components to help with security. Beyond the security kernel, you also need some way to verify the identity of subjects and objects. As mentioned previously, you also need an authorization database that is used to control access to objects. To know whether the reference monitor is behaving correctly, audit data must be produced to track its activities.

Taking a quick look back, you can see that the security model begins with subjects and objects and then incorporates an abstract reference monitor. The security model is now enhanced with the addition of three more components. The *identification and authentication* (I&A) component of a computer system interacts with the security kernel to positively identify subjects and objects. The authorization database component discussed earlier also is added to the security model. Finally, an audit mechanism is added for accountability and monitoring. With these three additions, the security model is complete enough to be useful for specifying a complete security policy. The *trusted computing base* (TCB) includes any hardware, software, or firmware used in the security kernel, the I&A subsystem, the authorization database, or the auditing subsystem to enforce the security policy.

### Identification and Authentication (I&A)

A secure computer system must provide a trustworthy component for identifying subjects and objects. Like the reference monitor and security kernel introduced earlier, the I&A component should be tamper resistant and simple. If the I&A programs or hardware can be compromised, the confidentiality and integrity of the system will no longer be guaranteed. After penetrating your system, one of the first things a hacker will do is plant Trojan Horse routines for the real I&A programs. One of the oldest tricks is to leave a password grabber running on a computer terminal. The grabber pretends to be the real operating system login program, but its sole purpose is to trick an unsuspecting user. Because I&A is the first step in getting into a computer, it is obviously where a hacker will probe for weaknesses.

A confounding behavior of computing systems is *on behalf of semantics*. When a person wants to access a computer, the first step is typically I&A. What really happens after this initial phase will be described in detail in the next chapter for both UNIX and NT. However, unless you are starring in the motion picture *Tron*, you can be sure that you don't physically enter the system yourself. Instead, things happen inside the computer on your behalf.

After a user authenticates to a computer, the operating system usually creates a process, a running program, that performs actions for the user. During a single interactive session, numerous other processes may be started for the user. Attached to each of these processes is a set of *credentials* that are used to uniquely identify the user. Credentials are not limited to computer environments. Spies have long carried some form of a credential in order to verify each other.

Computers and networks consist of hundreds and thousands of different processes. Something as simple as clicking on a Web link can result in dozens of interactions between different processes. Often a task you want to perform requires access to objects for which you have insufficient authorizations. To accomplish these tasks, the process representing you interacts with another process that *does* have the appropriate authorizations to complete the task. These specially privileged processes are performing tasks on your behalf. For example, your normal login session on a server is unlikely to be empowered to directly speak with the network adapter. Instead, various privileged programs are asked to do this on your behalf as you surf the Internet.

Notice that I&A is part of a particularly weak boundary between humans and the computer. The assumption is that the person who possesses the information required to successfully complete I&A is indeed the rightful owner. That is, the login information is sufficient for representing the user to the computer. The computer does not care whether your facial features have changed, whether your last name changed this morning, or even whether you cannot remember anything except your login information. A number of threats at this boundary include password guessing, password theft, and human error.

Identification and authentication are two distinct tasks. In some computer systems, these tasks are combined into one single step. However, the normal case requires someone to enter identifying information such as a user name for identification. When this value has been entered, the user must provide authentication information. Three classic types of authenticating information exist. These three types are briefly described in this chapter and covered in more detail in the next chapter.

## How Are You Authenticated?

Authentication is typically based upon something you know, something you have, or something you are.

**Something you know.**    The canonical example of something you know is a password or pass phrase. You might type or speak the value. A number of schemes are possible for obtaining what you know. It might be assigned to you, or you may have picked the value yourself. Constraints may exist regarding the form the value can take, or the alphabet from which you are allowed to construct the value might be limited to letters only. If you forget the value, you may not be ableto authenticate yourself to the system.

**Something you have.**    Another form of authentication requires possession of something such as a key, a smart card, a disk, or some other device. Whatever form it takes, the authenticating item should be difficult to duplicate and may require synchronization with systems other than the one to which you are requesting access. Highly secure environments may require you to possess multiple things to guarantee authenticity. A nuclear missile launch often is portrayed in movies as requiring two different people to insert a key and simultaneously press red buttons. Have you ever been asked for two credit cards to cash a check?

**Something you are.**    Something you are is really a special case of something you have. The usual examples given include fingerprint, voice, or retinal scans. Other possibilities are implanted microchips that report to a *global positioning system* (GPS). Naturally, your fingerprints are definitely something you have.

### Authenticating Other Entities

I&A is not limited to login events by users. When two computers want to communicate across a network, some form of I&A occurs. Sometimes computers simply exchange their network addresses for I&A. The TCP/IP protocol suite uses this type of *address-based authentication* in a number of applications. Numerous security hacks have exploited this method of authentication. Stronger mechanisms based on cryptography can be used by computers to identify and authenticate each other. You'll learn more about these techniques in Chapter 4, "Traditional Network Security Approaches."

Often individual programs running on the same computer or running on different computers need to identify and authenticate each other. The *Distributed Computing Environment* (DCE) provides a way for arbitrary processes to use strong authentication techniques based on cryptography. Each program has access to a secret that can be used to uniquely authenticate it to other programs, similar to the way in which users authenticate themselves with passwords.

Some authentication models require the use of trusted third parties. In such a scenario, two entities who do not necessarily trust each other might trust a common third party. This third party is asked to verify that each party is indeed authentic. For example, John and Jane might know each other. Jane and Ralph know each other, too. John approaches Ralph and tries to sell him some land, but how does Ralph know if John is indeed who he claims to be? To solve the dilemma, both John and Ralph take a trip to meet with Jane. Jane tells Ralph that John is telling the truth, at least with respect to his identity. If John had asked Jane to conversely authenticate Ralph, the interaction would have involved *bilateral* or *mutual authentication*. Notice how the interaction crosses boundaries that might be exploited. For example, is it possible to somehow impersonate the trusted third party, to pass the third party bogus information, or to steal information from the third party?

Another example of bilateral authentication occurs during logins in highly secure environments. The user wants to know for certain that no malicious programs have been left behind by previous users to grab passwords. To establish a secure channel with the computer, the user depends on a *secure attention key* (SAK) that can be used to terminate all activity at the login terminal and to guarantee that no bogus login program remains from the previous user session.

## The I&A Components Must Be Trustworthy

Often, in large networks you will find that various software products are responsible for a different range of I&A services. The example given previously for database versus operating system user names is a classic division of responsibility. Both management domains require a storage location for the user names, one or more programs to maintain the I&A information, and interfaces for other security components to request I&A services or information.

Both the database manager and the operating system are responsible for I&A within a particular *security context*. A database user name has no meaning within the context of the operating system. Likewise, the user names stored in the operating system's repository are generally irrelevant for gaining access to databases controlled by the database manager. Products installed at your site are responsible for security only within specific contexts. A firewall has little to do with rules controlling which records in the payroll database someone can access.

The parts of a security product that are used to provide I&A services play a pivotal role in networked environments. Every entity must be able to be uniquely identified. Furthermore, the integrity of the software or hardware used in I&A must be guaranteed. Any mechanisms or procedures used to create, delete, or change I&A information must meet the requirements of the reference monitor. That is, I&A software or hardware must be complete, verifiable, and capable of being isolated. The reasons are quite simple. If the I&A process can be subverted or spoofed, then the reference monitor cannot guarantee that the security policy is enforced. Also, if you cannot uniquely identify entities in the computing environment, you will have difficulty assigning accountability for actions or regulating access control.

## Access Control

The security model now includes subjects, objects, a subsystem for identifying and authenticating these entities, and a reference monitor for controlling access between entities. Earlier discussions made reference to an authorization database used by the reference monitor for making decisions about access requests by subjects. In this section, access control is added to the other components in the security model. Access control is further divided into *discretionary* access control and *mandatory* access control.

### Discretionary Access Control

*Discretionary access control* (DAC) is the type most frequently seen. Commercial UNIX systems as well as NT rely on DAC. In systems based on discretionary access, the owner of the object is responsible for setting the access rights. As a side effect of many operating system designs, one or more privileged users also can change access rights for an object. A DAC implementation needs to be granular enough so that the owner can specify access control down to the level of an individual user or group. You should be able to state individual users or groups as subjects in the first field of the access control database entry.

### Mandatory Access Control

Rather than relying on the owner of an object to control access rights, *mandatory access control* (MAC) uses the system itself to regulate access rights. The object's owner does not even have the capability to assign access rights to other subjects or users in the system. The system controls access rights based on how subjects and objects are classified. In addition to the normal string of characters identifying the entity, such as a user name or file name, each subject or object is tagged with a sensitivity label consisting of two parts:

◆ An access class label
◆ A list of category labels

The access class label is chosen from a predefined, hierarchically ordered set of labels. Commonly found labels in military security policies include top secret, secret, confidential, and unclassified. Each label represents a level of information that is more restrictive than the previous label. Order is important. The labels cannot be arbitrary tags that have no relationship to each other. A precedence relationship must state, for example, that top secret is at a higher level than secret, that secret precedes confidential, and that confidential is more restrictive than unclassified. The purpose of labeling is to prevent a user who is classified at only the confidential level from accessing information at the secret or top secret level. Another property of MAC is that you cannot "write down" information or declassify it to a lower level in the system. If a disk file is classified as confidential, MAC will prevent anyone from writing secret or top secret information into the file.

Category labels are arbitrary tags that are *not* required to be hierarchically arranged. The category labels can be thought of as compartments. In many situations today, we must compartmentalize information. The military has long used compartmentalization to ensure that information is given out only to those with a "need to know."

Users, as well as other subjects and objects, can be associated with many category labels, but they may have only one access class label. MAC enforces accesses based on these sensitivity labels. Returning to the two basic access primitives, read and write, MAC works as follows: To read an object, the access class of the subject must be equal to *or greater than* the access class of the object, and the list of category labels for the subject must be a superset of (contain) the list of category labels for the object; to write an object, the subject's access class label must be equal to *or less than* that of the object, and all of the subject's category labels must be included in the list of category labels for the object.

This concept may seem confusing at first, but if you think about it, the rules make perfect sense. Consider access labels first. When reading from an object, you obviously must be cleared at a security level at least as high as that of the object. If your label is confidential, you cannot read information classified higher than confidential. Also, if the object is tagged with several categories, and you are not allowed to access all of these categories, you should not be allowed to read from the object. To prevent downgrading of information, writing to an object requires that you be classified at no more than the classification level of the object. If your classification is top secret, you might be able to write top secret information into a file classified at a lower level. The write rule is designed to prevent this from happening.

Commercial products have been developed supporting MAC. These products are used in some of the most security sensitive sites that can be found. There also are some interesting formal properties that can be derived from MAC. For example, you can show that MAC is resistant to Trojan Horse attacks. Only a few of the products discussed in this book offer MAC capabilities, though. One reason is that developing software that runs on top of MAC-enabled operating systems is difficult, as is implementing the product so that it truly follows the MAC model. Still, you can find firewalls and Web servers designed to run on operating systems supporting MAC.

Access control is one of the most important components of the security policy. However, how do you know whether your access control rules have been entered correctly? Did you consider all of the possibilities? Is the reference monitor implementation working as designed, or did the vendor make some mistakes? To verify that the system is behaving correctly, you need to monitor or audit all of the security-relevant decisions being made by the TCB.

## Auditing

The security model needs one other addition to complete the picture. Auditing is a trusted mechanism, a part of the TCB, that the reference monitor invokes to keep a log of its activities. Information logged by the reference monitor should include the subject and object identifiers, the access right requested, the date and time, and the result of the reference request (success or failure). Audit records should be stored in a manner that ensures trustworthiness.

Most operating systems provide an audit subsystem that is at least capable of logging every file accessed by a user. Because many other subjects and objects exist in an operating system, the auditing mechanism is also responsible for recording events such as starting a program, ending a program, rebooting a system, adding a user, changing a password, and attaching a new disk drive. A number of different logs are maintained by an operating system, but not all of them contain sufficient information to accurately identify the subjects, objects, and access request. If you expect to be able to assign accountability for system activities, a complete record describing each access control decision is needed.

**T**IP    *Only by actively auditing a system will you know that the intended security policy is correctly entered and enforced. Intrusion detection is based on this simple requirement. If you do not monitor systems and networks, you cannot detect intruders or misuse by insiders.*

> **T**IP   *Auditing has always been recognized as an important part of the classic security model. Intrusion detection improves upon the traditional notion of auditing by helping you look for known attack scenarios, combinations of suspicious activities, and patterns of events that attempt to identify malicious behavior.*

Auditing is important for another reason. Remember that the security policy at your site is implemented using a security model. A number of different products, with different reference monitors, participate to accomplish this task. Stating your security policy completely is extremely difficult, as is being sure that you have entered the policy into the computer products correctly.

A typical operating system is composed of several thousand files. Designing the access control rules for an operating system is exceedingly complex. History has shown that vendors have not always been successful at doing this. You are certain to encounter similar problems when entering your security policy into different products or parts of the same product. Auditing and monitoring can help you identify where you have made mistakes and can complete the feedback loop for improving your security.

To summarize, the classic security model consists of the following:

♦ Subjects and objects

♦ An authorization database describing how subjects can access objects

♦ A reference monitor that regulates *any* attempt by subjects to access objects

♦ A trusted subsystem for identifying and authenticating the subjects and objects

♦ A trusted subsystem for auditing the activities of the reference monitor

For each of the products you have at your site, you should be able to recognize each of these components in the security models they implement. When you do, you'll be able to see what a product can do for you and what it cannot.

## Classifying Security Products with a Nod to Intrusion Detection

Previous sections have emphasized how complex a secure computing environment can be. This environment may contain many products, each implementing some security model, each with strengths and weaknesses, and all communicating with each other. Information flowing between security components is subject to attack just as the underlying product implementations are.

If you deploy different security products at a site, what kinds of roles do they play? What are the boundaries within which they exercise control? What relative value do different products bring? To answer these questions, products are broadly grouped into the following four *complementary* categories: I&A, access control, scanners, and intrusion detection.

### Identification and Authentication

Identification and authentication products are designed to improve the existing I&A facilities you are currently using. Using the same password for years on end is a bad idea. In general, reusable passwords are threatened by people who watch network traffic or try to guess passwords. Plenty of other threats also exist and will be discussed in the next chapter. I&A can be improved with products that do not rely on reusable passwords—products that require the user to *have* something such as a smart card or products that require the user to *know* something that might be supplied by a smart card. Some products also operate based on something you *are*, such as fingerprint scanners.

### Access Control

A number of products are offered to enhance the way information access is controlled. Most of the products improve on limitations of out-of-the-box versions of operating systems. However, firewalls also can be thought of as providing access control functions. Access control products work precisely as described previously in this chapter. Subjects, objects, and access rights are defined. A reference monitor is implemented to control access requests. What feature is an access control product missing? Access control products do not necessarily tell you whether the security policy has been entered correctly. To know whether you have made any mistakes, you can either scan the configuration occasionally or monitor the system for problems.

### Scanners

Several products are available to inspect your system or network configuration for weaknesses. Most of these products are run on a scheduled interval. An advantage of this approach is that the scanner product can be customized for different applications. For example, if certain Web server configurations are known to open security holes, a scanner can read the contents of the configuration files and look for improper entries. The scanner also can make an appropriate change to the file to remove the problem.

What are some things a scanner is not designed to do? Scanners obviously are not responsible for the primary I&A activities of the system. Also, scanners are not responsible for deciding the outcome of all access control requests. Do you need a scanner? The answer is almost certainly "yes." Scanners provide a way for you to verify that your security policy is configured correctly and that the policy is being enforced correctly by the numerous security components at your site. Today, most scanners are marketed as intrusion detection products because they look for weaknesses in your system that can be exploited by an intruder or by a malicious insider.

## Intrusion Detection and Monitoring

Although the research community has been active with *intrusion detection systems* (IDSs) for more than a decade, products in this category have only recently received wider market interest. The purpose of an IDS product is to monitor the system for attacks. An attack might be signaled by something as simple as a program that illegally modifies a user name. Complex attacks might involve sequences of events that span multiple systems. Intrusion detection products are classified with system monitors because they usually depend on auditing information provided from the system's logs or data gathered by sniffing network traffic. One difference between scanners and IDSs is the time interval. A scanner is running in real time when it is started. However, a scanner is rarely run *all of the time*. Intrusion detection products are designed to run in real time and to constantly monitor the system for attacks.

## Additional Product Differences

Besides thinking about products based on the security services they perform, you can also differentiate between products based on other design tradeoffs chosen by the vendor. Some tradeoffs are binary because the vendor is faced with two conflicting requirements that cannot be met simultaneously. A common example is the conflict surrounding a product designed for novice users or for expert users. If a product is complex and provides features that a sophisticated user might want, such as the capability to configure access control rules containing many different variables, a novice user probably will be overwhelmed when configuring the security policy. If the vendor decides in favor of expert users, the novice user might buy a less capable but easier-to-use product. When you think critically about security products, watch for the following tradeoffs.

### Real Time or Interval Based

A product like a scanner runs on an interval. That is, you schedule the scan to begin at a specific time rather than running the scan continuously. A real-time intrusion detection product, on the other hand, would always be running and watching for attacks. Sometimes classifying a product as real time or interval based can be a confusing process because real time is always a relative concept. For example, a product might claim to detect events in real time. However, the operating system may be storing several events in a queue for seconds or minutes before releasing the events to waiting programs. The event monitoring program may not really *see* the event until long after it happened. In computer security, a few milliseconds can make a difference between disaster or success. Keep in mind that the perception of real time depends on your perspective of the system. Someone working at the level of the CPU itself has a different notion of real time than someone connected to a system across a network.

### Centralized or Distributed

Everyone who manages a network of computers wants some type of centralized administration and reporting. On the other hand, centralized decision making can often be slower. Finding the proper balance is a challenge for security vendors.

Centralized reporting of security incidents is advised for a number of reasons including cost, consistency, and accountability for actions. Conversely, you do not want automated responses, like disconnecting a hacker, to be adversely affected by network delays. The time it takes the attacked node to receive the "disconnect response" from a centralized response database could leave enough of a window for someone to plant a Trojan Horse. A middle-of-the-road approach would be to report security violations at a central console but to let each node in the network immediately carry out a predefined automated response using its own computing resources, rather than looking up the appropriate response in a centralized database. A configuration option for centralized reports but distributed responses would make this possible.

### System Level or Network Level

Some security products focus on improving network security, and others add value at a higher level of abstraction in the computer. A product that encrypts network traffic improves the confidentiality of data passed between systems at the network level. Programs controlling whether users are allowed to delete files operate at the file system level of abstraction, rather than at the network packet level. In the intrusion detection product area, vendors have tended to focus on either the network level or the system level.

### Augment or Replace

One of the basic reasons you buy additional security products is because something you already have is not sufficient. You buy another access control product because the operating system that came with your computer did not allow you to express the types of access control rules you need for your policy. The new product can either replace programs that shipped with the operating system, or it can augment these operating system programs, typically by intercepting them. The vendor may choose to replace programs or libraries because this leads to better performance. The tradeoff is obvious when the operating system provider ships a patch that reverts to the original program and wipes out the replacement provided by the security vendor. You need to perform some additional integration tasks after the patch is applied. If the operating calls are intercepted, the security vendor might be trading off performance penalties for a simpler implementation.

### Existing Data Source or New Data Source

A network monitoring program usually sits on the network and examines network traffic. The program does not add a new data source, rather it relies on data already being shipped throughout the network. Other programs introduce a new data source for making security decisions.

For example, you might want to monitor your Web site for suspicious behavior. In order to accomplish this, your Web server could write a log record each time a remote system accessed a file in a protected directory. These log records are currently not being kept but need to be stored if you expect to monitor activities. The program that monitors this log for suspicious activities depends upon this data to work properly. Thus, a new data source has been introduced into your environment. Consequences of adding this new data source include the need for additional storage and a possible performance degradation due to logging.

Note that all of these design alternatives involve tradeoffs. Know the tradeoffs and decide what you are willing to accept. You will be doing both the vendor and yourself a favor if you candidly discuss your opinions on the tradeoffs chosen. You do not want to invest time in a product that will not meet your needs In the long run, and no vendor is capable of satisfying everyone.

## Prevention, Detection, and Response with Intrusion Detection

Experienced security professionals realize the value of the triad *prevention*, *detection*, and *response* (Smaha and Winslow, 1994). One of the best defenses is to build formidable preventative mechanisms. However, in practice, prevention alone is insufficient. Program bugs and other human errors have resulted in numerous security breaches in the past.

A security policy also must be monitored for violations. That is, you want to detect any security breaches that are caused by configuration problems or slack policies. Finally, because security solutions must scale, it should be possible to define automated responses to security incidents. Care is, of course, needed. You do not want a response policy that tries to terminate all of the processes running on behalf of a perpetrator, especially if this affects availability of resources that are crucial to your business.

In addition to knowing whether a product falls into one of the four product categories, consider to what degree a security offering provides features for prevention, detection, or response. Preventative tools that improve upon I&A, access control, and network security are now being augmented with intrusion detection and responses. Connecting to the Internet at a minimum requires a firewall. To install the best solution, you also should use IDSs to scan for problems and detect intruders in real time. To successfully secure your environment, a mix of products is required. Understanding the benefits and features each product brings to your environment is the focus of the remaining chapters.

## Where to Go from Here

Now you see how intrusion detection enhances the traditional approach to security. You definitely need I&A solutions. Certainly, preventative tools are required to lock down your systems and networks. As you see in the first part of this book, ways to get around these traditional products still exist, and this is where intrusion detection can help. You need to add detection and response to your preventative techniques.

In this chapter, you learned the fundamental components needed to create a secure environment. Three primary goals of security were identified. A security model was gradually constructed from basic principles beginning with subjects and objects. The reference monitor concept was introduced to control access requests by subjects to objects. Identification and authentication, an access control database, and auditing were added to the model. The purpose of starting with these fundamentals is to provide a context within which to discuss products in subsequent chapters. When you read about products in chapters to come, continually ask yourself these questions:

- ◆ What are the subjects?
- ◆ What are the objects?

- How do they interact?
- Where is the reference monitor?
- How do you specify a security policy?
- How do you specify access control within the security policy?
- How are subjects identified and authenticated to the system?
- How does the product assist with confidentiality, integrity, and availability?
- Does the product interact with other products? Does it have trust relationships?
- What are the boundaries of the product? Are there weaknesses at the boundaries?

Only by critically examining these issues will you be able to carefully evaluate whether a product meets your needs. As you discover the answers to these questions when they are applied to traditional security products, you will see the value that intrusion detection can bring to your site.

# Chapter 2

# The Role of Identification and Authentication in Your Environment

Intrusion detection involves not only knowing that someone is trying to break into your system, but also identifying *who* the intruder is. This fundamental notion of *who* in computer environments is at the heart of regulating all of the system's activities. That is, the subject of an operation is determined by who is performing the act. In this chapter, you learn about weaknesses with authentication systems, what people have done to improve upon these weaknesses, and why intrusion detection is still needed even if you deploy strong authentication tools.

Initially, the focus is on the standard login process used to authenticate a user to the computer. After this material is covered, you will explore authentication between other entities, such as computers or software servers. An in-depth survey of network authentication requires a thorough understanding of network protocols. Although some of the discussion is about authentication across networks, this topic is not covered in detail until Chapter 4, "Traditional Network Security Approaches," in which you will explore network security.

The material in this chapter begins with discussions of UNIX and NT login procedures. Threats and defenses are identified for traditional password-based authentication. Following this discussion, you learn about alternative authentication servers.

Recall from the preceding chapter that *identification and authentication* (I&A) can be based on something you know, something you have, or something you are. Note that most operating systems or other products requiring authentication are now enabled to use a variety of techniques for verifying the identity of users. For example, IBM's AIX operating system is designed with an authentication grammar that enables you to plug in different commercial products. The Open Group's *Common Desktop Environment* (CDE) also includes a pluggable authentication mechanism. The IBM Firewall supports strong authentication with hardware tokens, too. These enhancements were added because of concerns about relying on a single password for authentication. You easily can add stronger authentication software or hardware to products such as operating systems, firewalls, and databases.

Knowing who is on your system is only part of the story. Knowing *what* the user did and whether the account has been compromised by an intruder is also important. I&A tools will help you improve upon problems like weak passwords. Intrusion detection tools are needed on top of these to track the activities of your users and to watch for intruders masquerading as normal users.

## Identification and Authentication in UNIX

Consider first a configuration that involves a stand-alone, multiuser computer with a directly attached terminal or display unit. After this simple scenario is described, we can elaborate on more complex cases involving network connections. The entities that are involved in UNIX I&A are *users* and *groups*.

### Users and Groups

In UNIX users are identified by a unique *username* composed of a contiguous string of characters including letters and numbers. For historical reasons, uppercase characters are not used. Special characters such as punctuation symbols are rarely found in usernames because applications running on the system may have trouble interpreting unusual characters.

Paired with each username is a numerical user ID or *UID*. The pairings are not required to be unique. The UNIX operating system does not require each username to be paired with a unique UID. However, a recommended security practice is to assign a separate UID to each user. Some versions of UNIX provide higher level commands or programs for adding users. As common practice, these programs assign the next UID value when a user is added or force the administrator to enter an unused UID. Even so, bypassing these administrative utilities and assigning the same UID to more than one user is possible. The mappings between usernames and UIDs are defined in the /etc/passwd file. This file usually can be edited directly by the machine's administrator, which is how one can pair two usernames with the same UID.

UNIX uses the UID as the subject identifier when performing many of its access control decisions. The username is rarely needed for anything other than the initial login I&A phase. Because the UID is the basis for many decisions made by the reference monitor, you can see why assigning duplicate UIDs might be a problem. If several users are performing tasks with the same UID, determining accountability for actions will be more difficult, though not impossible. For the sake of simplicity, the remaining discussions assume that a UID is assigned to only one user.

UNIX also provides a means for combining users into groups. Each group is identified by a groupname and *group ID* (GID). A user belongs to a *primary group* whose GID value is stored with the user's record in /etc/passwd. All groups defined on the system are stored in /etc/group. Users can belong to zero or more *secondary groups*, too. GIDs also are needed by the UNIX reference monitor for making some access control decisions.

Figure 2.1 shows a dump of the /etc/passwd file from a UNIX system. Each entry in the file is contained on one logical line. That is, an entry is terminated by an *end of line* (EOL) character. Fields in a record are separated by the colon character (:). Table 2.1 provides an explanation of the meaning of each field in a record. Entries in /etc/group have a similar format except that no password is associated with the group itself. Figure 2.2 shows the contents of an example /etc/group file.

The /etc/passwd file can be read by any user on the system. Because password information is stored in this file, someone may be able to guess or crack passwords. For increased security, most modern UNIX variants rely on a *shadow* password file that is stored in a directory which only certain users can read—notably root and perhaps a security administrator. The system then would rely on both /etc/passwd and another file, such as /etc/security/passwd in IBM's AIX version

---

**Figure 2.1**   Typical contents of the /etc/passwd file.

---

```
root:x:0:1:Super-User:/:/sbin/sh
daemon:x:1:1::/:
bin:x:2:2::/usr/bin:
sys:x:3:3::/:
adm:x:4:4:Admin:/var/adm:
lp:x:71:8:Line Printer Admin:/usr/spool/lp:
smtp:x:0:0:Mail Daemon User:/:
uucp:x:5:5:uucp Admin:/usr/lib/uucp:
nuucp:x:9:9:uucp Admin:/var/spool/uucppublic:/usr/lib/uucp/uucico
listen:x:37:4:Network Admin:/usr/net/nls:
nobody:x:60001:60001:Nobody:/:
noaccess:x:60002:60002:No Access User:/:
nobody4:x:65534:65534:SunOS 4.x Nobody:/:
terry:x:101:100:Terry Escamilla:/home/terry:/bin/ksh
```

**Table 2.1**    Interpretation of Fields in a Record in /etc/passwd

| Field | Contents |
|-------|----------|
| terry | Username |
| fC3/.rj29MBD | Hashed password value |
| 101 | UID |
| 100 | Group ID (GID) |
| Terry Escamilla | Full name of user |
| /home/terry | Home directory of user |
| /bin/ksh | Login shell for user |

of UNIX. In this shadow configuration, passwords are stored in the shadow password file and the other user information from Table 2.1 remains in /etc/passwd. Technically, user information for AIX is stored in /etc/passwd, /etc/security/user, and /etc/security/passwd. UNIX operating systems may depend on many different files for user and group data, but /etc/passwd is always present.

### Superuser

Most UNIX systems ship with a default set of usernames and UIDs. These accounts have special privileges throughout the system. Of particular interest is UID zero (0) which identifies the *superuser*. On most UNIX operating systems, this UID is associated with the username *root*. With the exception of a few operations, the root user is given complete control over the machine and operating system.

**Figure 2.2**    Contents of the /etc/group file.

```
root:Bauidel4.byQ:6445::::::
daemon:NP:6445::::::
bin:NP:6445::::::
sys:NP:6445::::::
adm:NP:6445::::::
lp:NP:6445::::::
smtp:NP:6445::::::
uucp:NP:6445::::::
nuucp:NP:6445::::::
listen:*LK*:::::::
nobody:NP:6445::::::
noaccess:NP:6445::::::
nobody4:NP:6445::::::
terry:fC3/.rj29MBD:10071::::::
```

The preceding comments assume that the version of UNIX you are using has not been modified in a special way that prevents root from controlling the entire system. Some UNIX variants implement a security model based on *privileges* that can be used to more tightly constrain the root user's actions. UNIX derivatives that have the majority of the market share implement only *discretionary access control* (DAC) at best, and as a result, suffer from the *root problem*. If a person can gain root access to a system, that person then can do almost anything on the system. This problem will be analyzed in more detail when you learn about access control in Chapter 3, "The Role of Access Control in Your Environment."

## What Are the Subjects in UNIX?

Although users and groups are important entities in the UNIX security model, the main subject in the model is the *process*. A process is a program running within the context of the operating system. Every process is associated with a UID and one or more GIDs. Technically, several UIDs and GIDs for each process are available, but it is better to momentarily consider a simpler model in which a process is associated with a single UID and with one or more GIDs. Each process also is assigned an integer process ID or *PID* to uniquely differentiate it from other processes. When the login phase is complete for a user, the operating system constructs a process to *execute on behalf of* that user. This user process is *tagged* with the UID and GIDs assigned to that user in /etc/passwd and /etc/group.

If the I&A step succeeds, the operating system will know both your UID and GIDs. To create a process, the operating system initializes several data structures in the kernel and starts a program for the user who is requesting access. The program started after I&A is the *shell* defined for the user in /etc/passwd. From the shell a user can start other programs or exit the system. Notice that the operating system assigns the initial UID and GIDs, or the *credentials*, for the shell process.

The operating system also provides interfaces for changing the UID and primary GID of a process. Because the UID and GIDs are used in access control decisions made by the operating system, changing your UID or GID can give you additional (or fewer) privileges on the system. As such, the mechanisms for changing credentials in an operating system must be tightly controlled. Numerous attacks have been made on systems as a result of implementation problems in this area. Briefly, here is what happens.

By design, a program with special privileges can be executed by arbitrary users. The program needs special privileges because it must access some portion of the file system or a device that a normal user cannot. Due to a bug in its implementation, the privileged program can be diverted into doing something that it was not supposed to do. In many cases, the program is tricked into giving the normal user enough power to become the root user on the system. If such a flaw exists and if local users can take advantage of that flaw, you have a serious security problem. If a remote user can exploit this weakness *without a login account on your system*, such as by supplying data to a form on your Web server, you have a catastrophic problem!

## UNIX Login

UNIX processes are related hierarchically. As part of the initial boot sequence, the UNIX kernel starts the *init* process, which is the parent of all other processes on the system. To enable logins into the system, init will start a *getty* program for each terminal (TTY) attached to the system. The getty program performs several tasks unrelated to I&A (setting terminal line speed, for example) and then displays a login prompt. Both init and getty run with root privileges. In other words, they have a UID of 0.

When a person finishes typing in a username at the terminal login prompt and then presses the Enter or Return key, getty will overlay itself with the login program and pass to it the username just captured. The login program *inherits* root privileges because it is started as a child of getty. One of the defining characteristics of UNIX is this notion of *process inheritance*. When a parent process starts a child process, as a default behavior in UNIX, the child inherits many of the data structures being used by the parent, including the parent's security credentials.

Login next prompts the user to enter a password. Any keystrokes made by the user are not echoed to the screen to prevent *shoulder surfing*—an old hacker attack. If the password entered is correct, the login program then adds the following:

- A record into /etc/utmp that contains the list of currently logged-in users
- A record into /etc/wtmp that is used to keep track of login histories

At this point, login calls the operating system routines, which *change the credentials of a process*. Specifically, login asks the kernel to change its UID and GIDs to the corresponding values found in /etc/passwd and in /etc/group for the logged-in user. This change prevents the child process, which login is creating, from running with root privileges. After the credentials are changed, additional initialization tasks are performed by login, including setting up the user's environment variables, displaying the message of the day from /etc/motd, and switching into the user's home directory. On more secure systems, the user's last successful and unsuccessful login times are displayed. As a last step, the login program overlays itself with the *shell* program defined for the user in /etc/passwd. The user is now free to begin executing commands or other programs.

You can see that it is the login process which starts the first subject, your shell, executing on your behalf in the system. The security kernel uses the UID and GIDs associated with this shell, and with programs started out of this shell, to make access control decisions. Interestingly, several access control decisions were made during the login procedure already, such as when the login program accessed the files /etc/passwd, /etc/group, and the shadow password file to compare password values.

## UNIX Password Mechanism

To recap, the username is the basis of identification, and the password provides authentication. How the initial password is assigned to a user varies between UNIX implementations. The recommended strategy is for the security administrator to pick an initial password for the user or to have the operating system generate one. The user is notified of this value *out of band*, such as verbally or via a courier service. The password can be set to expire after initial use, thus forcing the user to choose a new password after the first login procedure is completed.

The user's password must be validated each time a user performs a login. Early operating systems stored the username and password literally in a text file or database. During the login process, normal string comparisons were performed between the value entered by the user and the stored password. The obvious threat to this approach is that if the password file is read by an unauthorized user, that person will be able to login in as and impersonate any other user.

The login procedure described here is an example of *two-party authentication*. The user and the computer (or operating system) are the two parties involved in the authentication. This procedure is also an example of *unilateral* or *one-way authentication*. The user authenticates to the computer, but the computer is not required to authenticate to the user. In order for one-way authentication to succeed, both parties must share a *secret*.

You might think that the shared secret is the user's password, but in fact, the shared secret is a value *derived from* the password. UNIX operating systems, as well as other operating systems, do not store the password itself in an encrypted form. The rationale for adopting this approach lies in export restrictions imposed by the U.S. government. The U.S. government, influenced by concerns for national security, did not allow export of both encryption and decryption software (or hardware). The rather lengthy *International Trade in Arms Restrictions* (ITAR) is a federal document describing in detail what one can or cannot export with respect to cryptography.

To comply with the ITAR, UNIX computes a *cryptographic hash* based on the user's password and stores the hashed value in /etc/passwd or in the shadow password file. In other words, when you choose a new password, the operating system uses your password as the *key* for a cryptographic computation.

A hash is a *one-way function* that takes an input value and produces an output value. A one-way function has the property that it is computationally infeasible to compute the input value given the output value. That is, you cannot compute the hash in the reverse to find the corresponding input value given the output value. To be cryptographically secure, a hash must meet the following requirements:

◆ Given only the output value, it is computationally infeasible to determine the input value.

◆ It is practically impossible to find two input values that will hash to the same output value, even if one input value and the hash are already known.

UNIX relies on a cryptographic algorithm based on the *Data Encryption Standard* (DES) to encrypt a *plaintext* string of 0s into a *ciphertext* string by using your password as the *key*. The resulting ciphertext value is stored along with your username in /etc/passwd or in a shadow password file. During login, the system takes the password you entered and computes the hash again, comparing the result to the hash value stored with your username. The login program does not decrypt the entry in /etc/passwd and compare it to the value you entered.

DES was designed to encrypt 64-bit blocks of text using a 56-bit key. UNIX converts your password into a 56-bit key by taking the 7-bit ASCII value for each of the first 8 characters of the password and adding some parity checking. *This means that if your password is longer than 8 characters, the additional characters do not improve security unless the underlying authentication routines have been changed.* The algorithm used by most UNIX systems relies on a modified version of DES, which is an effort to deter attackers who have access to hardware capable of computing DES quickly. To accomplish this, UNIX adds a *salt* to the procedure to further perturb the encryption steps.

The salt is a 12-bit random number chosen by the operating system. When the encryption algorithm is run, the bits of the salt are consulted to determine how some of the steps in DES should be altered. If a user happens to rely on the same password on different systems, a different salt will result in unique hashed values on the two systems. Similarly, if two users unknowingly choose the identical password on the *same* system, the cryptographic hash will be different. The salt is stored as the first two characters of the hashed password value in the shadow password file. Adding the salt means that a single cryptographic hash output value computed by an adversary cannot be compared to more than one entry in the password repository. Instead, the computed hash is potentially a match only for a single entry. This defense translates into an increase in the number of computations a hacker must perform when trying to crack passwords. More details of the UNIX cryptographic hash can be found in several references (Kaufman, Perlman, and Speciner, 1995; Garfinkel and Spafford, 1996).

The security of the UNIX password mechanism depends on several defenses. First, the password file is protected by the operating system using access control. Only limited privileged users can read the file. Next, the cryptographic technique used by UNIX to compute the hashed value is computationally infeasible to break. That is, based on public knowledge of the algorithm, you cannot decrypt the ciphertext value without the key or find the key given the ciphertext, even if the adversary has unlimited computing time.

Often, the phrase "unlimited computing time" is interpreted as "equal to the known life of the universe." The source code for the password cryptography used by UNIX is readily available, and to date no accounts have been published of breaking the algorithm. Other threats and weaknesses exist, though, and these are discussed later in this chapter. For the moment, consider the next logical step. What happens if you have several users and several computers in a network?

## Storing Passwords in a Central Server

Now that you understand the basic login procedure for UNIX, consider what happens if you have several computers in a network. If every user needs an account on each system, the network administrator will have a difficult time managing all of the accounts. Individual users will either need to keep their passwords synchronized across systems or use different passwords on each system. As the size of the network grows, these problems become increasingly complex. The solution is to provide an authentication server that contains all of the user, password, and group information in a database. Note that at this point all that is being suggested is a central store for the I&A information.

### NIS and NIS+

Sun introduced the *Network Information System* (NIS) to act as a repository for I&A information and network configuration data to facilitate computing in a networked environment (Stern, 1991). NIS is configured on a chosen server to process information requests from clients. The NIS authentication database can be populated by importing the contents of /etc/passwd and other system files. Other NIS databases can be similarly initialized from standard system files.

By default, most UNIX operating system routines that handle I&A are modified to automatically work with NIS. Sun has licensed the implementation of NIS to other vendors for this purpose. That is, almost every major UNIX port includes NIS capabilities as part of the standard product. A configuration file can be modified to specify whether the local /etc/passwd file is to be searched before the NIS master database or vice versa. Notice that a user's UID and GIDs will be established based upon this search order. If a username is found in both the local /etc/passwd file and in the NIS database, the first entry found will determine which UID is used to create the shell process. For performance and redundancy, NIS supports a primary or *master* server and one or more *slave* servers. Programs are provided for synchronizing slave databases from the master copies.

A simplified example will clarify the interactions during login. Assume that a network administrator has initialized an NIS server. A user now sits in front of a computer on the network. The computer could be the same as the NIS server, but assume that the computer is a completely different client system instead. The user enters a username and password in response to the login prompts as before. The client system controls these login prompts, not the NIS server. After the client's login program has accepted the password, it computes the cryptographic hash as before, but instead of searching the local /etc/passwd file, the client sends a request to the NIS server for password verification. The password itself is never sent across the network, only the hashed value is included in the client's request. The NIS server performs a lookup to verify whether the hashed value matches the corresponding value stored with the username in its database. The NIS server does not need to compute the password hash separately.

The original implementation of NIS has been criticized for several reasons. The password database was readable by anyone in the network. The *ypcat* command was available to dump the usernames and passwords for anyone interested. Access to the hash password values opens the system to attacks described later in this chapter, such as password guessing attacks. To circumvent this problem, Sun launched NIS+ so that passwords were kept in a shadow database, and only designated users would be allowed to access the information directly.

NIS+ also provides for encrypted network traffic between the clients and the NIS server. Even with shadowed passwords, an attacker could watch network traffic and try to capture NIS client-server exchanges. Because the hashed password is sent from the client to the server, over time the attacker would be able to obtain the equivalent of dumping the contents of the password database. If the traffic is encrypted, monitoring will succeed only if the cryptographic scheme can be cracked.

Cryptography is also necessary for secure NIS in order for both the client and the server to establish their identities. Otherwise, a hacker may be able to impersonate either the client or the server and cause problems in the network. You'll learn more about this type of network authentication in Chapter 4, "Traditional

Network Security Approaches." Descriptions of these procedures are not detailed here because one need not purchase any additional software to take advantage of these enhancements; they are part of most standard UNIX distributions. For more details on NIS, consult Stern, 1991. NIS+ is covered in depth in Ramsey, 1994. One final shortcoming of NIS is that it relies on a network protocol that is not usually permitted through firewalls—UDP. Still, in private networks, NIS can be depended on for simplified account administration as the size of the network grows.

The important points to remember from this discussion are as follow:

◆ An authentication server can be used for storing usernames and passwords.
◆ The introduction of an authentication server into a network results in client-server, or peer-to-peer, interactions across the network.
◆ If you have client-server communications, authentication must be expanded to reliably verify the identities of clients and servers; otherwise someone may be able to impersonate one of these entities and spoof the I&A subsystem.

## Identification and Authentication in NT

Microsoft NT is based upon the Mach operating system, which also has its foundations in UNIX. Like the UNIX operating system, NT has entities such as users and groups. Although the internals of NT are not as widely published as those of UNIX, several attacks have been made against the I&A mechanisms of NT. Many books describing NT security contain strong statements praising the integrity of the cryptographic techniques used to hide password values. However, several NT password crackers have been created (L0pht, 1997; Anonymous, 1997).

NT authentication is first addressed from the simple perspective of a user sitting down in front of a single system. When login is understood from this elementary view, a broader authentication approach is considered. The architecture of NT also supports authentication from a central server or *domain controller*. In other words, passwords and usernames are not necessarily stored on the NT workstation or server that a user is attempting to access.

### Users and Groups in NT

NT stores user and group information in the NT Registry, which is a general-purpose repository for important system information. Sun put only a limited set

of information in NIS databases, but the NT Registry includes nearly all important data for the system. The security access controls on information in the Registry
have been widely debated on Internet news groups, and indeed several flaws
and recommend improvements can be found in the NTsec mailing archives and
on Microsoft's Web site (www.microsoft.com/security). The physical file corresponding to the registry key for the user and group database is currently found
in the %SystemRoot%\winnt\system32\config directory in the file named SAM
(*Security Account Manager*).

Each user in NT is identified by a username and authenticated with a password.
The password is hashed using MD4, and the resulting value is stored in the registry. Passwords can be up to 128 characters long. Some interesting subtleties
exist regarding different types of groups when a domain controller is used.
However, the specifics of NT group administration are not particularly relevant
for this discussion.

## Subjects in NT

As in the UNIX environment, the string name associated with a user is not the
basis for making access control decisions. The NT equivalent of the user's UID
is the *security identifier* (SID). Each group also is assigned a SID. When the user
or group is added to the system, NT generates a SID using the computer's name
(chosen at installation time), the current system time, and the cumulative time
spent by the current thread being used to compute the SID. Technically, it is the
thread's user-mode time, rather than kernel-mode time, that is consulted. In principle, this combination ensures that the SID is unique within a given network.

```
S-1-5-21-975380050-2111395089-755307947-1000
```

An example SID is shown here. Don't worry about all of the fields and their
meanings. Think of a SID as a unique number used to identify an individual user
or group.

## NT Login Security

The NT login procedure is controlled by several cooperating components.
*Winlogon* is a process that displays the initial login window and acquires the
username and password. The SAM is a set of routines responsible for managing
the database of user accounts and for validating user information against its database. The *Local Security Authority* (LSA) performs the actual user authentication
process. Other security tasks are performed by the LSA, such as auditing, but
these tasks are not relevant to I&A.

After you enter your username and password, Winlogon passes this information to the LSA, which in turn invokes an authentication routine (called MVS1_0). The SAM database routines are consulted by these authentication threads to determine whether the user exists, and if so, whether the hashed password value matches. If authentication is successful, the LSA constructs your credentials by composing a data structure consisting of your SID and the SIDs of all groups to which you belong.

The LSA then creates a desktop process with these credentials, performs some further initialization such as executing your custom profile, and then returns to a waiting state in anticipation of the next login request. You will now have a graphical desktop from which to interact with the system. Any access requests made by you will be analyzed by the reference monitor based on the SIDs attached to the desktop process. Similarly, any new processes started from the desktop will inherit the credentials assigned to you at login completion.

To be more accurate, the LSA assigns an access token to you at login time. The access token contains the following fields:

♦ Your user SID

♦ Your group SIDs

♦ A list of privileges that determine what you can do on the system

♦ A default owner SID to be assigned when you create objects on the system

♦ A default DAC list to be assigned for protecting objects you create

The access token is consulted when you try to access objects because it contains your user SID and your group SIDs.

## NT Authentication Using a Domain Controller

Now that basic steps are understood, consider a configuration in which user information is stored in an authentication server rather than on the login system. As in the case of NIS in the UNIX environment, this setup introduces a client-server interaction between the login workstation and the NT authentication server that is also called the *domain controller*.

The NT login panel enables you to choose whether you want to login using a particular domain controller or the local workstation. The distinction is that when logging in locally, your user information is verified against the local SAM database. If a domain name is entered in the login dialog box, I&A information is tested against the domain controller's database. If a domain login is chosen, you still must enter your name and password. As in the local login example given previously, the password is hashed using MD4. The difference occurs in the protocol between the login node and the domain controller.

When the LSA determines that domain login is in process, the LSA communicates this to the authentication module (MVS 1_0). Instead of calling the local SAM routines as before, the authentication threads invoke the Netlogon service to contact the domain controller with an initialization message. The domain controller responds with a random value or *nonce* to be issued as a challenge to the login node. The NT login node encrypts the nonce with the hashed key derived from the user's password. This encrypted value then is sent to the domain controller. Because the domain controller also has access to the hashed user password in its SAM database, the controller computes the same encryption. The two results are compared and login succeeds if there is a match. See Figure 2.3 for example NT logins.

Some additional variations require that administrators establish trust relationships between domain controllers. If a user chooses, a specific domain controller can be entered on the login dialog screen. In the case in which the login node relies on domain controller A for authentication, but the user has requested a different but trusted domain controller B, a protocol is defined for allowing the two domain controllers to work together to authenticate the user. The specifics of trust relationships are interesting but not particularly relevant for showing how one might improve the security of I&A in an NT environment. Instead, it is time to consider problems associated with depending on passwords for authenticating users.

For more details on NT login security, you might want to read Sheldon (1997) or Okuntseff (1997). The Microsoft Web site also contains security white papers that provide an overview of NT's features.

You should know that Microsoft plans to modify a number of security relevant NT features in NT V5.0. User accounts will be stored in a directory service rather than in the registry and support for Kerberos Version 5 authentication (see section later in this chapter) will play a major role.

## How Hackers Exploit Weaknesses in Password Security

With an out-of-box operating system, the same *reusable password* is entered by the user each time a login is performed. The biggest problem with reusable passwords is that they are susceptible to a variety of attacks that have a single goal: to uncover the user's password. In the preceding chapter, this kind of security boundary was cited as a source of concerns. The login boundary is affected by three factors: the strength of the data provided by the user, the integrity of the data

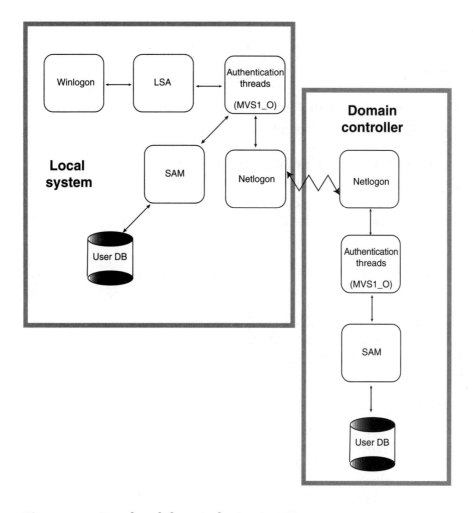

**Figure 2.3**    Local and domain logins in NT.

transmitted at the boundary, and safe communications at the boundary. A weak password is an example of the first factor. If the password is transmitted across a network, an adversary might be able to intercept and modify the value, validating the second type of concern. Finally, if the login programs are tampered with, and the boundary between the user and the computer becomes untrustworthy, the third factor is attacked. These three factors are targeted to varying degrees by the attacks described next.

## Easily Guessed Passwords

The first weakness lies in the composition of the password itself. Passwords to avoid include the following:

- Common names, especially relatives, coworkers, or dignitaries
- Jargon words often found in a specialty area, such as the name of a football play
- Simple strings, such as those composed of all the same character
- Words found in dictionaries
- Important numbers, such as your social security number, driver's license, birthdays, or vehicle tags

When choosing a password, pick one that is hard to guess and also easy to remember. Often, these two goals are contradictory. However, if you pick pronounceable strings mixed with numbers or special characters, you will be making the task of the attacker more difficult. Increasing the size of the space someone must search through to guess a password is your goal. Longer passwords are better because there are more combinations of letters to consider. Klein (1990) provides an interesting set of metrics on how easy passwords are to guess.

## Brute Force Attacks

The most basic attack that can take several forms is *brute force*. First, the hacker can sit down at the terminal and perform an *online attack*. The adversary enters your username and tries to manually guess your password. Given unlimited opportunities, an adversary may be able to guess the password. Login guessing attacks are thwarted by configuring the operating system to limit the number of failed login attempts allowed for each user. After a threshold is reached, the account will be locked and that user will be unable to log in until the system administrator intervenes by resetting the password or unlocking the account in some other way.

Unfortunately, this defense policy allows for a *denial of service* attack. A malicious person could cycle through each user account on the system, exceed the failed login threshold, and lock out all of the accounts. The policy should be configured so that the root user, or another privileged user, is always able to access the system from a designated, physically secure console in order to correct the situation. To generalize, any authentication system should be resistant to denial of service attacks that lock out the system administrator. On computers with an external media device, such as a tape or a CD-ROM drive, the administrator can always boot the system from backup media, enter a limited computing environment known as single-user mode in UNIX, and take corrective actions. One can further deter manual guessing by injecting some randomness into the login procedure. For example, if an incorrect password is entered, the system can delay for a time interval before presenting the next login prompt. The time interval can be computed as an increasing function of the number of failed logins from that terminal device or might be configured as a constant value such as always delaying for two minutes after three failed login attempts for a single user. If increasing interval delays are used, another configuration value is needed to determine when to reset the interval to its initial state. A variation on the interval delay is to change the input time between keystrokes used to read the password.

Another defense involves locking the terminal itself after a configured number of failed login attempts. As in the preceding case, the terminal can be reset only by an authorized administrator. Some operating systems also provide an option for configuring which terminal devices individual users are able to use for login. A failed login attempt at an unauthorized terminal is usually not counted against the failed login threshold. With today's ubiquitous networked computer environments, some operating systems extend the notion of "authorized terminal" to include a range of valid network addresses.

Notice that these attempts to defend against manual guessing attacks are used only to *deter* the hacker. Failed login thresholds, delay intervals, and other defenses will not *prevent* a brute force attack from occurring. However, they will discourage someone from instigating a brute force attack and increase the difficulty of successfully executing an attack. Preventing a brute force attack from happening is nearly impossible. It is highly probable, though, that one can prevent manual guessing attacks from succeeding.

To increase the sophistication of the online brute force attack, the hacker can write a program to carry out the manual guessing steps. A dictionary of passwords is compiled and perhaps even customized for the penetration attempt. The program consults the dictionary when attempting to crack an account. Heuristics can be used so that the program adapts to the targeted host. For example, guessing that the password is the same as the username is a plausible first attempt. The Internet Worm was able to crack a number of accounts throughout the Internet using the following heuristics for passwords (Ferbrache and Shearer, 1993):

- No password
- The username or the username concatenated with itself
- Variations on the user's first name or last name—uppercase, lowercase

- ◆ The username typed in backwards
- ◆ A dictionary of 432 words chosen by the worm's author
- ◆ The online UNIX dictionary if available

You might think that a programmed attack like this works only if the attacker is trying to login via a network using one of the many built-in ways in which operating systems provide for network logins. However, it is just as easy to detach a terminal from its cable and directly attach the cable into the back of a personal computer programmed to emulate a terminal. From this configuration, the hacker can run an automated attack that appears like a user attempting to physically login.

A more dangerous brute force occurs when the attacker is able to gain a copy of the stored password values. With this additional knowledge, an *offline* attack is possible. Two approaches are possible. In the first, the attack is still centered on repeatedly trying to guess the password on a victim machine. Your system will be unaware of any attempts by the user to guess passwords because all efforts are made on another system. If a UNIX password file is obtained, the attacker could use any number of collaborators to achieve offline guessing in parallel. Portions of the password could even be divided among the cohorts. Victim machines are configured by attackers so that the defense mechanisms, such as failed login thresholds, are disabled.

A second offline attack depends on a matching strategy. Instead of guessing passwords, the attacker computes a number of hashed password values in advance. The attack succeeds when a user's hashed password value matches one of the precalculated hash values. Tools to facilitate this approach are readily available for both UNIX and NT. *Crack*, developed by Alec Muffett, is widely relied upon by professional penetration testing teams to probe the suitability of user passwords on UNIX systems. Crack has been very successful at breaking many passwords. The arrival of L0phtCrack from Mudge (www.l0pht.com) showed that NT also was subject to the same kind of offline brute force attack. You might find it interesting that the infamous Internet Worm (which does not seem so infamous given the sensitivity of sites recently broken into) traveled with a mini-dicitionary and password cracker.

You must assume that an attacker has more time to devote to hashing potential passwords than you have for managing your systems. Thus, this attack is particularly threatening if your users are choosing passwords from a small search space, such as passwords of only three alphabetic characters. Various statements about the difficulty of breaking the UNIX password hash have circulated in the community for years. Often one will encounter a statement describing the probability that a password can be cracked to be nearly impossible. Such statements are made from a theoretical basis and cite the length of the password, usually in bits, and how hard it would be to exhaustively search the entire space of these bit strings. Indeed, the usual phrase is that an exceedingly powerful computer running for the known life of the universe would not be able to complete the search. What these statements do not consider are the *practical* aspects of password guessing.

Users repeatedly choose weak or easily guessed passwords. *Hackers and password crackers use this information to narrow the search space and substantially reduce the complexity of the problem.* Although in theory, guessing an 8-character password from the universe of 8-character passwords is impossible, in practice hackers are quite successful at it!

A good defense against offline brute-force guessing is to use stronger passwords. You also need to protect the password repository, whether it is a file on a local computer or database on a central server. If the computing environment in which you are working will support encryption of the password file or database, you should take advantage of this feature, too. If the password file is stolen, mounting offline attacks against an encrypted file will be much more difficult.

If a user is required to remember different passwords for several systems, chances are that the passwords will be written down. Hackers who physically reconnoiter a site have favorite places they inspect for written passwords such as under the keyboard, on a nearby filing cabinet, or on the back of the monitor. Needless to say, passwords that are written down are fairly easy to crack.

It is interesting that despite the many additional defense mechanisms in operating systems to deter brute-force attacks, many computers today are cracked because of weaknesses in the password itself. Ignoring pleas from security experts, countless books, and trade magazines, users still continue to choose passwords that are easily guessed.

## Social Engineering

Not all password threats are based on guessing or cryptographic techniques. Many hackers report that the easiest way to break into a system is *social engineering* (Littman, 1997; Knightmare, 1994). You would be amazed at how freely information is given over the phone without proper authentication between the parties. The lore of hackers is filled with tales of gullible users being conned into giving away their passwords, the passwords of their superiors, or other information that can be used to penetrate a network.

Sometimes, the social engineering attack requires physical surveillance of the work site. To accomplish this surveillance, an opponent impersonates someone from a maintenance company, courier service, or even a pizza delivery person to gain access to the site. Once inside, personal information about the target person can be gleaned from pictures on the desk, by sifting through the trash, or by listening to careless office gossip. Some even go so far as to dig through trash containers on the company's premises. Security guards who stumble upon these sifters are easily repelled when the hacker explains the activity as collecting aluminum cans, searching for a lost article such as a watch, or desperately trying to retrieve a lost report. Stories have been told of security guards helping a hacker find useful information in these situations (Knightmare, 1994).

The shoulder surfing technique identified earlier is also a favorite technique. Try watching a friend type in a password. You will be surprised how easy it is to pick up at least a few characters. Remember, any information is useful. Knowing the password length and a few of its characters also can help reduce the search space. If the password is particularly difficult to type, or if the user is unaccustomed to keying in the password, shoulder surfing is made easier by the slow keystroke pace. Social engineering tricks also include distracting a user while the password is being entered. Verbal information processing can reduce the keystroke rate of a user. In other words, if the attacker is chatting in your ear about last night's football game, the time it takes you to enter your password will be increased.

When sufficient background material is obtained, the fun begins. The biggest problem the hacker faces is deciding which approach to use for social engineering. A particularly successful approach is for the attacker to call the target user and impersonate a superior. If the perpetrator can act convincingly, the hapless employee probably will respond automatically to any request. An alternative is to call a powerful network or system administrator over a period of time and build rapport by appealing to this person's ego. For example, hackers have reported calling site experts with faked problems only to gradually develop a "friendship" with the unsuspecting soul on the other end. Enough trust has been built up to trick the victim into divulging information useful for penetrating systems, even if passwords were not obtained. At one recent hacker conference, a successful social engineering attack was carried out via telephone as part of a keynote address. In order to avoid breaking any serious laws, the speaker disconnected the victim only seconds before some useful secrets were disclosed.

The purpose of a social engineering attack may be to simply gain additional information that makes password guessing easier. Almost any information is useful to an attacker. Names of children, favorite hobbies, project names, birthdays, and other personal data can help narrow the search space for a brute-force password attack. A popular but predictable technique that some people use to "improve" the strength of passwords is to replace some characters with numerals. For example, the password "cocoon" would instead be "c0c00n". With respect to computer search speeds, this additional twist does not add significantly to the password combinations the cracker must test. Notice that the only defense, if you rely on reusable passwords, is to educate site users. Periodic reviews and trials can ensure that employees are complying.

## Trojan Horses

Every computer science major has learned how to leave a login Trojan Horse on a system. Before logging off the system, the perpetrator starts a problem that displays a login prompt and waits for a victim. The username and password entered into the Trojan Horse are logged to a file or mailed to a collecting account. Usually, the Trojan Horse fakes some type of problem and exits. The operating system then takes control and displays the true login prompt. Most users would assume that they had entered a password incorrectly or that some other glitch occurred in the system. Not surprisingly, this attack can be very fruitful.

The temporary Trojan Horse login succeeds because of a flaw in the login authentication protocol described so far. The user is required to authenticate to the computer, but the login program is assumed to be legitimate. To circumvent this problem, secure operating systems provide a *secure attention key* (SAK) sequence. The NT operating system instructs the user to enter Ctrl-Alt-Del to initiate a *trusted path* with the operating system. Most UNIX systems also provide a SAK. When this special key sequence is pressed, the user is assured that a clean environment is made available for login. For example, the system will detach any processes that are attached to or running on that terminal. What happens to these processes depends on the operating system implementation. The net result is that there will not be a chance for the previous user's processes to act as a login impostor.

A more serious threat is replacement of the login program in the system itself. This attack depends on circumventing the system's access control mechanisms because login and other I&A routines are part of the TCB. A hacker who manages to install a permanent login Trojan Horse can gain multiple username and password pairs. It is unlikely that only the login program was replaced. Trojan Horse versions of other security enforcing programs are certain to be found as well.

## Network Sniffing

Many network protocols were designed with the assumption that users could be trusted or that the network was trustworthy. Precautions in protocol design were not always taken for defending against network eavesdropping. Network traffic monitoring is the electronic equivalent of shoulder surfing. A *network sniffer* is a program, or dedicated device, capable of capturing all traffic made available to one or more network adapters. Any data sent in the clear across the network is captured and inspected for usefulness. Countless network sniffers are running throughout the Internet today.

Network sniffers are freely available in the public domain (see Anonymous, 1997 for a comprehensive list) or can be purchased as part of products such as RealSecure from Internet Security Systems. A user who has access to a personal computer connected to a network can easily install a sniffer program. Most sniffers are sophisticated enough to selectively find passwords used for network logins. The attacker does not need to monitor *every* packet traversing the network. Assuming that the communicating systems rely upon reusable passwords for authentication, the person sniffing network traffic can effortlessly gather passwords to be used for later attacks. No evidence of this activity will be found on the attack targets, as was the case for online brute-force attacks.

Network sniffing is not limited to watching for passwords used during the authentication phase of a network login session. Because e-mail and other document delivery systems might contain lists of passwords, it is worth the effort to capture and scan these data forms as well. Remember that a new user must acquire the initial password from the security officer in an out-of-band manner. Often, the method chosen is e-mail, especially inside of private corporate networks. Employees are often required to sign agreements declaring that they will not engage in network sniffing or scanning. Because many computer crimes include an insider, the threat of legal consequences does not always outweigh the opportunity for financial reward.

Many private corporate networks also are accessed by contract vendors, who in turn may not adhere to the same restrictions. A successful social engineering attack could land a planted a network sniffer on your network. The sniffer could periodically send passwords via e-mail to an external system. *For these reasons, you should assume that passwords which are sent across a network in cleartext form have been compromised.*

## Electromagnetic Emissions Monitoring

Electromagnetic emissions also have been exploited as a means for sniffing passwords, albeit in a different wave spectrum than network traffic. Despite efforts by various standards agencies to limit emissions from monitors and even storage devices, surveillance of these data sources is a very serious threat. The U.S. TEMPEST standard is one guideline that manufactures must follow to reduce electromagnetic emissions in an effort to eliminate this attack. The general idea behind TEMPEST is to shield devices from emitting a strong signal. In some cases, an individual room or an entire building is built to the TEMPEST standard.

## Software Bugs

Sometimes, the operating system does all the hard work for the hacker. Software bugs continue to be a major source of security problems. For example, a recent bug in the Solaris operating system made the hashed password values available to anyone on the system. One of the network application programs could be forced to end abnormally, and as a consequence, that program would dump its memory contents to disk in a *core* file (to aid in debugging the crash). Users with no special privileges could force the program to do this. The core file contained copies of the hashed password values that normally were stored in a shadowed file. The information could be used as input to *Crack* for an offline brute-force attack.

### Ideas for Improving Reusable Passwords

If you are constrained to relying on reusable passwords for I&A at your site, consider these ideas. Good security practices dictate that each password be subject to an aging rule, such as expiring the password when it becomes 180 days old or after it has been used 265 times. Similar rules should be followed for password composition, requiring that passwords include uppercase, lowercase, numeric, and even some special characters. Another composition recommendation is to limit the number of repeated characters in a password, whether serially repeated or not. To ensure that an attacker must search a large number of alternatives, the password should be the maximum length permitted on the system. Unfortunately, most UNIX systems only support 8-character passwords.

Another password rule is to limit similarities between the user's previous password and the newly chosen one. You could require that at least six of the characters in the password be different from those used in the previous password. Controlling password history is also a good idea. Some operating systems allow the administrator to configure how many password changes a user must endure before the same password can be reused. To prevent the user from choosing a temporary new password several times until the threshold is reached, a configuration value also is provided for a minimum password age. The user cannot change the password until the minimum age has expired.

The system also can generate passwords for users. Two problems are encountered with this approach. If the password is difficult to guess, the tradeoff is that you will find users writing down the complex strings. On the other hand, if the password generator creates pronounceable strings that fit a particular grammar, an attacker can use this information to narrow the search space. A hacker also can proactively check for passwords as they are chosen by users. Ideas for proactive password checkers can be found in the literature (Stallings, 1995; Bishop, 1993). Logical choices include modifying the change-password routines to invoke programs that compare the user's choice with dictionary entries.

One additional idea is to require each user to enter more than one password value. That is, authentication would be based on something you know *and* something you know. Although this method is stronger than a single reusable password, it still suffers from the problems already described. In terms of algorithm complexity, guessing twice as many passwords is negligibly harder for a password cracker.

As you probably have guessed, significantly improving the security of I&A at your site means foregoing reusable passwords. For example, instead of requiring a user to know two passwords for authentication, it would be better to base authenticate on two values selected separately from something you know, something you have, and something you are. Perhaps, you have seen movies in which an employee first inserts a badge into a reader and then also keys an access code into a keypad. Here, authentication is based on something the user has *and* on something the user knows. Either single authentication item alone is insufficient for gaining access to the target environment.

You will learn about mechanisms that avoid reusable passwords or require multiple authentication values in a few moments. Before doing so, let's pick up the earlier discussion path and expand your knowledge of authentication servers. Because many improvements to I&A require authentication servers, knowing how a server such as Kerberos works will help you evaluate alternatives. Before reading about Kerberos, you might want to glance through the sidebar, "A Cryptography Primer," if you are a novice to cryptography. More thorough treatments of cryptography can be found in Schneier (1996), Denning (1983), and Koblitz (1994).

## Improving upon I&A with Authentication Servers

In this section, you learn how authentication servers can be used to solve I&A problems in distributed systems. Specifically, third-party authentication based on Kerberos and X.509 certificates is described.

### Third-Party Authentication

The goal of a third-party authentication system is to provide secure communications between previously unknown entities. When MIT started the Athena project to deploy a number of distributed systems across a large network, they immediately realized that I&A was the initial weakest link in security. To solve their problems, researchers developed the Kerberos authentication system. Now widely deployed at various sites, Kerberos provides a third-party authentication server across heterogeneous operating systems.

## A Cryptography Primer

Because cryptographic concepts are used throughout the remaining sections of this chapter, a few definitions will be helpful. Cryptography can be used to provide confidentiality, integrity, authenticity, and nonrepudiation. To begin with, cryptography relies on encryption to provide confidentiality of data. A secret key is used to encrypt the data according to some algorithm. The concerned party assumes that the details of the cryptographic algorithm are publicly known. Therefore, confidentiality is maintained only if the secret is not divulged or discovered and if the algorithm is sufficiently strong to resist attacks. More specifically, the algorithm must be such that decryption without the secret key is computationally infeasbile and that discovery of the key is equally difficult even if the attacker is given significant amounts of cleartext and ciphertext.

A distinction is made between *symmetric* cryptography and *asymmetric* cryptography. The same secret key is used for both encryption and decryption in symmetric cryptography. Different keys are used for encryption and decryption in asymmetric cryptography. Thus, symmetric cryptography requires that the communicating parties share a secret key; whereas asymmetric cryptography requires at least one key pair for successful communication.

Many popular symmetric encryption algorithms are used, although DES is the most widely known and deployed. RSA public-key cryptography based on work done by Rivest, Shamir, and Adleman (1977) is the famous example of asymmetric cryptography. A recurring and difficult problem in cryptography is distribution of the initial shared secret. With symmetric cryptography, the complexity of the problem increases as the number of communicating parties grows. Public-key cryptography partially eliminates this problem because the keys used in the key pair have interesting mathematical properities. One member of the key pair, the *public key*, can be broadcast to a broad audience in any desired fashion. The other half of the pair, the *private key*, is kept secret by its owner. The keys are mathematically related so that if one key is used for encryption, the corresponding key can be used for decryption using the RSA algorithms. Also, it is computationally infeasbile to derive one key given the other.

To communicate with a stranger in a secure fashion, you would first obtain this person's public key, encrypt the message, and forward the message using any preferred means including unsecure networks. The recipient decrypts the message using the private key. A message sent from the stranger is encrypted with your public key and decrypted by you with your private key when it arrives.

Because no key pairs are alike, you can first encrypt a message with your private key and then encrypt the result with the sender's public key. The doubly encrypted message after being delivered to the addressee is first decrypted with the private key of the recipient and then decrypted with your public key. In addition to other benefits, this protocol can be used to assert that no one other than you could have possibly sent the original message (nonrepudiation). Cryptography also is used to provide *digital signatures* using this technique. That is, if you sign a message using your private key and a cryptographic hash function, or if you encrypt a message with your private key, you cannot later disclaim the results.

Because public-key algorithms are not as fast as symmetric algorithms, both approaches are often employed in communications protocols. Public-key techniques are used to deliver a limited secret key that is then used for the communication session. Depending on the amount of secrecy required, you can even change the key on each message exchange to obtain one-time password support.

An interesting post to the Internet suggests that the U.S. and U.K. governments were working on public-key techniques in 1970 and possibly earlier (www.cesg.gov.uk/ellisint.htm).

Another third-party system described in this section is based on X.509 digital certificates. One of the drawbacks of Kerberos is that to date it has relied on secret-key technology, or symmetric cryptography, for I&A between entities. Lately, though, extensions have been proposed to Kerberos to support X.509 certificates. The X.509 standard is part of a large body of standards developed by the *International Standards Organization* (ISO) aimed at solving distributed computing problems. X.509 certificates are based on public key, or asymmetric cryptography, which overcomes some of the critiques of Kerberos mentioned in the following section.

## Kerberos

Kerberos is a centralized server for authenticating entities and for enabling secure communications between entities in the network. To accomplish this, Kerberos provides an *Key Distribution Center* (KDC) that fulfills two roles. First, the KDC contains hashed password values that are used to authenticate users during login. Next, the KDC also distributes a shared secret to communicating parties when a secure session is needed. The secret is used for encryption or message integrity computations when the parties exchange messages. The Kerberos server is assumed to be running on a physically secure server in the network. To prevent password cracking attempts, information stored in the server's database is encrypted using a secret chosen at installation time. Remember that this type of encryption was one of the recommendations for improving the security of reusable passwords.

Kerberos relies on reusable passwords to initially authenticate entities such as users in the network. When a user completes the login process, though, the password is no longer needed. Instead, the KDC generates a unique *session key* that is the shared secret between communicating entities. A given session key might encrypt several different messages between the two ends of the communication channel. However, when the last message is sent, and the session is terminated, the session key can be discarded. This process is more secure than relying on the same secret for each communication session between two endpoints. Also, the Kerberos server "forgets" any session keys it has generated for other entities to use.

Unlike NIS, which is really just a different data store for the same information found in /etc/passwd or /etc/group, Kerberos is an alternative I&A repository that *introduces its own notions of subjects and objects*. The authoritative scope of a Kerberos authentication server is called its *realm*. The subject in Kerberos is called a *principal*. More than one *instance* of a given principal can exist, so the pair {principal, instance} uniquely defines a subject in a Kerberos realm. Principals are identified using a string name, just like the username in UNIX or NT. The KDC server shares a master key secret with each principal in the realm. For simplicity and without loss of generality, the remaining discussions assume that a single instance of each principal is in the realm. By introducing its own notions of subjects and objects, Kerberos is adding a new security model to your site. For this reason, you will want to critically examine how Kerberos works and how it is integrated into your site.

The KDC is further divided into an *Authentication Server* (AS) and a *Ticket Granting Server* (TGS). The responsibility of the AS is to authenticate the identity of entities in the network. Secure dialogues in a network are accomplished when the communicating parties share at least one secret that can be used to encrypt and decrypt the information they exchange. The Kerberos TGS is responsible for generating a unique session key to be shared between two parties. The parties then use this session key to encrypt their messages or to guarantee the integrity of messages sent. Both the TGS and the AS are combined into a single server in Kerberos. The distinction between the AS and the TGS is conceptual and based on the role being played by the Kerberos KDC server at any given time.

Therefore, the term KDC sometimes will be used to jointly refer to both the AS and the TGS.

### Third-Party Authentication Steps

Consider the high-level steps and requirements for authenticated and secure communications between two entities using Kerberos. Assume that $X$ wants to communicate with $Y$ in a network. $X$ and $Y$ could be users, software processes, or workstations. $X$ contacts the KDC with a request for a secure session with $Y$. Because the KDC knows the secrets for both $X$ and $Y$, and neither $X$ nor $Y$ knows the other's secret, the KDC can rely on cryptography to fulfill the request.

1. A random session key $SK_{x,y}$ to be shared by $X$ and $Y$ is generated by the KDC.

2. Several values are combined to form a ticket that is needed to prove $X$'s identity to $Y$ and to deliver the shared secret securely to $Y$. The ticket includes $SK_{x,y}$, the principal name for $X$, and some other fields. Finally, the ticket is encrypted by the KDC with $K_y$, the secret key of $Y$, so that only $Y$ can decrypt the result.

3. $SK_{x,y}$ and the ticket are encrypted by the KDC with $K_x$, the secret key of $X$, so that only $X$ can decrypt the result. The encrypted ticket and session key are sent from the KDC back to $X$. Let the notation { $SK_{x,y}$}$K_x$ represent the encryption of the session key with the secret key of $X$ and the converse for $Y$.

4. The KDC has sent $SK_{x,y}$ and { $SK_{x,y}$}$K_y$ encrypted with $K_x$ to $X$, who decrypts the message to obtain the session key $SK_{x,y}$. Using the preceding notation, the message received by $X$ is { $SK_{x,y}$ and { $SK_{x,y}$}$K_y$ }$K_x$.

5. $X$ sends { $SK_{x,y}$}$K_y$ and the rest of the ticket encrypted with $K_y$ to $Y$, who likewise decrypts this message to obtain the session key. In looking at the contents of the ticket, $Y$ also deduces that this message could have been created only by the KDC, and that $X$ is indeed legitimate. For example, part of the ticket, encrypted with $K_y$, contains the principal name $X$. When $X$ sends the ticket to $Y$, the principal name $X$ also is included as part of the message header. $Y$ compares the value in the header with the decrypted value from the ticket to help verify the identify of $X$. Again, because the ticket was encrypted by the KDC using $K_y$, and only the KDC could have known this secret, $Y$ can trust that the identity of $X$ is authenticated by the KDC.

$X$ and $Y$ now share a secret $SK_{x,y}$ which can be used for secure communications. $Y$ knows that the session key received in the message from $X$ must be valid because only the KDC, which shares $K_y$ with $Y$, could have appropriately encrypted the ticket containing the session key. Notice how both $X$ and $Y$ must trust the KDC to authenticate each other. How did the KDC verify the identity of $X$ in the first place?

### Kerberos Login

Because the Kerberos KDC acts as an authentication server, it controls its own security domain or model. A user or entity that wants to communicate in the domain of Kerberos must first establish an identity with the Kerberos server. The Kerberos administrator adds names, passwords, and other information for each of the principals in the realm. Only the system administrator of the secure Kerberos server should be allowed to modify these entries. After a user is added as a principal in the database, login to the Kerberos environment is possible.

Assume that $X$ is a user. The login process begins in the familiar fashion when the user sits down in front of a terminal displaying a login prompt. $X$ enters a username that the login program captures. The login program klogin, in the role of Kerberos client, sends an authentication request containing the username and current timestamp to the KDC. The KDC and the login workstation could be the same system, but it's more interesting to think of them as different nodes in the network. If the user enters an incorrect username, the KDC responds to klogin with an error.

If the user enters a correct username, the KDC sends to klogin a response message encrypted with $K_x$, the secret key of $X$. As you might suspect, $K_x$ is a DES key derived from the user's password and stored in the KDC database. At this point, the AS component of the KDC has fulfilled its role. That is, the KDC is not involved from this point forward in completing the authentication process. The program klogin assumes responsibility for completing authentication by asking $X$ for a password and then converting the password into a DES key. The result will be equivalent to $K_x$ if $X$ entered the correct password. An attempt is made by klogin to decrypt the message received from the KDC using the hashed value computed from the password. If the decryption is successful, $X$ has been authenticated and can proceed to use the system. Note that the password itself is never sent in the clear over the network to the KDC.

Of special importance in Kerberos Version 4 is the protocol requesting the user's password. This step is not initiated until *after* klogin receives the first response from the KDC. When the user enters an invalid username, the KDC responds with an error to klogin. When the user enters a correct username, the

KDC responds with a message encrypted with the secret key of the user. Only after this response is received will klogin prompt for the password. Kerberos V4 introduces this delay in retrieving the password in an attempt to limit the amount of time the password string is kept in memory. This approach is laudable because storing a password in memory even for a short time might enable a concurrently running rogue program an opportunity for password theft. However, as you will see, this protocol also opens Kerberos V4 to password guessing attacks.

### A More Detailed Analysis of klogin

The login scenario described previously is actually more complex than the overview indicates. In this section, you learn additional details about the messages exchanged in Kerberos.

Recall that the TGS is the part of the Kerberos server responsible for generating shared session keys. The TGS is itself a secure Kerberos server, named krbtgt, which shares a secret with the KDC. Anytime $X$ wants to initiate a secure conversation with another entity in the network, X must contact the TGS and ask for a new session key and ticket. In order to communicate with the TGS, $X$ must establish trust with the TGS by completing the login process. The TGS is the only place where a principal can obtain a session key, and the only way to gain the right to request a session key from the TGS is by logging in to the KDC. Remember, too, that the TGS is just a special part of the KDC. So, when you read that a message is exchanged with the TGS, it is really the KDC that receives all of the messages for the Kerberos server. Here are the login steps assuming again that $X$ is the user attempting to authenticate to Kerberos.

1. $X$ enters the username $X$ in response to the login prompt. For simplicity, assume that the Kerberos principal name for $X$ is the string $X$.
2. klogin sends an authentication request to the KDC. *The message is not encrypted.* Fields in the message include the current timestamp on the login workstation, the principal's username $X$, and the name of the principal service with which klogin wants to communicate. The service name is krbtgt, and this string value is included in the message. This process will be important later when you learn about one attack against Kerberos.
3. The KDC verifies that $X$ exists in the database and obtains $K_x$, the secret key for X. A reply message is encrypted with $K_x$ and returned to klogin. The encrypted message contains the principal name $X$, the server name krbtgt, the original timestamp sent in the request from klogin, and some other fields that enable $X$ to verify that the response

came from the KDC. The encrypted message sent by the KDC also contains a session key $SK_{x,tgs}$ and a *ticket granting ticket* (TGT). The session key $SK_{x,tgs}$ is used by $X$ to securely communicate with the TGS.

The klogin program obtains the password from $X$ as before and attempts to decrypt the message received from the KDC. One of the indicators for successful decryption is when the name of the requested service sent back by the KDC matches the string krbtgt. If decryption is accomplished, login is complete, and the user $X$ now starts communicating with other principals.

### A More Detailed Look at a Session

At some point in the future, $X$ will want to talk to another principal such as $Y$. The TGT plays an important role in this process. Normally, when two principals exchange a ticket, the lifetime of the ticket is very short to prevent *replay attacks*. If the ticket's lifetime is too long, an attacker might be able to use the ticket at a future time, impersonate one of the principals, and trick the other principal into divulging information. Therefore, tickets normally expire within a few seconds, although the limit is configurable by the Kerberos administrator. On the other hand, the TGT has a longer lifetime because a principal needs to reuse it each time a new session key is needed. When a TGT is renewed or when a new TGT is obtained , the user must complete the I&A process again with the Kerberos server. This process requires reentry of the password. Most sites limit the TGT lifetime to eight hours or less for a login user.

When login is complete, a principal has both $SK_{x,tgs}$ and the TGT. At a minimum, the TGT contains the value $\{SK_{x,tgs}\}K_{tgs}$, or the session key for use between the TGS and $X$ encrypted with the secret key of the TGS. All of this information was obtained from the KDC. What happens when $X$ wants to communicate with $Y$?

1.  $X$ sends a request to the TGS asking for a session key to communicate with the principal $Y$. The message that $X$ sends contains several fields. First, it contains the TGT that can be decrypted by the TGS using $K_{tgs}$ to obtain the shared session key $SK_{x,tgs}$. The message also includes information, such as the principal name of $Y$, encrypted with $SK_{x,tgs}$. When the TGS gets the shared session from the TGT, it can decrypt this additional information.

2.  The TGS generates a new random session key, $SK_{x,y}$, to be shared between $X$ and $Y$ for their session. The TGS asks the KDC to use $K_y$ to encrypt this new session key $SK_{x,y}$ and some other values into a ticket $T_y$. The TGS then returns to $X$ the new session key and the ticket $T_y$

encrypted with $SK_{x,tgs}$. To be clear, $SK_{x,tgs}$ is the session key for secure exchanges between $X$ and the TGS. $SK_{x,y}$ is the session key to be used for secure exchanges between $X$ and $Y$.

Having received both $SK_{x,y}$ and $T_y$ from the TGS, $X$ now can start the dialogue with $Y$ as before. One detail that needs to be mentioned is that the initial message $X$ sends to $Y$ includes $T_y$ and an *authenticator*. An authenticator is used for $X$ and $Y$ to prove that they are who they claim to be. Principal $Y$ decrypts $T_y$ and obtains the session key $SK_{x,y}$. The authenticator was encrypted by $X$ using this session key and therefore can be decrypted by $Y$ only through using the same session key. The authenticator includes the sending principal's name $X$ and the current timestamp. $Y$ verifies the identify of $X$ by comparing the decrypted timestamp with its own synchronized timestamp. Because the timestamp only can be decrypted with the same session key used for encryption, $Y$ verifies $X$.

If bilateral authentication is required, $X$ can request this of $Y$. To meet this requirement, $Y$ takes the timestamp from the authenticator, increments the timestamp by one, encrypts this value with the session key, and sends the result back to $X$. The incremented timestamp can be decrypted and verified by $X$ using the session key. Figure 2.4 provides a graphical simplification of how two parties use a KDC to begin a secure session.

To summarize, Kerberos provides for two-way, third-party authentication. The key points are as follows:

- A KDC shares a secret with each principal.
- Each principal authenticates to the KDC using this shared secret or password-derived value.
- When an originating principal wants to securely communicate with a receiving principal, the originating principal obtains a new random session key from the KDC.
- The KDC also sends the originator a ticket that is the session key encrypted with the secret of the receiving principal.
- The originating principal sends the ticket and an authenticator to the receiving principal.
- The receiving principal decrypts the ticket and obtains the session key. This key is used to decrypt the authenticator and to verify the identity of the originator.
- If bilateral authentication is required, the receiver can demonstrate knowledge of the shared session key by encrypting a modified

timestamp from the authenticator and returning this value to the originator.

### *Integrating Kerberos and UNIX Login*

This login process identifies and authenticates the user *X* into the Kerberos environment, but what does this have to do with a login session on UNIX or NT? Recall from the previous discussions that in UNIX, for example, your UID and GIDs determine who you are on the system and what you can do. In the Kerberos login described, your identity is based on your principal name and your Kerberos password. Environments that integrate UNIX or NT with Kerberos can be confusing because you can have two identities. Because both Kerberos and UNIX implement their own security models, a separate identity is used in both security domains depending on the situation.

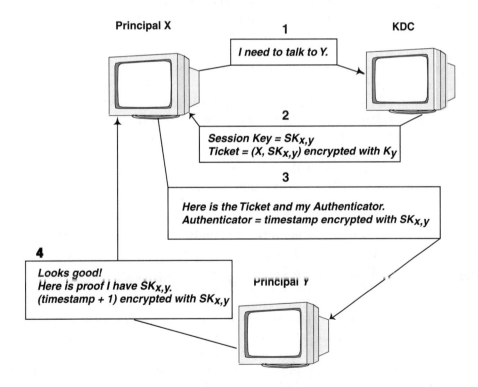

**Figure 2.4** Interacting with a Kerberos KDC to initiate a secure communications session.

Consider the following scenario. If you have a personal UNIX workstation, you will have an account on that system. When you login and start running programs, the UID and GIDs assigned to you form your credentials. All of the programs on that system look at your UID and GIDs to decide what you are permitted to do on the system. Kerberos is a completely different environment. In order for a program to take advantage of the features in Kerberos, that program must be *instrumented to* or *enabled for* Kerberos. For you to interact with a Kerberos enabled program, you must have a Kerberos credential. The only way to obtain a credential is to authenticate to the Kerberos server. None of the programs delivered with your UNIX system will by default be able to do anything with your Kerberos credential unless they have been modified to do so. Although, Solaris provides some UNIX network applications that are enhanced to work with Kerberos.

Because the operating system security kernel does not make decisions based on Kerberos credentials, think of Kerberos as an *application level* framework. Applications are written specifically to work with Kerberos, and these applications sit on top of the operating system. Many of these applications are servers that run with root or special privileges on the operating system. To show you how confusing this can be, the Kerberos enabled application understands and interacts with Kerberos security internally, but the application itself is running within the security context of the UNIX operating system! When you remember that Kerberos is made of several different programs running on various operating systems, this concept does not seem so hard to grasp. Still, it's an interesting dichotomy that surfaces with security products. Using terminology from Chapter 1, Kerberos augments the security of most operating systems, rather than replacing operating system components. Because Kerberos was designed to improve distributed systems security, it's not surprising that this is the case.

Operating systems that have been integrated with Kerberos rely on modified login programs or procedures. If the change is transparent to the user, then login will create a shell with your credentials *and* obtain your Kerberos credentials from the server. In this way, programs that make access control decisions based on your UID and GIDs will work as usual, and any programs needing your Kerberos credentials can obtain these where they are stored on the local system. If integrated properly, the authentication step will not rely on finding your password in /etc/password (or the shadow file), but will use the Kerberos server to verify identity. In this way, the integrated system is taking advantage of a centralized store for user passwords. A word of caution is needed, though. Unless all login paths to the operating system have been modified to query the Kerberos server for authentication, leftover entry points into the system will exist. These leftover paths will use the information in /etc/passwd and might introduce weaknesses into your system.

### Benefits of Kerberos

Notice a couple of the security features provided by Kerberos. No passwords are shared between any of the principals. Only the KDC knows the hashed password values for the principals. The KDC additionally encrypts the hashed password database to strengthen security. A different shared session key is used when $X$ communicates with the TGS than when exchanging messages with $Y$. Similarly, if $X$ were to initiate sessions with other principals, the shared session keys would be random and different. Assuming that the technique used to generate random session keys is sound, it is computationally infeasible for an adversary to guess a session key.

Identities are verified by showing knowledge of a shared secret without divulging the secret itself in the clear over the network. Both $X$ and $Y$ possess the same shared secret distributed by the trusted KDC server. Cryptography and checksums are used to protect the integrity of the tickets. Thus, an attacker cannot attempt to modify a ticket in transit to trick one of the principals into using the wrong session key. Although the improvement beyond standard UNIX or NT login authentication is not that significant with Kerberos, the features it provides for secure communications between principals in a distributed network are substantial.

### Complaints and Attacks against Kerberos

One of the chief reasons for analyzing Kerberos in detail is that many of the topics discussed in the remainder of this book require authentication protocol exchanges between two or more entities in a network. Kerberos is really a simple system to learn first. Many more complex cases and environments need to be considered. Knowing problems with distributed protocols can help you avoid costly mistakes. To see how intricate distributed authentication protocols can be, consider some of the following arguments against Kerberos (Bellovin and Merritt, 1991; Kaufmann, Perlman, and Speciner, 1995).

- Each software component must be modified to work with Kerberos. If you want to use only Kerberos to improve login security for your UNIX or NT box, you are getting more than you need. Kerberos is designed for much broader tasks than this.

- File systems such as the *Andrew File System* (AFS) have been built around the Kerberos protocol. However, Kerberos itself does not provide access control or authorization services. Of course, it was never intended to provide this feature.

- Systems in a Kerberos network require synchronized time clocks. Secure distributed time services are thus a prerequisite for Kerberos to operate properly.

- You should be able to easily see how a Kerberos user principal can enter a password to authenticate to the KDC. Kerberos was designed to provide trusted third-party authentication for other principals, such as software servers and workstations. For these inanimate principals to prove their identity to the KDC, the principal's password must be stored on disk in the /etc/srvtab file. This file could be compromised if the system is attacked.

- On multiuser systems, principals' tickets are stored in a temporary directory that can be read by any user. This information could be useful to a hacker for offline password cracking.

- Kerberos relies on the *User Datagram Protocol* (UDP), which is often blocked at the firewall. As such, it is difficult to run Kerberos between sites protected by a firewall.

- Kerberos V4 binds tickets to a single network address for a workstation or server. Thus, a system with multiple network adapters will have problems using tickets.

A few problems with the protocols described in the preceding list also affect Kerberos V4. The most often lamented feature is the login protocol.

Remember from previous comments that klogin will send an initial request to the KDC containing the principal's name and some other values. If the principal name is valid, the KDC sends a reply encrypted with the secret of the principal. Because the initial request information is transmitted in the clear, and the Kerberos code is freely available, an adversary who knows the names of principals can send this initial request and obtain the encrypted reply. This reply then can be used as input for an offline password cracking attempt. If the decrypted reply contains the string krbtgt, the attacker has uncovered the principal's password. Someone using a network sniffer also can capture the entire initial request packet containing the principal name and current time to further validate decryption. Principal names also can be obtained through techniques such as social engineering, network sniffing, or electronic mail. Once again, the system is only as strong as the reusable passwords chosen by users.

Kerberos V4 also suffers from a bug that allows one to perform offline password cracking even if the name of a principal is not known (l0pht 1997). If the KDC receives an improper UDP packet, it will return an error containing the name of the last principal to request a TGT along with the realm name. To acquire a list of principal names just repeatedly query the server with incorrect UDP packets and store the resulting messages. These names can be used to attack the system as described previously.

If the AS is not configured to limit online password guessing attempts, you can try password cracking interactively. Should this approach fail due to limits on failed login attempts, the attacker can always turn the hack into a denial-of-service attack by sequentially locking out all principals.

Some characteristics of Kerberos have not been discussed in detail. For example, Kerberos servers in different realms can establish trust relationships and perform cross authentication services. Because the cooperating KDCs cannot dynamically enter a password as a user might, cross-realm authentication relies on the stored secret problem already identified.

Another problem with Kerberos lies in the authenticator. Bellovin and Merritt (1991) describe how an attacker might be able to use an authenticator in a replay attack. Also, any successful attempts to alter the allowable time skew between nodes opens up possibilities for authenticator replay attacks. Previously expired authenticators could be used again.

Incrementing the timestamp by one for bilateral authentication also is not without its problems. A better choice would be to use a challenge-response mechanism. When a Kerberos client wants to verify that a Kerberos server holds the session key, the client should ask the server to generate a random challenge or *nonce*. The server would encrypt the nonce with the session key and send it to the client. The client responds with some function computed on the nonce, encrypts the result, and returns the value to the server to prove knowledge of the session key. Of course, the client and server must agree on the function (which is "increment by one" in Kerberos V4). *A general rule of thumb for mutual authentication is that something in a message should differentiate which side it came from* (Kaufman, Perlman, and Speciner, 1995). Either each side should use two different keys (one for sending and one for receiving), or each side should perform a different algorithm when responding to a challenge.

In Kerberos, there is no way to adequately determine whether the first reply from the KDC to klogin is genuine. Therefore, at least a denial-of-service attack can be launched against the login workstation by sending "principal not found" from another node. The hacker succeeds when the forged message arrives at the login workstation before the KDC's response. This is an example of a *race condition*. With today's open network protocols, it would be possible to flood the KDC with network packets to slow its response time. An attacker who knows the secret keys of the principal and the TGS can trick both into using a compromised session key by spoofing the login process.

Finally, weaknesses in the random number generator of Kerberos V4 allowed secret keys to be guessed rather easily in some circumstances (Dole, Lodin, and Spafford, 1997). Clearly, creating a secure, distributed authentication system is difficult. The keepers of Kerberos listened to these criticisms and problems and made many changes in Version 5.

### Kerberos Version 5

The core of Kerberos was completely rewritten for Version 5. The goals and overall design remained the same. A third-party KDC was used to generate session keys in the manner already described. However, Version 5 relies on greatly enhanced message formats based on *Abstract Syntax Notation 1* (ASN.1). A programmer can use ASN.1 to accurately identify the data type and length of all data values used in a message. This capability improves the integrity of data in Kerberos messages as well as allowing for more options in message formats.

Rather than describe all of the advantages and new features of Kerberos Version 5 here, you are advised to visit the Kerberos ftp site at ftp://athena-dist.mit.edu for papers and copies of the Kerberos documentation. Commercial versions of Kerberos can be obtained from Cygnus (www.cygnus.com), Veritas (www.veritas.com), and Cybersafe (www.cybersafe.com) to name a few.

One important difference between Kerberos V4 and V5 is the way login occurs. In Version 5, the user is required to prove knowledge of the password before the first message is sent by klogin to the KDC. Therefore, without network sniffers to grab the KDC replies, an attacker cannot easily carry out a password-guessing attack. No KDC replies will be encrypted with the user's secret unless a password has been entered. Instead of entering just the principal name as in V4, the user must enter both the principal name and password before klogin sends the authentication request.

Numerous other improvements can be found including enhancements to the authenticators. Most of the criticisms identified previously are addressed in Kerberos Version 5. For example, the Kerberos V5 authenticator can be a complex data structure for a challenge-response dialog as recommended by Bellovin and Merritt (1992). Kerberos V5 also enables a client program to choose to which network address the ticket is bound, in cases in which the client program is running on hosts with multiple network adapters.

Two other interesting features of V5 tickets are the capabilities to perform ticket *forwarding* and *delegation*. A ticket is forwarded if it is obtained at one network address but is to be used by the principal at another network address. The ticket essentially can be passed between network nodes until it is consumed on the appropriate machine. Delegation is an option that allows a second principal to be able to use a ticket on the ticket owner's behalf. Principal *X* could obtain a ticket by authenticating to the KDC but request that the ticket be usable by principal *Y* instead. A number of other ticket qualifiers have been added such as predating a ticket so that it becomes valid on a future date.

One final component of Kerberos V5 deserves mention. Included with this release is a set of programming interfaces that vendors can exploit for application-level encryption. The *Generic Security Services API* (GSSAPI) has been implemented on top of Kerberos V5 and relies on the DES algorithm for security. GSSAPI includes routines that a vendor can call for providing authenticity, privacy, and message integrity in communications. If a vendor's product is required to provide secure communications across insecure networks, GSSAPI interfaces are available to deliver the necessary security services. The implementation obviously would require the existence of a Kerberos V5 server to satisfy the calls made to the GSSAPI.

## X.509

A digital certificate can be thought of as an electronic passport, which is uniquely used to identify entities in a network. Certificates are most commonly associated with system users, although a certificate could be created for software servers just as Kerberos creates principal secrets for these entities. The most common form of digital certificate is the one defined by the X.509 ISO standard. An entire suite of ISO standards is targeted at providing secure, distributed communications in a network. X.509, which is part of the X.500 series of standards, is concerned with the precise format of digital certificates. This section describes how X.509 certificates provide for significant improvements in I&A for networked environments.

### The Lure of X.509

A major benefit of certificates is that they are based on public-key technology. One of the problems with Kerberos is that the principals and the Kerberos server must share a secret key. No such requirement exists for the X.509 approach to authentication. Public-key cryptography takes advantage of the relationship between the public key and private key. Because the keys can be used for complementary cryptographic operations, entities in the network do not have to share a secret key to prove identity. An example will help clarify how this works.

Let $P_x$ be the public key of user $X$ and $S_x$ represent the secret key of the pair. To verify the identity of user $X$, $Y$ chooses a random nonce $N$ value and encrypts it with $P_x$. $Y$ then transmits $\{N\}P_x$ to $X$. To prove identity $X$ decrypts $\{N\}P_x$ using $S_x$ and transmits this value $N$ back to $Y$. Only $X$ who secretly knows the mathematical inverse key $S_x$ for the public key $P_x$ could have successfully decrypted the challenge. As a final twist, if two-way authentication is required, $Y$ can be challenged to prove knowledge of $S_y$ in a similar fashion. To improve the protocol $X$ could encrypt $N$ with the public key of $Y$ before sending the response. Even this change is not sufficient for a complete protocol, because an attacker between

$X$ and $Y$ can still modify the messages in transit. More detailed protocols that also provide *message integrity* are covered in Chapter 4, "Traditional Network Security Approaches."

To see how public-key cryptography can be further utilized for establishing secure network communications, consider that the nonce value $N$ can become the session key between $X$ and $Y$. Not only is authentication of the entities accomplished, but they also now share a secret key for encrypting exchanged messages. Another consequence of the inverse relationship between the key pairs is that $Y$ can ask $X$ to digitally sign some message $M$ with the secret key $S_x$. At a future time, it can be shown, by decrypting *the digital signature* $\{M\}S_x$ with $P_x$ to obtain $M$, that only $X$ could have provided the signature. To be precise, the digital signature is not computed as an encryption function as the notation $\{M\}S_x$ implies. Rather, the signature is normally derived with a cryptographic hash algorithm.

### Contents of an X.509 Certificate

The X.500 standard defines a naming syntax for a universal directory structure that can be used to store information about important entities in a network. An X.500 name consists of several *attribute-value* pairs. The syntax of a *distinguished name* uniquely identifying an entity, such as a user, would like something like the following:

```
C=US, O=IBM, OU="Software Security", CN="John Doe"
```

Names of entities or objects are derived in a hierarchical fashion. Because the standards are international, different portions of the naming tree are assigned to various registration authorities who are responsible for further assigning subtrees to other authorities. In the example, the root of the naming tree is the attribute $C$ representing the *country*. Other attributes are $O$ for *organization*, $OU$ for *organizational unit*, and $CN$ for *common name*. Internally in a program, the representation of a distinguished name is much more complex, and like Kerberos V5, the naming is based on ASN.1 data types. For the purposes of this discussion, though, all you need to know is that each digital certificate is created for a particular entity identified by the distinguished name.

The certificate also includes the public key of its owner, an expiration value indicating when the certificate is no longer valid, a serial number, and other administrative fields. An important field appearing in the certificate is the digital signature of the *Certificate Authority* (CA) which issued the certificate. The signature could have been computed with any one of several cryptographic hash algorithms, so the certificate also includes information identifying which algorithm was chosen.

### Certificate Authorities

Why are certificates issued by a CA? Although X.509 certificates simplify the process of distributing shared session keys and authenticating users, a trusted third-party authentication server is still needed for strict verification of identities. Certificates are designed to be public and published in a way that makes them easily accessible to other network entities. In some environments, the data store or directory used to publish certificates might be tightly controlled. Also, two users wanting to communicate over an insecure network may already trust each other and gladly exchange certificates without hesitation. However, in public networks, you should be concerned about whether a certificate is genuine. Products are readily available for creating X.509 certificates, and any user may be able to advertise a certificate claiming to be another party. Only by verifying the authenticity of the X.509 certificate can one be sure that impersonation is not a threat.

Various companies including IBM and Verisign currently offer CA services. The belief is that if a certificate is generated and signed by a respectable authority, users of the certificate can trust its authenticity. The CA generates the digital signature by using its secret key and then publishing its public key. The signature can be verified because of the relationship between the secret and public keys of the CA. The important points include the following:

- *X* wanting to communicate with *Y* obtains *Y*'s X.509 certificate.
- *X* verifies the authenticity of the certificate by verifying digital signature of the CA that issued it.
- When satisfied that the signature is legitimate, *X* can use the contents of *Y*'s certificate to communicate securely.

You are not limited to having a single X.509 certificate. Indeed, you can obtain multiple certificates from different CAs and decide where to publish each one.

If the secret key for a user is compromised in some way, the CA must *revoke* the corresponding certificates. Each CA must maintain a *certificate revocation list* (CRL). Before a certificate can be employed as the basis for secure communications, it should be compared to the CRL at the CA to verify validity. Creating a usable public key infrastructure, which includes providing CAs, is a major challenge facing many companies and governments today.

### Why X.509 Is Popular

The X.500 family of standards has been around for quite some time. Still, not many software products used these standards until the explosion of interest in the Web. The *Secure Sockets Layer* (SSL) is widely relied upon for secure communications across the Web. A commonly used implementation of SSL is delivered by RSA, Inc., now part of Security Dynamics. The founders of RSA (Rivest, Shamir, and Adelman) were some of the original researchers in public-key technology. Consequently, it is not surprising that SSL is based upon public-key techniques and X.509 certificates. Web browsers and servers that carry out secure communications across the Internet primarily depend upon SSL for security services.

Like GSSAPI in Kerberos V5, SSL is available separately as a set of library routines from RSA. This means that arbitrary applications written by vendors can be enabled to take advantage of SSL features for secure distributed communications. Because the UNIX sockets interface is a common programming abstraction for thousands of programmers, you can reasonably assume that SSL will be a popular tool for distributed security in many products to come. Higher level programming interfaces, such as Microsoft's CryptoAPI and Intel's *Common Data Security Architecture* (CDSA), also fit nicely with the X.509 and SSL approaches.

### Comments on X.509 Security

The weakest component in the X.509 approach is still the reusable password. If you have a Web browser that supports certificates, you already know that the certificates are stored on your system's disk. Before writing the certificate to disk the system first encrypts it using a password hash. The password is reusable and chosen by you when configuring your browser. For unattended operation of servers that rely on certificates, a data store is also needed for the server's secret key or keys. In this case, a password chosen by the system administrator is the basis for the hashed key used to encrypt the server's secret key. If an adversary can capture the encrypted value, an offline password cracking attack can be undertaken.

It is practically impossible to break commercially available public-key implementations, assuming sufficient key lengths and discarding experienced cryptanalysis. However, the system is still threatened because if the secret key of a key pair is disclosed, an attacker can impersonate the certificate's owner or decrypt private messages. Because the secret is protected by the fallible reusable password, we have sufficient reason for concern.

Note also that with respect to identity within the context of a local operating system, X.509 certificates are not replacements for UIDs and GIDs. Like Kerberos, X.500 and X.509 introduce their own subjects and objects, and even bring along a separate access control mechanism. It's not hard to find UNIX network applications that are enabled to work with Kerberos. Discovering a freely available or commercial version of one of these applications that has been modified to use X.509 is less likely today but should change in the near future. Given the widespread interest in certificate-based authentication, it is advisable for operating system vendors to support integrated login with X.509.

Some important concepts can be summarized from the previous discussions on authentication:

- ◆ Authentication involves proving knowledge of a shared secret.
- ◆ Reusable passwords are *not* the most reliable value for authenticating users.
- ◆ A shared session key, regardless of how it is obtained, can be used for secure communications between parties. The session key can also be used to establish the authenticity of the parties.
- ◆ A session key that is used only once is very desirable because it is highly resistant to cryptanalytic attacks.
- ◆ An authentication server can be used to distribute shared secrets to parties, and such a server is an administrative necessity in large networks.
- ◆ Frameworks such as Kerberos and X.509 do not replace the subjects and objects in an operating system, although they can be used to augment the I&A process.

Now that you understand some alternatives for secure authentication and communication, it's time to make some additional recommendations for improving login security at your site.

As you have seen from the previous discussions, traditional I&A security is weak in a number of ways. Intrusion detection products are designed to assist by monitoring the system for password attacks and other suspicious behaviors. Even if you have an authentication server such as Kerberos, RADIUS (Rigney et. al. 1997), or TACACS (Finseth 1993), you will want to add an IDS to monitor the authentication server. Weaknesses in Kerberos implementations or protocols (some identified earlier) as well as published exploits for RADIUS implementations should encourage you to monitor the activities of your authentication servers with an IDS. After all, I&A is the first step in securely accessing your system.

## Ideas for Improving I&A Security

Now that you know about weaknesses of reusable password authentication, it's time to check into alternatives. In this section, you learn about stronger techniques for authenticating users and other entities in networked environments. You should know in advance that even though you can eliminate some problems with better I&A tools, you will still need other security products, such as IDSs, to complete your solution.

## One-Time Passwords

The first improvement to I&A is to depend upon one-time passwords instead of reusable passwords. In practice, this approach requires the use of cryptography, although one can easily envision a simpler case. For example, two people could decide to sequentially use all words from an encyclopedia as the authenticating values for communicating. Each time authentication is needed, the originator sends the next word in the encyclopedia as the authenticator value. The recipient merely checks the value against another copy of this readily available code book if the authentication is unilateral. For bilateral authentication, the originator sends the next available encyclopedia word, and this word's successor is sent as a response by the recipient.

Several problems exist with the encyclopedia protocol as described. The universe of passwords is easily cracked if an adversary determines which volume of the encyclopedia is serving as the code book. Also, it is recommended that a more complex algorithm than the successor function be used to authenticate the recipient. For example, the second party in the conversation could begin choosing passwords for the return messages by working backwards from the last page of the encyclopedia. Of course, both parties would need to know this variation in the protocol.

Still another problem is that you must assume that the communication channel between the originator and the recipient is not secure. If an adversary can capture and modify the message in transit, authentication will not be reliable. Attempts by an attacker to replay a previously used password are not a threat because each password is unique and used only once.

The basic idea is that the two parties share a secret, or secrets, chosen from a predetermined universe of values. *Each secret is used only for a single authentication*. If a secret were to be reused, a number of confounding issues would be introduced, such as the need for an expiration time on a secret  The strength of one-time passwords depends on the secrecy of the password generator and naturally on the secrecy of the storage device for the passwords. Cryptography is preferred when deriving or using one-time passwords because cryptography is more resistant to a variety of attacks.

## Strong Authentication

Rather than transmitting the secret value itself, whether in unilateral or mutual (bilateral) authentication, *strong authentication* prescribes that an entity *only*

## One-Time Passwords and One-Time Pads

The strongest cryptographic protection comes from using *one-time pads*. A onetime pad is a randomly generated string of characters to be used as the key for encrypting plaintext. For the moment, think of the plaintext and the one-time pad as binary strings. Encryption is accomplished by XORing the plaintext with the key. Each bit in the one-time pad key is used to encrypt a single bit in the plaintext, and each bit in the key is used *exactly* one time. Reusing any portion of the key reduces the strength of the cipher. Therefore, bits of the key are discarded after they are used. The accomplice receives the ciphertext and reverses the operation using the same one-time pad. Both parties must have agreed on the contents of the one-time pad in advance. Additionally, if either party loses synchronization with the other, the message will not be decrypted correctly.

Spies have long relied upon one-time pads, actual printed sheets with keys, to exchange small amounts of super-secret information. Unless the pad used to encrypt the message cannot be found, deciphering the message is computationally infeasible. Although no formal proof exists for guaranteeing that a cryptographic algorithm is unbreakable, intuitively the one-time pad is the most secure method because any string of 1s and 0s is an equally probable key. The search space is practically infinite.

Because the key length must be identical to the message length, one-time pads are impractical for general cryptographic communications. Also, the approach is only as safe as the technique used to generate the random numbers of the key. In practice, random-number generation has often been the weakest component in a security product. The random-number generator of an early Netscape product was cracked not long after Netscape offered a reward for doing so. For a thorough treatment of randomness in computing see Luby (1996).

A one-time password is similar to a one-time pad in that the password is used only once for authentication. After the user or other entity is authenticated, the password is discarded.

*prove knowledge of the secret.* In other words, strong authentication involves demonstrating that you know a secret without actually *revealing* the secret. Obviously, login passwords are not a form of strong authentication because you must actually enter your password to authenticate to a system.

Imagine a modified UNIX I&A procedure in which you do not enter your usual password. When the system prompts you for the password, you provide a value that is derived from your password. For example, assume that your password is an integer or that the password can be converted into an integer value. In response to the password prompt, you multiply your integer password by a predetermined constant value, such as the integer 4, and key in the result. In this way, you are not revealing the secret you share with the system. Unfortunately, this simple approach is not much stronger than relying on reusable passwords because the example algorithm is too simple. Again, cryptographic techniques commonly underlie commercial implementations of strong authentication.

## Two-Factor Authentication

Recall that authentication can be proven by demonstrating something you know, something you have, or something you are. Combining any two of these to form two-factor authentication markedly adds to the security of the authentication system. For example, if you must know a secret key sequence and if you are required to possess a badge to access a secured area, this method is better than relying on only one of the two values. The Security Dynamics Inc. (SDI) ACE/Server was one of the first commercial products to combine one-time passwords with token devices.

### Security Dynamics ACE/Server

SDI provides a variety of token devices, the most familiar one in the form of a small electronic card. The token card displays an integer value to use as a one-time password. The value is not random but is instead computed as a mathematical function of the token's unique ID and the current time. The ACE/Server knows the unique ID of each token as well. Before a token is distributed to the user, its time and unique ID are synchronized with the ACE/Server. At any given instant in time, the token card and the ACE/Server are locked onto the same one-time password value. The details of the mathematical computation used to generate the unpredictable integer values are not public. Like most time-synchronized systems, some amount of clock skew can be tolerated by the communicating systems. The skew value is configurable in the ACE/Server for each token device registered in its database.

In Figure 2.5 you see the basic SecurID card. A software token device was designed to operate the same way as a physical card but overcomes previous complaints about cards such as cost. Some tokens require that the terminal support a token reader device. For example, a token could be combined with a physical key that must first be used to unlock the token reader. Only after this step is complete can the user proceed to use the token card for authentication.

**Figure 2.5**    Standard card for a SDI token authentication device.

The ACE/Server contains a database of users, in which each user is associated with a *personal identifier number* (PIN) and individual token card. The PIN can be chosen by the user, and thus hidden from the administrator, or it can be assigned by the ACE/Server depending on site policy. PINs can be composed of numbers only or both numbers and letters. The PIN length is an important security factor, and SDI recommends a minimum length of six. Notice that the ACE/Server has introduced another repository for storing user information. This database must be kept in sync with the /etc/passwd file, for example, if SecurID cards are being used to replace reusable password logins in UNIX.

To authenticate to the ACE/Server the user enters both the PIN and the current number displayed on the token device. Together these values are called the *passcode*. This type of authentication is much stronger than using a single value such as a password.

What happens if an attacker manages to steal a PIN and somehow guess a token value, without possessing the token card? If the attacker tries several values before the guess succeeds, the ACE/Server detects the guessing attack and prompts for a second token value. Someone probably cannot guess two successive token values in sequence or the original token value in a single guess. The guessing threshold can be configured by the administrator. A separate threshold can be configured to limit the number of total failed passcodes allowed before a card is inactivated.

A stolen token card is useless without the user's PIN. If the ACE/Server detects a sequence of events consisting of repeated incorrect PIN guesses with the appropriate token value, the server assumes that the token card has been stolen and ignores future authentication requests from that card. Someone who steals a token card and also uncovers the user's PIN can impersonate the user. Because time synchronization between the server and the token cards is critical, the server will alert the administrator if its time is set back. A replay attack is possible with a previously used passcode if the server clock is set back. An adversary could shoulder surf to obtain an old token integer value. The PIN alone would be insufficient for a replay attack.

### Attacks against ACE/Servers

Although SDI created a very strong authentication mechanism, successful attacks against the server have been documented. Two threats are faced by one-time password systems. The first problem is the *man-in-the-middle attack* in which an adversary sits on the network between the client and the authentication server. The attacker attempts to capture the packets for future replay or merely monitors packets in an effort to launch the second hack based on a *race condition*.

Because most authentication systems have defenses for replay attacks, the race condition is a greater threat. SecurID cards are configured to return or display a fixed-length value. This is true whether the token value is returned directly or the card is used for a challenge-response protocol. The default is 10-digit integers with no alphabetic characters. With enough effort, an attacker can discern the length for a given card that is the target of the hack. Early ACE/Servers were subject to the following weakness assuming that the length of the token value is $D$ digits.

An opponent on system $O$ first would detect that the login user has initiated an authentication session from the client to the ACE/Server. $O$ then opens up $D$ simultaneous authentication request connections with the server, too. The attacker watches each keystroke entered by the user as it is sent in a packet to the server. Assuming that the login user's system is not buffering the token value and sending it in a single packet, each digit of the integer will be sent in a separate packet. As a digit is seen in a packet from the client to the server, $O$ similarly packages up that digit and sends it to the server in each of its $D$ connections. After the second to last digit (D-1) is sent by $O$, one each of the digits 0–9 will be sent by $O$ on each of the $D$ connections. This represents an attempt by the attacker to guess the appropriate last digit and send it to the server before the client. Network jamming techniques could be employed for slowing packet delivery from the client, so the attacker has a strong possibility of beating the client to the server. In addition, the attacker now has a 1-in-$D$ chance of successfully authenticating to the server. Note that if the guessing threshold is set low enough, the token card will be disabled.

SDI modified the ACE/Server to deter this type of attack. For example, a token card can be used only in a single authentication dialogue. The same token cannot be used in simultaneous login attempts, although the same card can be reused within a short, configurable time interval. This fix is reasonable because it is unlikely that the token card can be in two distinct physical locations at once. Also, because network traffic between the clients and ACE/Server are encrypted and digitally signed, this attack is more difficult to carry out.

Unfortunately, if a token card is subjected to the preceding attack, the user now is exposed to a denial-of-service problem. An adversary can attempt to launch login sessions shorter than the allowed interval. The ACE/Server will disable a token card if this is detected, even if the card's legitimate owner accounts for one of these login sessions.

Note that these attacks are really targeted at the protocol used between the client and the server. Although the SecurID card is backed by some expert security designers, it is inherently difficult to devise secure, distributed authentication protocols. Other protocol exploits can be found in the paper *securid.ps* found at www.secnet.com. Note that many of these problems have been fixed since the paper identified them. Still, it is interesting to read how complicated it can be to safely deploy strong authentication systems. As noted in the introductory chapters, a product will help you solve one class of problems, but by adding new protocols and security models, it also might open your system to attacks not previously possible.

## Challenge-Response Authentication

To strengthen I&A further, the authenticating system displays a randomly chosen integer each time it shows the password prompt. Instead of merely keying in your password, you calculate some mathematical function using this *challenge* value and *respond* with the computed result. If the mathematical function used is cryptographically strong, you significantly improve I&A beyond the reusable password method. NT uses a challenge-response technique for authentication with domain controllers, although this authentication is not based on two separate factors by default.

Some commercial products, such as Digital Pathways (now part of Axent) combine challenge-response with hand-held token devices. The authentication software chooses a random value and sends it to the user as a challenge. A shared secret between the authentication server and the user is stored inside the token. The user keys the challenge into the token device that computes the response. To authenticate to the server, the user enters the response, which is verified at the authentication server.

You want to avoid some potholes with challenge-response systems. The challenge should come from a random source. Timestamps do not make good challenges because they come from a predictable sequence of numbers. Also, if the time values are not fine grained, you may be able to replay previous values or to trick one of the parties into computing responses in advance, which could be later used for a reflection attack. Finally, if authentication is mutual, each side of the protocol should use a different challenge, each preferably from different domains—such as the initiator always sends an even number, and the responder sends an odd number. This simple addition in complexity reduces the threat of replay attacks and reflection attacks (Kaufman, Perlman, and Speciner, 1995).

## The Need for Intrusion Detection

Here is a recap of what is to be a recurring theme in the book. Your environment requires different software and hardware tools for solving security problems. Even as you add new techniques for reducing risks, you will find that enhancements you deploy also have their own weaknesses—either in implementation or in the way they might be configured. Therefore, you want to add IDS tools to detect and respond when other tools in your environment don't work perfectly.

In this chapter, you have learned how the out-of-the-box configurations of UNIX and NT support I&A of users. Both operating systems rely on reusable passwords for authenticating users, although integration with other authentication servers is widely supported. Third-party authentication servers, such as Kerberos and Certificate Authorities, were introduced to show how I&A can be scaled for large environments. These discussions also highlighted the importance of correct protocols for proving identities in a distributed environment.

### Biometrics

Space does not permit a thorough coverage of the explosive field of biometrics. It seems that a new biometric product alliance is announced every day. A few years ago security product vendors rushed to alter their products to work with authentication devices from Security Dynamics or Digital Pathways. The same now can be said of biometric authentication. I&A systems based on fingerprints, voice, facial features, and keystroke patterns are available today. For more information, you can start by visiting the International Computer Security Association's Web site and looking at www.ncsa.com/hotlinks/biometric.html.

The two key recommendations for improving I&A security are to user either one-time passwords or strong two-factor authentication with token devices as a replacement for reusable passwords. Although the cost of deployment might be more, the added security is well worth the expense.

Finally, even though more secure authentication products, such as the Security Dynamics ACE/Server, can be added to your site, avenues of attack will still be open for a hacker. Some examples of attacks against the ACE/Server were described to emphasize this point. An authentication product will not deter, prevent, or detect many attacks. For example, an I&A product will not detect someone who maliciously deletes files or otherwise violates your security policy once logged in to the system! If you want to catch intruders who have hacked through your I&A system or insiders who are misusing corporate resources, IDSs are needed to detect and respond. Also, because systems like Kerberos introduce additional security models, you want to monitor their activities for intrusive behavior such as password guessing attacks.

Now that you understand how to improve the initial I&A step in computer interaction, it's time to take a look at how access control decisions are made after you are connected. In the next chapter, you will learn about the underlying access control models of UNIX and NT, their weaknesses, and how you might overcome some of the problems.

# Chapter 3

# The Role of Access Control in Your Environment

Recall from Chapter 1, "Intrusion Detection and the Classic Security Model," that the reference monitor is the portion of a computer model that performs access control decisions. After you have logged in, *everything* you do after that moment is regulated by the access control routines. The purpose of this chapter is to ensure that you have a clear understanding of the role that access control fulfills and to understand why intrusion detection is needed even if you think your reference monitor is doing its job. To accomplish this goal, you will learn about the types of access control features provided in UNIX and NT by default. Then, you'll see why preventative access control techniques do not eliminate all of your problems.

Access control, like I&A, is a common place for hackers to attack. You know that I&A is imperfect and not completely successful as a preventative mechanism. Access control also leaves security exposures for two reasons:

**Configuration Problems.** Access control rules are not defined properly, thus providing the hacker a pathway for attacks. In general terms, the system is improperly configured.

**Program Bugs.** Flaws are found in the implementation of programs that enable an adversary to circumvent access control.

In the next two sections, you will find a quick overview of how configuration problems and program bugs lead to weaknesses in access control. To understand specific examples of these flaws, you need to understand how UNIX and NT implement access control. When this material is covered, you will see specific examples of how hackers get around access control systems and why you need intrusion detection to catch these events.

## Configuration Problems

One of the most challenging tasks in building and shipping a complicated software product is the process of assigning ownership for files and configuring access control rules for all of the files in the product. Many system administrators have installed commercial products from shrink wrap media only to find that the default configuration is not secure. As the complexity of the product grows, so does the difficulty of properly defining default access control rules for the product.

The most common mistake occurs when the vendor sets file or directory access control rules that are too permissive. For example, a privileged program might be provided with a software product. The program should be run only by administrators. The flaw is that the default permissions enable *any* user to run the program. A definite security problem exists here.

A variation on this situation occurs when a privileged program reads information from a data file and alters its behavior according to the values it reads. If the directory or file permissions enable *any* user to modify the contents of the data file, then a lowly user with no special rights on the system can trick the privileged program into doing something it should not. Notice in both of these cases that the reference monitor is acting in a perfectly valid way. The reference monitor looks at the credentials for the subject, looks at the access control rules on the object, and allows the operation to proceed. *The hole exists because the access control rules are not configured to accurately reflect the security policy for the site.*

You might think identifying default configuration problems during product testing would be easy. However, if the product is developed by dozens or hundreds of programmers, you cannot always find a single individual who understands all of the security issues and interaction effects of the product. Not all programmers keep security at the forefront of their hot list, either. Sometimes, just getting the program or subsystem to function properly is challenging enough. Like software documentation, security issues are often left for the end of the development cycle when little time is available for thoroughness.

A related and equally important cause of system hacks is the system administrator configuration error. Someone who administers hundreds or thousands of users and a similar number of files and resources and has responsibility for many other tasks is bound to occasionally make a configuration mistake. These errors also can lead to security breaches.

## Program Bugs

Access control rules, even if perfectly configured, are not sufficient for securing a computer system because the possibility of programming errors always poses a threat. Computer operating systems divide users into two broad categories—privileged users and normal users. To be precise, various types of privileged users exist, but for the moment, two categories will suffice. A privileged program is often invoked by a normal user to perform a task *on behalf of* the normal user. The privileged program runs under the identity of a privileged user.

Sometimes programmers make mistakes. You may find mistakes in software a lot more frequently than "sometimes," but this is a topic for a different book. When a mistake sneaks into software, it can take several forms:

◆ The programmer forgets to check the input parameters passed to the program.

◆ The programmer forgets to check boundary conditions, particularly when dealing with string memory buffers.

◆ The programmer forgets the basic principle of least privilege. The entire program is run in privileged mode, rather than running only a limited subset of the instructions in privileged mode and all other statements with reduced privileges.

◆ A programmer creates a resource, such as a file or directory, from within the privileged program. Instead of explicitly setting the access control rules for the resource (least privilege), the programmer assumes default permissions would be set properly. Often, the programmer never even stops to think about setting permissions for privileged resources created by a program.

All of these weaknesses have been used to attack systems. Improper input parameters have been used to trick a privileged program into doing something it should not. *Buffer overflow* attacks are implemented by providing to a privileged program an input string that is too long. The programmer does not check the length of the input string. In the bogus input string are executable statements that the privileged program accidentally puts on the instruction stack. The program fragment is specially written to give increased privileges to the hacker or to an account that has been compromised. For example, a buffer overflow attack can be used to add a user to the system and to give that user superuser privileges. Generally, the first step in a buffer overflow attack is to gain access to a root shell on UNIX systems.

Nothing in the access control system will detect these problems. Only by monitoring your systems and looking for specific security policy violations will you detect errors such as these. Intrusion detection systems look for event patterns, such as the creation of world readable resources by a privileged program.

## What Is Access Control?

In some sense the login process itself is a form of access control, too. The login process limits who can *access* the computer. Unfortunately, this is not the type of access that was defined in the basic security model. Recall from that introductory material that access control in the security reference monitor is limited to the simple notions of read and write reference requests. The remainder of this chapter deals with how you access resources and accomplish tasks after you have survived the login steps.

The confusion about what precisely constitutes access control stems from various interpretations that appear in marketing literature. You might read a brochure claiming that a particular product can help limit access to your critical resources. Reading further, you find that the advertised solution is really a badge card reader that limits physical access to systems. In some respects, a router that regulates network traffic also performs access control functions because it will drop packets that do not satisfy configured routing rules. Still, for the purposes of this chapter, access control is considered only in the context of the operating system itself and its reference monitor.

Recall also from Chapter 1 that access control is the primary function of the reference monitor. An access request by a subject for an object is checked by the reference monitor against a conceptual database of access control rules. In theoretical computer discussions, entries in the access control database describe what is *not* permitted. In practice, and in the rest of this book, access control statements instead state what is permitted. The three values of interest in the access request are the *subject identifier*, the *object identifier*, and *the type or mode of access* requested. Changing one or more of these three values can generate a different result when the request is evaluated.

Think about that last statement again in more detail. *Who* the system thinks you are is the basis for deciding *what* you can do. When you log in to a computer, your subject identifier is created from your account information stored in the system. If you want to access a resource on the system, your subject identifier is passed to the reference monitor in the request. *If you find a way to impersonate another subject or a way to change your subject identifier, you might be able to access a resource in a manner that normally would not be allowed.* In most systems, this is both a design feature and a threat.

UNIX security features are provided for changing subject identifiers in a controlled fashion. These subroutines are the primary means of temporarily increasing privileges for a user, but they also provide avenues for hacker attacks if the implementation is not properly coded by the programmer. NT defines a special privilege that allows a process or thread to impersonate another user. Later in this chapter, you will see how subject identifiers can be changed in UNIX. To keep the issues from getting too confusing, Chapter 10, "Intrusion Detection for NT," covers impersonation.

---

**N**OTE *Remember that you sometimes must request access to a resource that you cannot regularly reference. To accomplish your task, the system magically invokes a process with higher privileges to carry out the job on your behalf. Because this latter process has higher privileges, the boundary through which your process communicates with this privileged process must be tightly controlled. Otherwise, you might be able to send this privileged process information that tricks it and enables you to hack the system.*

---

### How Are Access Control Decisions Made?

When you have logged into a system, *everything* else that happens seems to be regulated by access control. If you want to print a document, access to printers and documents must be granted. You can accomplish something after you have logged in and started a shell, desktop, or some other type of session in one of two ways:

First, you can create new programs that operate on your behalf. Many commands that you type into a shell are interpreted and executed directly by the shell. However, the majority of commands that you type into a UNIX shell will create new programs, even if these programs run for only a few moments.

Second, you can have your shell send a message to another program that already is running on the computer. This latter form of activity on the system is called *inter-process communication* (IPC) because two running processes are communicating with each other. Instead of creating a new process to execute some commands on your behalf, you can send an IPC message to another program that performs the task for you.

An example of this process is the print spooler on most systems. The spooler is a program running constantly on the system. You might use a direct communication channel to ask the spooler to print something for you, such as sending a print request through an IPC. You also can communicate with the spooler indirectly by storing a file in a special location that the spooler checks. In either case, you can communicate to the spooler that you want some action to occur—printing.

Depositing *data*, such as a file to print or mail, is a technique hackers have used to gain additional privileges on a system. *Common Desktop Environment*

(CDE) had a bug in its mailer that gave peon users the capability to write any file into the mail directory. In some cases, a normal user could create a empty mail box in this directory for the root user. The mailbox would be owned by the normal user, not by root. At any later time, the peon could read the contents of the root user's mailbox. Access control worked as designed; the access control rules just weren't configured properly.

When you perform activities on the system, the credentials associated with your process (UID and GIDs) are checked to see whether the requested operations are permitted. If you run a program, the program has your credentials. If you communicate with another process using an IPC, the credentials of your process are checked by the receiving program. If you deposit data into a directory for a privileged program to act upon, the owner and group IDs for the file represent your credentials, and the privileged program inspects this information to make security decisions. These behaviors show access control at its most fundamental level of analysis—identifiable subjects request access to objects.

## Access Control Lists

Access to objects or resources on a system are regulated by *access control lists* (ACL). At an abstract level, each object in the system is associated with an ACL. The ACL contains zero or more *access control entries* (ACE). An ACE contains enough information for the reference monitor to be able to decide whether the access request is permitted. Because an access *request* at least consists of the subject identifier and the access mode, the ACE contains this information at a minimum. For example, if a user with a UID of 7 wants to have write access to an object, the ACE conceptually contains at least the values {7, write}.

Although architectures vary, a generally accepted security principle is that the ACL should be stored with the object. That is, wherever the object is stored on the system, the ACL for that object also should be stored. Not all security models adhere to this idea. For example, DCE stores all ACLs in an ACL database. When an object, such as a software service, receives a reference request from an object, the object receiving the request performs a lookup in the database to evaluate the request. One reason this approach was adopted for DCE was to provide a general purpose access control framework for software servers. Object replicas could be located in multiple locations for redundancy and high availability, and all copies of the object could use the same single storage location for performing access control lookups. If you think this looks very much like a design tradeoff, with advantages and disadvantages for both approaches for ACL storage, you're starting to understand the complexities of security models.

## Who Are You?

An access control decision must be based on knowing the subject of the request. How does the system know "who" you really are? Unfortunately, the answer is complex, and because it is, systems get hacked. If a security model implementation could perfectly control access to resources, it would not be subject to attacks. You already know this type of control is impossible because of design flaws, programming errors, or administrative errors. Two of the most common ways to break a system are to change who the system thinks you are or to increase the privileges you have on the system. These themes will recur throughout the chapter as you explore access control in UNIX and NT.

## Access Control in UNIX

In the UNIX operating system, access control can take many forms. Files and directories have permission bits that control how users and groups are allowed to access them. The subjects are the UIDs and GIDs that represent the users and groups, and the objects are the files or directories. UNIX also supports a number of IPC types including message queues, semaphores, and shared memory segments. Like the previous chapter, the scope of access control is considered here only in the context of a local computer without network connections. In the next chapter when you explore network security, both I&A and access control topics will be revisited to broaden their meaning to include network concepts. For the moment knowing "who" the system thinks you are, how you want to access a resource, and what access modes are supported by that object are the important items regulating access control.

### Who Are You in the UNIX Environment?

In the preceding chapter, a simplified view of UNIX credentials was presented. You were told that the credentials consisted of a UID and one or more GIDs. In fact, several IDs are associated with a UNIX process, such as your login shell. These values include the *effective user ID* (EUID), the *real user ID* (RUID), the *effective group ID* (EGID), the *real group ID* (RGID), and secondary group IDs. In UNIX when your account is created, you are assigned to a primary group and one or more secondary groups. Your primary group value is copied into the RGID and

EGID credentials fields when your login shell is started, and a separate field in the credentials data structure is set to contain the list of secondary, or supplementary, GIDs. Similarly, the RUID and EUID are initialized to the UID assigned to you when your account is created.

The RUID and RGID represent who you really are because these values are set by login and normally never change. The EUID, EGID, and supplementary GIDs are the values checked when you try to read a file or access another resource. These values primarily represent the subject of the request. In some cases, a programmer may want to check an access request for a resource using the RUID and RGID instead. The access() function is provided in UNIX for this explicit request. Generally, the EUID, EGID, and supplementary GIDs are automatically examined when access to a resource is needed.

On some versions of UNIX, two additional IDs are provided. The *saved set-user-ID* (SSUID) and *saved set-group-ID* (SSGID) are stored copies of the EUID and EGID, respectively. These values can be used to reset the UIDs and GIDs when the credentials for a process are changed during execution. More will be said about these fields later.

Finally, when you log in, an *audit ID* (AUID) is attached to your shell as well. In almost all cases, the AUID is equivalent to the UID reserved for you in /etc/passwd. When system auditing is turned on, your AUID becomes the prefix for every audit record logged for actions you perform. Auditing is discussed further in Chapter 8, "UNIX System Level IDSs." With few exceptions, the AUID is *really* who you are on the system. During a normal interactive session with the computer, your EUID and EGID might change; your RUID and RGID are less likely to change but still might. *Your AUID never changes unless a kernel service is explicitly requested to do so.* Rarely does this occur, and when it does, an audit record is logged to show that the change occurred.

IDs associated with a process can change during the course of program execution. The importance of this capability in UNIX and similar security models cannot be overemphasized. The ability to increase your security privileges by changing your EUID, EGID, RUID, or RGID is one of the basic notions in the UNIX security model. This privilege escalation mechanism is at the root (pun intended) of many UNIX hacks. The chief goal of most hacking attempts is to gain root privileges to exercise total control over the system. If you do not know or cannot guess the root password, the quickest path to becoming root is to log in as another user and find a way to change one of the UIDs to zero—the UID of the root user. Related hacks involve changing one of the IDs to *any* user or group on the system other than the current user. Even incrementally increasing your privileges to those of nonroot users might lead to eventually compromising the root account.

You can change *who* a UNIX system thinks you are in two ways:

◆ You can explicitly change the IDs associated with a process by invoking library or kernel routines.
◆ You also can let the system automatically change your identity based on access permissions that are set for program files on the system.

This latter technique is the one you will explore first as you investigate access control rules for UNIX files and directories.

## UNIX File and Directory Permissions

The UNIX operating system provides a hierarchical virtual file system that might consist of multiple physical storage devices. Each entry in the file system represents a file or directory. The file abstraction is used in the normal sense as a container for data, but in UNIX, the file abstraction also encompasses other concepts such as sockets, character and block devices, and even system memory. Many major UNIX entities are implemented in the file system in one way or another.

The basic storage identifier is an *inode* that contains information about a filesystem object. Each inode is associated with an owner UID and GID. These values are assigned when the file is created but can be changed later using the chown or chgrp command or with a corresponding library routine if invoked from a program. An inode can have only a single owner and a single group ID associated with it.

Traditional UNIX systems support DAC through the use of permission bits. Stored with each inode is a 16-bit mode word that controls access to the files represented by the inode. The least significant nine bits are the most important. Access control in UNIX can be specified for either the file's owner, the file's group, or all others. The three primary access modes are *read* (R), *write* (W), and *execute* (X). The interpretation for these modes varies for files and directories as shown in Table 3.1.

**Table 3.1**   Standard UNIX File Permissions

| Permission | Allowed Action If Object Is a File | Allowed Action If Object Is a Directory |
|---|---|---|
| R (read) | Read contents of file | List contents of the directory |
| X (execute) | Execute file as a program | Search the directory |
| W (write) | Change file contents | Add, rename, create files and subdirectories |

**Are You Remembering to Ask Tough Questions?**

Are you periodically stopping to ask yourself how a hacker uses information you are learning? You should be. Hackers do. Here are a couple of ideas.

You might have a program that scans your system occasionally looking for executable programs created by users. A hacker can use knowledge of when you scan to keep the execute bit turned off, turning it back on only before running the program. To automate the task, the hacker can put a *wrapper* around the program that first turns the execute bit on, runs the program, and then turns the execute bit off.

A hacker can leak information to someone else by setting the permission bits so that *everyone* can read a file. Although in some cases, UNIX (by poor design) requires world-readable or world-writable directories, the general rule is that there should be no permission bit settings of this type.

Certain user files and directories control security aspects of the user's login session. If the permission bits of one of these files has been set so that others can write to the file, a security breach is imminent. If the permission bits have been changed by *another user*, get a cup of coffee or tea. You have some work ahead to discover the trail of activities.

If you're running a real-time IDS, you can catch these events as they occur.

Notice that these interpretations lead to some interesting conditions. If you have execute permission for a directory but not read permission, you can run programs but only if you know the name of the program. You cannot search the directory or list its contents to find the name of the program. In addition, if the file or program you want to access is nested deep within several subdirectories, you must have execute permissions to traverse the directory path.

The ls command displays the permission bit settings for a file or directory. Additional arguments for ls cause it to reveal other inode attributes including file create date, last access time, and last change of any value in the inode (such as the file's length). See Figure 3.1 for an example of a directory listing.

In this example, the file entry for the file gunzip divulges important security information, such as the following:

◆ The user who owns the file, the one whose name is "bin."

◆ The group owner of the file is also group "bin" (although it could have been a different group).

---

**Figure 3.1**    Sample UNIX directory listing.

---

```
-rwxr-x-x   1 bin      bin         110 Mar 09 17:28 gunzip
-rwxrwx-x   1 bin      bin      120931 Mar 13 08:19 gzip
-r-xr-xr-x  1 bin      bin      596549 Mar 26 1997  perl
-r-xr-xr-x  1 bin      bin      113300 May 06 1997  rftp
-r-xr-xr-x  1 bin      bin      158734 May 06 1997  rtelnet
-rwxr-xr-x  1 bin      bin      233378 Apr 29 1996  ssh
-rwxr-xr-x  1 bin      bin       92047 Apr 29 1996  ssh-keygen
```

- The file is composed of 110 512K blocks.
- The last modification time of the file was Mar 09 at 17:28.
- The file's inode has a *link count* of 1, meaning that no other files on the system reference this inode (such as through a hard link).
- The permissions are read, write, and execute for the owner; read and write for anyone in group bin; and only execute for any other user.

Another value that can be set in the inode's 16-bit mode field is the *sticky bit*. The original design of UNIX required that some directories be writeable by all users on the system. In general, this feature is not desirable in a software product. Nonetheless, the /tmp directory has always been writeable by anyone. To prevent users from deleting files that they do not own, the directory's sticky bit can be set. A command for setting the typical permissions for the /tmp directory would be as follows:

```
chmod 7777 /tmp
```

The first 7 sets the sticky bit and the remaining 7s respectively enabled read, write, and execute permissions for owner, group, and world (or user, group, and other). World-writeable directories are not recommended. If you must use them, at least set the sticky bit to prevent the malicious deleting of files.

Other mode bits that can be set include the set user ID and set group ID bits, SUID and SGID respectively. When a file's SUID bit is enabled, program execution can result in increased privileges for the requesting user. Recall that as a normal user on the system, you do not have sufficient privileges to perform all tasks on a system. For example, normal users are not allowed to write a new password directly into the shadow password file. Instead, to change your password, you must execute a privileged program that changes the password on your behalf. Hopefully, the program is well behaved. If not, the flaw can be exploited by you or any interested hacker.

### Link Counts, Hard Links, and Symbolic Links

The standard UNIX file system is divided into a number of storage chunks. Two important chunks are the areas set aside for the inodes of the file system and the data blocks making up the contents of the file system entries. A file and a directory are both entries in the file system, even though a directory can contain one or more files or subdirectories. Each file or directory defined in the data blocks area is associated with an inode, so the file has a pointer back to the inode that describes it.

Two or more different files can refer to the same data bits making up a file. This process is accomplished by creating one of two types of links. You first create file A. At this point, the inode for A has a link count of 1. Next, you explicitly create file B by declaring that it is a *hard link* to file A. This can be done from the command line or through a subroutine. A directory entry is created for file B; the contents of file A are not copied. Instead, the directory entry for file B points back to the inode for file A. When B is created, the link count in the inode for file A is incremented by one. You can repeat this process as many times as you like.

A *symbolic link* is stored differently in the directory. If you had created B as a symbolic link, it would have the string name of the target file, namely "A," stored in the directory entry for B. Symbolic links were originally cre-

---

The interpretation of the SUID bit is as follows. When a program is executed, the file's mode bits are examined. If the SUID bit is enabled, the kernel obtains the UID of the file's owner. When the process context is being initialized for the program to run in, the EUID and SSUID are set to the UID of the file's owner. If you run a SUID program, the EUID and SSUID of the new process will be set to the owner UID, but the RUID remains the same. If the program is owned by root, you will have gained root privileges on the system.

The passwd program used to change your password is an example of an SUID program. Other programs, such as the notorious UNIX sendmail daemon, might be configured as SGID for group *mail*. Because SUID root programs effectively give the requesting user root privileges, these programs need to be well written.

Note that you should never have SUID shell scripts on a system. A race condition attack is possible in which the hacker can trick the operating system into executing an arbitrary shell script with root privileges instead of the SUID root shell script stored on the system. Some operating systems, such as IBM's AIX, do not even allow you to create SUID shell scripts. If you need to write privileged

ated to overcome a limitation in early UNIX systems that did not allow you to define hard links across different file systems. POSIX allows an option for the creation of hard links across file systems. *Therefore, you should consult the reference manuals for your specific UNIX version to learn about the limitations of hard and symbolic links and how various system routines behave when a link is passed as a parameter.*

The type of link—symbolic or hard link—affects the way access control routines behave. For example, the system call access() will follow the symbolic link and operate on the file named in the link. Using the files shown previously, access(B) really is interpreted as access(A). Other routines do not follow the link and work with the file it points to, but operate on the symbolic link itself. If you call chown(B), the owner of the symbolic link will be changed, *not* the owner of file A. This may seem like a confusing mess, but if you do not understand these internals, you will not understand the potential threats.

Can a hacker exploit link counts? If you *delete* file B, the data bits are still accessible via file A! Are there other hacks that exploit the intricacies of hard links and symbolic links? Yes, and you'll see some of these in Chapter 8, "UNIX System Level IDSs." Will access control mechanisms protect you from these configuration problems? If they could, you wouldn't need to install intrusion detection systems.

scripts, learn Perl and write your scripts in its more tightly controlled environment. Unfortunately, in at least one published attack on Perlin which its similar SUID capabilities are exploited.

The UNIX operating system is full of SUID and SGID programs. You can easily display a list of these programs using the find command. If your environment consists of many commercial products, too, it's likely that additional SUID or SGID programs will be installed. Escalating privileges in programs through the use of SUID and SGID semantics is a common programming practice in UNIX. Sadly, these programs are the most commonly exploited items on computers today. Privileged programs executable by arbitrary users can be probed in a number of ways. If you try sending a range of invalid parameters to a program, and the program crashes, a buffer overflow attack probably is lurking in that program.

One defense is to diligently monitor SUID activities on your system. Access control does not provide a complete security solution in itself. You should regularly inspect your system for new SUID or SGID programs. *Also, you should install intrusion detection products that monitor privilege transitions in real time and alert you when one of these programs changes or is executed by a user.*

If you prefer, tools such as Tripwire from COAST are available for interval monitoring of important files such as SUID and SGID executables. With Tripwire, you can compute cryptographic checksums on files and store the results in a database. Periodically, you can recalculate the checksums again on the files to see whether they were modified.

## Increasing Your Privileges or Capabilities

In addition to using file permission bits such as SUID or SGID to change who you are on a system, UNIX variants provide library or kernel routines for changing UIDs and GIDs associated with a process. When SUID or SGID bits are set, the system automatically calls one of these routines on your behalf when setting up the process' context before execution. Because changing credentials can lead to increased capabilities on the system, limitations exist on how UIDs and GIDs can be changed. Two commonly available routines are setuid() and setgid(), which are passed a single integer parameter to change the UID or GID of a process respectively. The outcome of invoking one of these routines depends on the credentials associated with the calling process:

- All three IDs—RUID, EUID, and SSUID—are changed if the process has superuser (root) capabilities.
- If the value passed in as a parameter is the same as either the RUID or SSUID, the EUID is changed to the parameter value. To change the EUID to the RUID, pass in the RUID as the parameter. Setting the EUID to SSUID is accomplished similarly.
- If neither case is met, the routine returns an error.

Depending on whether your version of UNIX supports POSIX or is derived from BSD or System V UNIX, other ID manipulation routines are available including seteuid() and setegid(), which set only the effective UID and GID respectively. As before, the outcome of the request depends on the privileges of the requesting process. Normal users can set only the EUID to the value stored in RUID or SSUID. When called by a privileged user process, these routines set only the EUID or EGID, unlike setuid(), which changes the RUID and SSUID, too.

The RUID, EUID, and SSUID are set to your assigned UID by the login process, which is a privileged program. The RUID normally never changes. Under usual circumstances, the EUID is changed only by the exec() routine when the SUID bit is set for a program file, and you execute that file. An unprivileged user cannot set the EUID to an arbitrary value. Therefore, when you start another process or run a program from your login shell, the EUID is inherited and remains unchanged unless the file's SUID bit is set. The EUID value is copied into the SSUID field by exec() after interpretation of the SUID bit for the file. In other words, if the file's SUID bit is set, the UID of the file's owner is stored into both the SSUID and the EUID. The EUID then can be set to either the RUID or the SSUID depending on the needs of the program. Why is this necessary?

Good programming practices dictate that SUID and SGID programs escalate privileges only for the fewest program statements necessary. A program requiring SUID should first set the EUID to the value stored in the RUID (the invoking user's ID). Privileged resource accesses are not permitted with these settings, and the program is relatively safe from exploits with these settings. Only when the privileged operations are needed should the program call setuid() using SSUID as the parameter to increase the program's privileges. When the privileged section of code is complete, the EUID should be set back to the less powerful RUID. Similar comments apply to changing GIDs associated with a process.

*You should know that many UNIX hacks originate with SUID or SGID programs.* Buffer overflow attacks against SUID or SGID programs appear almost daily, especially when the file's owner is the root user. The typical attack is to overflow a buffer for the program in a way that loads executable statements onto the stack. The common attack is to load statements that will start another shell from the SUID program, essentially launching a shell or window with root privileges.

One of the most important aspects of your access control policy is to tightly limit which users are allowed to run SUID or SGID programs. This control can be very difficult to maintain with only permission bits. A user normally may not have access permissions for a SUID program. However, if that user *does* have access to a SGID program whose group in turn has permissions to run the SUID program, the transitive behavior will violate your policy. These types of complex relationships are difficult to protect against using only permission bits for files and real (or effective) user IDs. What is more desirable is a mechanism for always tracing the access request to the a particular initial user regardless of transitions in EUID or EGID.

Another choice is to remove all SUID and SGID programs on the system. This process is essentially what happens on multilevel operating systems that rely on itemized privileges for users. The file and directory permission bits are not overloaded to include SUID or SGID semantics in these systems. If multilevel solutions are not feasible, other improvements are still possible. The discussion on Memco SeOS later in this chapter describes one alternative.

SCO UNIXware is equipped with a more granular notion of capabilities than most UNIX variants. Specific privileges can be granted to users, such as the following:

- The right to start and stop print services
- The right to create, change, or delete users
- The right to mount or unmount devices

Many other privileges, usually defined for management tasks, exist as well. The purpose of this feature is to provide more flexibility in delegating administrative tasks. Thus, a user can have increased privileges on a system for performing some administrative tasks without knowing the root user's password. A little known feature of IBM's AIX operating system is that it also contains a data structure supporting privileges, although the design was never implemented as fully as in SCO UNIXware. Products, such as those provided by Tivoli, discussed briefly at the end of this chapter, have been introduced to layer this feature on most versions of UNIX.

## Background Processes and Credentials

In Chapter 2, you saw how to control who can log in and begin interacting with the computer. Many processes already are running on the system before you even log in. These processes and applications, of course, have a security context. That is, they are tagged with UIDs and GIDs so that appropriate access limitations can be enforced. How does such a process get its security credentials or context?

Most operating systems have a common startup process. The details naturally vary across manufacturers, but the following high-level description should suffice. When the computer is turned on, the system's hardware performs various *power on self tests* (POST). These checks look for memory, processor, and bus problems. Usually, a programmable ROM (PROM or EPROM) has been set to look into a special memory location called *nonvolatile random access memory* (NVRAM). The NVRAM contains various types of configuration information for the system, especially data on how to boot the operating system. The CPU loads this boot information that typically points to further boot instructions stored on disk in a special *boot record*. The boot record points to a minimal version of the operating system kernel that is then loaded into the CPU. This kernel then overlays itself with the full kernel found on the disk.

The kernel typically initializes a process from which all other processes are created. This *init* process starts with the root user ID. When other processes are started as children of this initial process, their security credentials will be the same unless the operating system is configured to run them with other privileges. For example, the mail daemon on most systems is usually run with a GID for the group *mail*. The default UNIX /etc/passwd file shown in the preceding chapter should give you an idea of the possible UIDs that background processes might be launched with when a UNIX system boots. There really isn't any magic in how this works. The system is still using the basic notions of process inheritance or explicit system calls to establish the credentials of these special programs.

## Access Control in NT

In NT every access control reference goes through a single reference monitor (except for applications that implement their own reference monitors). In the long run, this architectural model is better to use for security. The same architecture is found on mainframe computers and implemented by products such as RACF, ACF/2, and TOP SECRET. Even though the architecture is good, the implementation can still be flawed. NT has had its fair share of hack attacks.

Like UNIX, NT makes decisions based on subjects, objects, and access control lists. To begin with, the NT reference monitor must know the subject of the request in order to evaluate whether to permit the operation.

### NT Rights and Privileges

What you can do in NT is a combination of the rights you have and the access control rules defined for objects you want to manipulate. The NT operating system contains more than 27 specific rights. The rights you have are formed

---

**Who Are You in NT?**

In the preceding chapter, it was shown that the NT login process finishes by creating a desktop process for you and associating with it an access token. The access token contains your unique *security identifier* (SID), your primary group SID, and the SIDs for any other groups to which you belong. Access control rules in NT specify the subject using the SID of a user or the SID of a group. See Chapter 10, "Intrusion Detection For NT," for a peek at the contents of an access token.

from the union of any rights assigned to you as an individual plus any rights defined for groups to which you belong. Example rights include the ability to log in to a system from the network, the ability to log in locally to a system, the ability to impersonate other users, the ability to back up files, and the ability to create new users. A particularly powerful right is the ability to act as part of the operating system. Naturally, you would not want everyone on your system to be able to have this right.

To simplify administration of the environment, default users and groups are enabled as part of the standard NT installation. These users and groups are assigned sets of rights to perform tasks on the system. For example, the default group Backup Operators have the ability to back up and restore files but not the right to add or change users. Like default settings for file and directory permissions, no proof that the default settings are secure exists. A weakness in NT, or in a privileged application running on NT, which can be used by a hacker to increase access rights, is a serious problem. The widely publicized *GetAdmin* hack is an example of how an arbitrary user is able to gain Administrator rights. In this hack, a normal user was able to write a global memory variable in the NT address space, which gave the user Administrator rights after the next login session.

## Permissions for NT Files and Directories

The *NT file system* (NTFS) supports granular DAC. Each file in the NTFS is an object. Every NT object has a security descriptor consisting of the object's unique identifier and a pair of access control lists. The security descriptor for an object is initialized when the object is created. Figure 3.2 shows the components of the security descriptor.

The security descriptor contains a DAC ACL component and a SYSTEM ACL component. Normal NT user and group access rights for an object are stored in the DAC ACL. Each entry (ACE) in a DAC ACL identifies a particular user or group SID along with the access permissions granted to that subject. The special NT user SYSTEM, which represents the operating system itself, has a separate ACL. These two distinct ACLs are described in the next few sections.

### DAC Access Control Lists

NT distinguishes between *standard* permissions and *special* permissions. Access permissions for an object are normally defined using the standard permissions that are logical groupings of special permissions. Consider the more low-level special permissions first.

Special permissions are similar to permission bits found in UNIX with two additions. First, an explicit option enables the subject to change the object's access

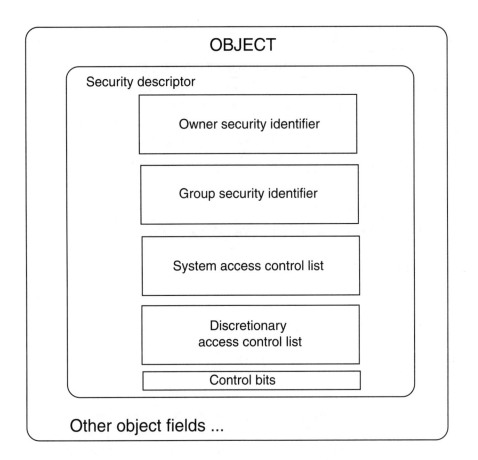

**Figure 3.2** Contents of the NT security descriptor.

permissions. If you have this permission for an object, even if you are not the object's owner, you will be allowed to modify its permissions. Unlike most UNIX systems, NT allows for the possibility that the object's owner may not be the only user who is allowed to change the permissions of an object. For example, user Joe may want users Bill and Jane to be able to set permissions on files that they work on together. Next, special permission can be granted to take ownership of an object. By default, the owner of the object controls its permissions. Taking ownership of an object is a powerful permission and is normally limited to the object's owner. The Administrator is allowed to take ownership of any object. Table 3.2 describes the special NT file permissions.

**Table 3.2**   NT Special Permissions

| Permission | Allowed Action If Object Is a File | Allowed Action If Object Is a Directory |
|---|---|---|
| R | Read contents of file | View file and subdirectory names |
| X | Execute file as a program | Can change to subdirectories |
| W | Change file contents | Add, rename, create files and subdirectories |
| D | Delete file | Delete directory and subdirectories |
| P | Change file permissions | Change directory permissions |

**Table 3.3**   NT Standard Permissions

| Permission | Allowed Action If Object Is a File | Allowed Action If Object Is a Directory |
|---|---|---|
| No Access | None | None |
| List | Not applicable | RX |
| Read | RX | RX |
| Add | Not applicable | WX |
| Add & Read | Not applicaable | RWX |
| Change | RWXD | RWXD |
| Full Control | All | All |

Standard permissions are summarized in Table 3.3. Notice that the intent is to provide more meaningful terms for users to administer access permissions than the granular special permissions. Whether in practice these higher level abstractions are easier for systems administrators is a matter of opinion.

Notice that the List and Add permissions have no interpretation for individual files. These permissions are meaningful only for directories. Recall from the discussions on UNIX permissions that a number of special meanings are applied to the permission bits depending on whether the object is a file or directory. The interpretations for the NT standard permissions are shown in Table 3.4 for files and Table 3.5 for directories.

Why not simply itemize all of the permission interpretations and allow users to individually grant or deny these? The NT and UNIX designers alike were making a tradeoff for simplicity over granularity. Rather than explicitly creating a permission for more than a dozen different access rights, grouping and overloading were allowed to *simplify* the administrator's task.

You also can assign the permission Special Access for a file that gives the designated user the ability to explicitly specify individual special permissions (R, W, X, D, and P) for the object.

**Table 3.4**    Interpretation of NT Standard Permissions for Files

| Permission | Interpretation |
| --- | --- |
| No Access | Under no circumstances is the user allowed access to the file. |
| Read | Permission to execute the file, open the file, or display the file's attributes. |
| Change | Permission to append to or change data in the file, to display the file's owner and permissions, plus the Read permissions. |
| Full Control | Equivalent to Change with the additional capability to take ownership of the file. |

**Table 3.5**    Interpretation of NT Standard Permissions for Folders

| Permission | Interpretation |
| --- | --- |
| No Access | Under no circumstances is the user allowed access to the file. |
| List | Users can list files and subdirectories to which they have access but cannot list files or subdirectories to which they do not have explicit access in this folder. |
| Read | Permission to list files or subdirectories, execute programs, change into subfolders, and display attributes of files or subfolders. |
| Add | Files can be added to the folder. Neither Read nor List are implied by this permission. |
| Add & Read | Includes Add permissions and Read permissions combined. |
| Change | Permissions granted by Read augmented to include creation of subfolders and files, changing file or folder attributes, and deletion of the folder's files and subfolders. |
| Full Control | Equivalent to Change with the additional capability to change permissons of the folder itself and to take ownership of the directory itself. |

The Windows NT interface for viewing or changing permissions can be confusing to read. When you view the permissions for an object, the permissions are itemized for each subject (user or group). Each line in the lower portion of the display shows the subject and the access permissions. The access permissions include the standard permission name and two sets of special permissions. The first set itemizes special permissions allowed on subfolders (subdirectories), and the second set lists the special permissions for files within the current folder. These sets are not always equal as Tables 3.4 and 3.5 show.

A user can gain access either through permissions granted individually to the user or with permissions defined for any groups to which the user belongs. Access permissions are interpreted with the least privilege principle. *Any expressly denied permission overrides any granted permissions.* For example, if a user belongs to a group that has read access, but the user is explicitly entered in an ACE with No Access, the user will not be allowed to access the object. No Access overrides any other permissions.

You should know that access control can be specified for other objects in the NT environment including printers. Not all of the access control options identified are available for all objects, however.

### NT Registry Permissions

The NT Registry is the main repository for storing system configuration information. As applications are added to the system, additional Registry entries are created. It is safe to say that the Registry is mysterious to even experienced systems administrators. Microsoft has responded to some security advisories by creating new Registry entries or by recommending changes to default values stored in the Registry.

Because the Registry is so critical to the operation of NT itself, a set of access control permissions is defined for Registry entries. Each entry in the Registry consists of a *key* and a *value*. Technically, the value can be a complex expression such as a string of characters. Entries are arranged hierarchically, much like a file system. Unfortunately, many parts of the Registry must be readable by all users. Not all users should be allowed to change Registry entries. Just as the NTFS supports standard and special permissions, the Registry has three *standard* access permissions and 10 *special* access permissions. Table 3.6 summarizes the standard Registry permissions, and Table 3.7 describes the special permissions.

Just as file access permissions are set by default for NT, Registry permissions are also configured when NT is installed.

## How Hackers Get around Access Control

Postings in cyberspace as well as recent books have detailed some of the attacks and recommended configurations for NT systems (Sheldon, 1997; Anonymous, 1997; Klander, 1997). Chapter 10, "Intrusion Detection for NT," is devoted exclusively to describing what can go wrong on NT systems and why intrusion detection is needed despite NT's C2 rating. The literature on problems with UNIX systems is immense, with Garfinkel and Spafford (1996) on most recommended reading lists.

In Part 2 of this book, some specific hack attacks will be detailed. For the purposes of this chapter, it is sufficient to state that access control problems can be narrowed down to one of two cases:

**Table 3.6**  Standard Registry Permissions

| Permission | Interpretation |
| --- | --- |
| Full Control | Edit, create, delete, or take ownership of Registry entries |
| Read | Read any key value |
| Special Access | Any combination of the 10 special permissions |

**Table 3.7**  Special Registry Permissions

| Permission | Interpretation |
| --- | --- |
| Query Value | Read a value for a key or subkey |
| Create Subkey | Set the value of a subkey |
| Enumerate Subkeys | List all subkeys within a key or subkey |
| Notify | Receive notifications generated by this key or subkey |
| Create Link | Create symbolic links to subkeys |
| Delete | Delete keys or subkeys |
| Write DAC | Modify the DAC for this key |
| Write Owner | Take ownership of key or subkey |
| Read Control | Read security information for a subkey |

◆ Access control rules defined for an object are too permissive, and the hacker exploits a weakness introduced by this configuration. This situation can be the result of a configuration problem by the vendor, by the administrator, or by a program when it creates the object.

◆ A user can increase rights or privileges, with the goal of gaining Administrative or root access. Remember, this is usually the result of a software bug.

A couple of solutions to the first problem exist. You can diligently try to analyze every possible access permission for objects in your environment and hope that you set them properly. In practice, this approach has not been completely successful, which is one reason the marketplace is so interested in intrusion detection for finding leftover weaknesses. Because your site also contains many custom or purchased applications, properly configuring the NT or UNIX operating system settings alone will not secure your site. For example, if you run a Web server on your system with exploitable bugs, and the operating system is locked down tightly, hackers will still be able to penetrate your defenses. Unfortunately, only time will tell whether your configurations are adequate. The other approach, monitoring your systems, is the only way to know for sure that your access control policies are defined correctly or have been modified without your knowledge. *Intrusion detection products are expressly designed for this purpose.* Among other things, they look for evidence indicating that a user has created a SUID root program, accessed a normally unavailable directory, or altered resources belonging to another user.

System monitoring also can help solve the second problem. By watching privilege increases for users, you can be alerted when a security policy violation occurs. Already mentioned are two famous techniques for gaining additional privileges—the GetAdmin hack on NT and the buffer overflow attack (Aleph One, 1997) now so common in UNIX. (The *Phrack* article written by Aleph One contains material originally posted by Mudge at the L0pht Web site www.l0pht.com). Other flaws in privileged programs have been exploited by users to gain additional privileges.

## How to Improve upon Access Control

Only by monitoring your systems will you know that your security policy is being enforced properly. Intrusion detection can solve security problems that I&A, access control, and even firewalls do not. Before launching further into these discussions, though, you can improve access control on out-of-the-box UNIX and NT systems by installing other products. Several access control security products are available to sit on top of UNIX and NT operating systems. Many of these products merely provide a thin veneer over the existing features in UNIX and NT.

One particular product, Memco's SeOS, adds significant value. Portions of SeOS have been incorporated into Tivoli's Security Manager product. What is SeOS?

Monitoring and intrusion detection products work by identifying *who* performed *what* action. The *who* is determined from the AUID of a process or by deducing the AUID from a series of events. One of the problems with the UNIX operating system is that access control decisions are made most of the time by using the EUID or EGID. In some cases, the RUID and RGID might be the basis for the decision. SeOS limits access based on the AUID and provides stronger protection. IDSs use the AUID to assign accountability because it is a reliable indicator of *who* is performing the action. SeOS uses the AUID to regulate access control for the same reason.

SeOS also provides for the capability to limit accesses based on the *path* of access. For example, SeOS can limit access to a resource depending on the program that a user is running to get to the resource. These two features are among the best advantages of SeOS.

## Memco SeOS

SeOS is a real-time access control product that *intercepts* a subset of system calls, performs a *user exit* routine, and then either rejects the access request or passes control to the kernel for processing. In the user exit, SeOS compares the parameters of the request (UID, GID, file name, or resource name) to its database of access control constraints. If no constraint is violated, the user exit completes with success and the request is forwarded to the requested system call. SeOS does not replace any system calls.

Each SeOS enabled node has a local database. Several daemon processes are run on the node as well. The database can be updated from a remote system if configured to accept inbound commands. The managed nodes may subscribe to a central policy manager to obtain database updates. The SeOS environment is managed by a SeOS administrator and a SeOS auditor. Both of these users are distinct from the root user.

Managed resources can be assigned labels and categories that are used to enforce *mandatory access control* (MAC). This feature is also applicable to network resources such as hosts or services. No capabilities are provided for MAC on System V IPC semaphores, message queues, or shared memory. Communications between distributed systems are accomplished via DES encryption between nodes. The entire encryption library can be replaced and example code is provided. For example, if someone wanted to substitute weak encryption for export, SeOS supports extensions. No key distribution framework is provided for ensuring that all communicating parties share the same secret.

### Access Control Constraints

To summarize SeOS in one sentence, it is best described as RACF mainframe security on UNIX. SeOS terminology comes from both UNIX and RACF, but SeOS is sometimes summarized as an attempt to provide traditional mainframe administrators with familiar concepts for specifying a security access control policy when working with UNIX and NT systems.

Many systems are configured to allow root access only from a physically attached terminal. The only way to gain root privileges remotely is by using the su command to switch from a normal user to the root user. The AUID is not changed by the su command. That is, the su command does not hide who the user *really* is. SeOS uses the AUID to make access control decisions and is not fooled by su transitions. Even if a hacker guesses the root password and can su to root, access to a resource will not be granted if SeOS is configured properly. This feature goes way beyond the access control security features supplied in UNIX and NT by default. In a typical UNIX configuration without SeOS, the su operation would give the remote user full access to the system.

The commonly used terms in SeOS are subject (or *accessor*) and resource. Access control features include the following:

- Login limits varying time of day, day of week, source network address, or physical terminal.
- Limits on which programs can be killed, *even by root*.
- TCP/IP packet filtering by services, host, host-groups, network address, hostname patterns, or port number (firewall-like services).
- TCP/IP access control by user or group combined with the preceding variables, including inbound and outbound connections where applicable. (Joe cannot telnet out; Joe cannot accept a connection.)
- For almost every access control constraint, one can specify time of day, day of week, and controlling terminal. (Joe can run /bin/vi but only on Wednesday from 9–11 and when logged in from IP address 1.2.3.4.)
- Trusted computing base (Tripwire type) protection for SUID/SGID programs that the administrator defines; if the TCB signature changes, the program is no longer trusted and cannot be run until *retrusted* by the SeOS administrator.
- Division of privileges so that root cannot tamper with auditing or audit files.
- Watchdog daemon that ensures SeOS daemons are running.
- *Program pathing* that limits access to a resource only when the user is doing so from a particular program name. (Joe can change /etc/hosts but only when done through the /bin/trustme editor.)
- Password quality rules.
- SUDO for root privilege granularity, giving unprivileged users the ability to run a subset of administrative commands (start/stop printers or user management, for example).
- Locking of idle terminals or *X*-stations after *N*-minutes of inactivity.
- Full CLI or GUI.
- Resource protection, such as files and directories, even from the root user.

## APIs

Program APIs are provided for nearly all of the functions SeOS contains. An arbitrary resource can be defined; access control rules for this resource can be declared; and access requests can be queried by the resource controller using these APIs. Note that this is very much like DCE in that it represents a general-purpose access control framework and is not limited to UNIX semantics like "file on a disk." In other words, a resource's controlling program may view different parts of a normal UNIX file as different access control regions, and SeOS can be used to regulate which users (or other accessors) are permitted to access various regions of the file independent of its UNIX permission bits. The resource has a dual identity: (1) as a file with UNIX permission bits and SeOS access control constraints and (2) as a resource whose contents are subdivided into SeOS access control regions that are only meaningful to the program subsystem which *owns* the file. This idea is *very* powerful because access control can be applied to concepts that are more granular than traditional UNIX or NT resources.

## Impact of SeOS on Base Operating System Security

Because the system call that SeOS intercepts is eventually executed when access control is permitted, the base operating system's auditing features are generally unaffected by SeOS. One exception to this occurs with root privilege division.

Most UNIX systems do not support a standard mechanism for dividing root privileges among multiple users. SeOS includes a program that executes as a root process but performs tasks on behalf of unprivileged users. The SeOS database is configured to control which users are permitted to run special privileged programs. Here, a *privileged program* means one that is usually not accessible by the ordinary user because it is in a protected directory or because its permission bits do not allow access. This definition does not necessarily include SUID or SGID programs that are addressed separately by SeOS.

Privilege granularity, in which ordinary users can be given limited root privileges, is an exception to base system auditing in that the audit record shows UIDs (real, effective, and audit) that represent *root* rather than the login user. The UIDs belong to root because SeOS is executing a process on behalf of a requesting user. In other words, this *new* function is not normally available in UNIX systems. For a monitoring system to assign accountability for a behavior that occurred during privilege delegation, the monitor would need to look at SeOS audit logs as well as the operating system logs.

IDSs are affected in other ways by SeOS and other software products that intercept system calls. You'll learn more about this concept as you dig into intrusion detection in Part 2, "Intrusion Detection: Beyond Traditional Security," of this book.

## SeOS Auditing

SeOS emits its own audit trail for security tracking. Even without a security policy, SeOS reports on important activities, such as login, logout, password changes, fork, exec, and so on. The types of events reported include the following:

- Access control success and failures
- Additions, deletions, and changes for the SeOS database
- Individual commands run at the SeOS console window (that exists on each managed node)
- Logins (failures and successes)
- System startup and shutdown
- Audit startup and shutdown

Like the base operating system audit services, an audit ID (AUID) is added to each audit record.

Audit records are logged in either binary or text form based on the configuration. Logs can be consolidated to a central audit server based on scheduled parameters. The audit server consolidates the distributed audit logs into a single file by adding the hostname to the beginning of each record. This consolidation enables the user to be able to filter based on hostname at the audit server. On each audited node, one can configure audit filters that determine the types of audit events forwarded to the audit server. This feature can help reduce bandwidth on the network and reporting time at the audit server because unimportant records are not forwarded.

Audit consolidation is performed by the emitter daemon running on each node and the collector daemon on the audit server. Both daemons support configuration files in which the output format, filters, and log file characteristics can be defined. Audit records include a sufficient amount of information, roughly equivalent to what is found in audit records from the base operating system. APIs are provided for accessing the audit records in binary form. The events reported in normal auditing of SeOS are primarily access control events or login events.

How does SeOS decide what to audit? When users or resources are defined, the security administrator sets the audit characteristics for those entities. Again, the events for users might be successful or unsuccessful logins. For resources such as files, events include access successes or failures. Individual file auditing is thus supported. Resource access can be set to *notify* so that each time someone accesses a particular file, for example, e-mail can be sent to a set of addresses. At this time, the response capability does not seem to be configurable, although custom responses are possible in the TME Event Console when SeOS is used as part of Tivoli's Security Manager product.

Audit logs can be scanned or reported on using CLI or the interactive GUI. A separate audit server is not required. The audit logs can be examined on each system. Filters include the following:

♦ Login/audit ID

♦ Terminal or workstation (if network attached)

♦ Originating host (for consolidated logs)

♦ Resource class

♦ Start/stop dates and times

♦ Status (success, failure, warning, and notify)

♦ IP service name, port

♦ Trusted program name

♦ Startup/shutdown

♦ SeOS administrator name

Filters for viewing audit records can be wildcards or specific entries. Indeed, for many of the fields in a given access control constraint, wildcards are accepted. Possibilities include "Joe can access file /home/foo only when requested through program /bin/v*."

The Trace log is similar to the audit log and can be configured to store its output in the audit log. Trace logs include more detailed information including process create, fork, exec, process death, setuid() calls, setgid() calls, and more as the documentation claims. Many of the Trace events are SeOS related. These events include administrator activities such as "user XYZ ran the seadmin command with these parameters . . ." The entire set of Trace messages provided is contained in roughly 25 pages of documentation in a SeOS publication appendix.

## Other SeOS Features

SeOS protects against su, SUID, and SGID escalation with access control rules. Individual SUID programs can be limited with the types of variables described in this chapter (user, group, time of day, and so on). SeOS will scan the system for SUID programs, for example, or you can enter names individually. This additional level of access security addresses some of the concerns regarding SUID and SGID programs. An administrator can specify some very complex predicates that are used to limit normal user access to privileged programs. Because hackers often look for privileged programs to exploit, this feature is valuable. One simple approach is to disallow running of privileged programs from users that login remotely. This approach actually requires some fine tuning, because programs such as e-mail fall into this category.

Many customers complain about UNIX because it permits the same user to log in more than once simultaneously to the same system. Others see this feature as an advantage. In any event, like mainframes, SeOS can limit individual users to a single active login session per node.

SeOS can be configured to disable logins based on failed login attempts. Flexibility exists in how this can be done. For example, N failed logins from a given source would block logins only from that source IP address, terminal, or X-station. Although most operating systems support login disabling after a configured number of failures, blocking from a specific source is designed to reduce the denial of service threats due to login failures. (Remember this from Chapter 2?)

## Going beyond SeOS

The *Tivoli Management Environment* (TME) layers a uniform security model on heterogeneous operating systems. Like the individual privileges or rights that a user on NT can be assigned, the TME security model supports granular privileges using a *role-based model*. Role-based access control is both a practical and a research topic, meaning that you can find both commercial products and formal papers about the area. Essentially, a role is a collection of operations or privileges. A user can belong to one or more roles. When an operation is initiated by the user, various access rights are verified based on the roles assumed by the user.

A role-based architecture, such as the one provided by TME, is flexible enough to permit arbitrary definitions of roles beyond the predefined set in NT, for example. Roles can be defined for the operating system as well as for application-level programs. Depending on the situation, a program may need to be modified to be aware of the role-based model, or the model can be layered over an existing environment including much of the UNIX operating system. Unfortunately, when layered over UNIX, the root access problem still persists. That is, you or a hacker can always bypass the processes on the system implementing the layered approach and work directly with system programs or processes. Still, role-based architectures provide promise for access granularity for systems management and application programs beyond what is delivered in off-the-shelf operating systems today.

## Why You Still Need Intrusion Detection

One of the main points to remember from this chapter is that the success of access control depends heavily upon knowing the subject of the request. Who the system thinks you are is controlled at login time by I&A processes detailed in the preceding chapter. In this chapter, you also saw how you could change *who* you are in the system through privilege escalation in UNIX and impersonation in NT. As part of the normal activities on a system, various programs increase and decrease their privileges on a regular basis. *This basic behavior is one of the most often exploited characteristics of systems. Hackers look for weaknesses in privileged programs to gain superuser access to a system.*

Even if the access control rules are correctly set, it is possible to abide by these constraints yet still hack a system and gain complete control. The net is *that access control is not sufficient for securing your environment.* A few years ago, it was not hard to find people who would argue that preventative access control techniques were enough to block attacks. Now, awareness of the importance of monitoring and intrusion detection is slowly creeping into the marketplace.

One weakness of SeOS is that it does not regulate access to traditional IPC constructs, such as semaphores, message queues, or shared memory. No audit trail events are emitted by SeOS for these resources. Not many hack attacks are launched from IPC components, but it will not be long before weakness in IPC security result in system compromises. If you're using an IDS, you have a higher chance of catching hacks if they occur at this low level in the system.

Although it is not a weakness of SeOS, a computer with only SeOS can still be hacked when someone accesses a resource that is not managed by the SeOS reference monitor. How is this possible? Because SeOS is an access control environment that requires the administrator to specify access rules, administrators may make mistakes. Also, an administrator may not put all system resources under the control of SeOS. Not all buffer overflow attacks will be intercepted by access rules in SeOS. Thus, although SeOS significantly improves the access control security for most systems, it must be complemented with monitoring products.

As noted before, it is extremely important that you monitor your system's activities to fine tune both your I&A and access control configurations. In the next chapter, you will see how these same issues affect network security. Both I&A and access control for networks will be described. Adding a firewall to better control your site security will definitely increase your perimeter security. However, you will see that intrusion detection is still required because firewalls and other network security mechanisms do not completely eliminate successful hacker attacks.

# Chapter 4

# Traditional Network Security Approaches

So far you have seen that I&A and access control for systems are not enough for a complete security solution. You learned that intrusion detection is needed to monitor your systems because I&A and access control, even when augmented with other products, still leave your system vulnerable to attacks. Intrusion detection will not prevent these attacks, but it can help you detect trespassers when they enter your site. If your responses are configured properly, an IDS can help stop hackers before they get too far.

The last two chapters dealt with I&A and access control mostly from the perspective of a single computer without network connections. Now that you understand the basic issues in I&A and access control, let's move forward into network security. As the first section shows, network security is a bit more complicated because it introduces new sources of threats.

Next, you'll examine the important entities in network security. When you examined I&A in the basic stand-alone model, the user was the chief entity of interest. The user was represented by subjects such as processes or threads that operate on the user's behalf. In access control decisions, the subject was represented by a set of UIDs and GIDs. In some network communications, these credentials are still important, but new entities must be addressed as well. Examples of other entities include network nodes and software processes that communicate over the network. Therefore, in this chapter, you will see how I&A and access control are implemented for these entities, too. You also will learn about the weaknesses in some widely used Internet protocols, although many improvements to these standards are being implemented in commercial products today.

Like stand-alone systems, network attached systems must meet the three security goals identified in Chapter 1 (confidentiality, integrity, and availability). Stand-alone systems primarily use a combination of I&A and access control to meet these three goals, although cryptographic methods are sometimes employed to protect files on a disk. As you move into the network space, you will find that these same basic mechanisms—I&A and access control—are equally important for ensuring network security. However, you eventually will see that cryptography provides the best security for network communications.

Because one of the most commonly used access control products for networks is the firewall, some time will be spent describing firewall architectures and features. *As in the case of I&A and system access control, you will see that firewalls still do not complete the security picture for your site.* Knowing the limitations of firewalls and other network security techniques will complete the foundation necessary for understanding the need for intrusion detection.

## Layers of Network Security

One of the reasons that network security is harder is because the channel over which two entities communicate may be unsecure. On a stand-alone system, when two programs want to exchange information, the operating system provides a variety of secure mechanisms. The programs can communicate using shared memory, message queues, pipes, or files. All of these techniques are handled by the operating system, which the programmers assume to be trustworthy.

When two programs need to communicate across a network, the assumption of trustworthiness is not always valid. By default the Internet does not provide a secure network transport. Because the network is open to just about anyone, a number of threats arise—threats that are not seen in stand-alone systems. One of the best ways to visualize why these threats occur is by looking at an abstract model of networks using a layered architecture.

The ISO model of networking defines seven layers in the network stack. Widely deployed network technologies, such as the *Internet Protocol* (IP), Novell's IPX, Microsoft's SMB, and IBM's SNA, all implement variations on this seven-layer model. The basic ideas behind the layered model are simple.

Consider an example in which two computers want to communicate with each other over a network. At the lowest layer of the network is the Physical layer on which the electronic impulses flow. At successively higher layers, communication protocols are stacked on each other. Each layer has a very specific purpose and plays a well-defined role in that it provides services that layers above and layers below need. The main theme here is *encapsulation*. A layer is responsible for providing a certain set of abstractions in the form of interfaces. Think of a given layer as providing services to the layer above and services to the layer below. Layer N provides services to layer N-1 and to layer N+1. Breaking the model into layers simplifies both its architecture and its implementation.

Because information flows in both directions in the network stack, layer N has responsibilities that include sending information to and receiving information from layers N-1 and N+1. Smaller numbered layers typically begin at the physical network layer, and numbers increase as you move up the stack. Also, at each layer in the model is a conceptual communication channel that exists with the peer (same numbered) layer on the other network node. That is, layer N on node A is communicating with layer N on node B even though the data they exchange must actually pass through lower layers on the respective nodes.

Consider a simple three-layered model shown in Figure 4.1. In this example, Layer 3 represents an application program running on the system, Layer 2

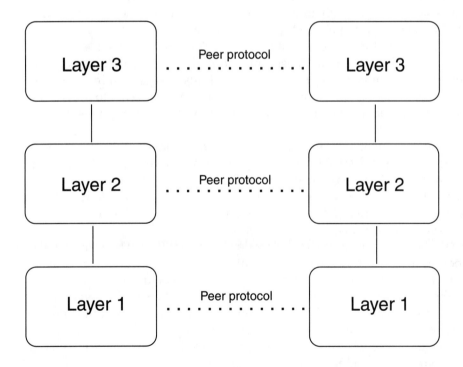

**Figure 4.1**    A simple three-layered network model.

represents a network software layer, and Layer 1 represents the physical network layer. For network packets to be sent at Layer 1, a restriction may indicate that each packet be a maximum of 10-bytes long. Any information sent to Layer 1 from Layer 2 must be fragmented into 10-byte packets. If Layer 1 of node A receives a packet longer than 10-bytes, not only must it be broken apart to be transmitted at the Layer 1 level, but some type of meta-data must be added to the packets so that they can be reconstructed by Layer 2 on the receiving system B. This meta-data is commonly referred to as *a packet header*.

In general what happens is that layer N asks layer N-1 to perform some service by calling interfaces provided at the *boundary* between the layers. Generally, layer N is asking layer N-1 to help transmit some data. Other interfaces might exist for checking the status of requests or querying the state of a layer. When a transmission request is sent from layer N to layer N-1, layer N-1 takes the information packet(s) sent by layer N and *wraps* them with a packet header to construct a meaningful packet for layer N-1.

Each layer of the network model has a data structure or packet that it understands. The data structure includes the actual data value to transmit and information describing the packet being transmitted. If you want to send your mailing address, the data value would be the character string for your postal address. Other information in the packet might include the length of the data, a sequence number, a protocol identifier, a timestamp, and perhaps some I&A information. The peer layers on communicating systems need this header data in order to be able to assemble, disassemble, and interpret packets. Another way to think about this is that the packet created at layer N and sent to layer N-1 becomes the *data* in the packet created at layer N-1.

When a message needs to be sent between systems, layering is employed to wrap the message as it passes down through the layers so that peer layers on the receiving system will have the necessary information for handling the packets. When Layer 1 on node B receives the packet from Layer 1 on node A, it performs various checks to ensure that the transmission was successful by inspecting the Layer 1 packet. If no transmission errors have occurred, Layer 1 on node B unwraps the packet and captures the data portion that it then passes up to Layer 2 (on node B). Layer 2 receives the data sent from Layer 1, which is of course a full packet meaningful to Layer 2, and processes the packet. If the packet was fragmented, the data from the Layer 2 packet may need to be cached and concatenated with other incoming packets from node A. At a given layer of the network model, a number of complex processing steps may occur including retransmission of lost packets, special messages for synchronization with the peer layer on the other node, or coalescing of fragmented packets.

## Security between Layers on a System

How do you know that layer N and layer N-1 are communicating securely? Because it is assumed that layer N and layer N-1 run on the same node, whatever access control mechanisms ensure communication integrity *as part of the standard operating system* are assumed to be sufficient for implementation of the network layers on a given node. Network security is not generally concerned with how layers on the same system communicate with each other. Instead, access control facilities supported for communicating processes on the same system are used between layers.

Access control for IPC such as semaphores, message queues, and shared memory work much like file system permissions. Different users or groups are allowed to read, write, create, or perform other operations on message queues depending on how the access control rules are defined for the queue. The layers could communicate just by calling subroutines or library routines. In this case, security of the message exchanges between layers also is handled by the operating system's security kernel.

A subtle issue about network security within node layers is worth mentioning. The design of most network protocols allows one process on the system to communicate with another process on the *same* system *as if they were talking across a network.* You probably are familiar with how this works because the same network node can be running both the client and server programs for a database. On that node, you can access the database server by invoking the database client. As far as the client and server are concerned, they think communications are occurring over a network.

## Security between Peer Layers across Systems

The interesting aspect of network security is secure communications *between peer layers* on different systems. Most network security threats occur during communications between layer *N* on node A and layer *N* on node B.

You should know that each layer of the network model is not required to implement the same security architecture as all other layers. Figure 4.2 shows an example in which each layer is using a different technique for network security. Each layer might require an independent security model from the other layers. This practice is actually common. A company with two sites might connect the sites using an encrypted physical connection (the lowest layer). Applications running on the system, such as e-mail, additionally could provide encryption to protect the privacy of messages exchanged between employees. The Application layer

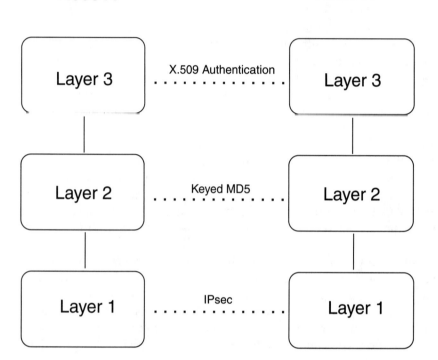

**Figure 4.2**    Different layers with alternative security solutions.

and the Physical layer are likely to be using two very different cryptographic implementations, but both are part of the network security solution. Of course, peer layers are required to implement the same security model.

Recall that packets are wrapped and unwrapped as they are passed between layer N and layer N-1. The security information needed in the packets of layer N will be encapsulated along with the rest of the header when processed by layer N-1. Layer N-1 is unconcerned with the *peer security* needs of layer N. This notion is a logical extension of the layered model, which is based on the theme that a layer provides services for adjacent layers without understanding the intricacies of packets from those other layers.

From a site security officer's point of view, this practice can lead to some very complex implementations. Network software layers might each be protected using a different security solution. One reason this is not unusual is because of the way in which systems evolve. The person responsible for secure network communications between two different endpoints, perhaps representing two different sites for the same company, is probably not the same person responsible for all of the applications that run between the sites. If a database transaction system is enabled between the sites, the project administrator for the database probably decides whether the nature of the transactions requires secrecy. The network administrator might want to have some input in the decision process, but most of the time various islands of authority exist in a company responsible for the security of individual application subsystems.

## I&A for Network Security Entities

Chapter 1 recommended that each time you explore a security topic, you begin by asking simple questions: Who are the subjects? What are the objects? How does access control work? To understand how network security can succeed, you need to list the entities—the subjects and objects—that interact in the model.

### How Hackers Exploit Protocols

When two layers on the same node communicate, or when peer layers communicate, they rely on a well-defined *protocol* and precisely stated *message formats*. The protocol states who initiates the connection, how the session is terminated, the order of messages, what to do if an error occurs, and other characteristics of the session that are necessary for the exchange to succeed. A protocol also can be thought of as an algorithm because most protocols are defined as state machines.

As with other algorithms, order is important. If you want to bake a cake, getting the right ingredients is just one part of the process. Mixing and cooking the ingredients in the right order are required to achieve an edible result. The same is true for network communications protocols. If one half of the session decides to get creative with the protocol, the results will not be guaranteed.

Getting the order of messages right is important, but you also need to format the messages properly. A baking recipe is useless if the order of the steps is clear, but the steps are not accurately defined. For example, if the recipe is incorrectly copied from a friend and asks for one unit of butter instead of one unit of flour, you will end up with a different dessert. Similarly, in network message exchanges, if message integrity cannot be guaranteed, any dialogue between the peers will not succeed.

Designing a secure distributed protocol is more of an art than a science. When someone at your site invents a new distributed security protocol, alarm bells should sound. Unless this person is knowledgeable and has studied a number of references, a better-than-average chance exists for the protocol to have weaknesses. Here are some examples from real-world situations:

- A distributed authentication protocol was designed using a challenge-response technique, but the challenge and the response were the same value. A hacker impersonating the recipient could just replay the challenge when asked for the response.

- A protocol was designed to accept incoming messages of a fixed length. Unfortunately, the program did not check the length of incoming messages (sound familiar?) and, because the system was a public Web server, any anonymous user on the Internet could crash the site.

Both of these examples appeared in commercial products developed by well-known companies with corporate offices on the West Coast. Network security is a complex beast. The merit badge for network security is earned only after years of study and trial-and-error. Designing network protocols is tough. Designing a *new* network security protocol is for experienced practitioners only.

## How Many Network Entities Are There?

How do you think it is possible for peers at layer N on communicating systems to implement appropriate security? Well, you know that the first requirement is to have some form of information that uniquely identifies the peer layer on each node (the subject). In some cases, the identifying information could be the same as that used at other layers in the network. More often, an entity's identifying information is meaningful only at one particular layer in the model. Unlike the single system that you investigated in Chapters 2 and 3, networks can contain a complex collection of different entities.

You should take a few moments to digest that last paragraph. If you think about the simple three-layer model introduced previously, you can see that up to six different entities can exist just to support the example. There are two network nodes. Each node has three layers. The two nodes communicate using a protocol, and peer layers between nodes communicate using unique protocols. That makes six different entities. Each one must be uniquely identifiable. Each entity also must be authenticated. Compared to a login session for a single user on a system, *there are quite a few more places where things can go wrong in network security*.

A peer layer does not necessarily rely on the entities of the operating system for its security. For example, an e-mail application runs *above* the operating system on a computer. On any two nodes in the network that support this mail protocol, some form of I&A exists, which at a minimum identifies the recipient of a mail message. If standard UNIX mail is used, the identities are the same as those found in the password files. If the application is Lotus Notes, the *users* are entirely different entities from those found in /etc/passwd. Lotus Notes relies on a client-server protocol in which the users are defined on the server and each user has a public key certificate. Therefore, the mail application uses a different security model than the network stack itself. *This is a perfect example of how multiple security models can reside on the same system at the same time*. Each security model offers opportunities for hackers for the two familiar reasons:

- Something can be configured improperly.
- The implementation of one of the models is flawed and is thus susceptible to protocol attacks, buffer overflow attacks, or other hacks.

How do you know when you have an application security model in addition to your operating system security? The distinction between an operating system and an application is often blurry. Some applications are delivered with the operating system and work with operating system security entities such as users and groups. When these applications communicate across a network, other entities become relevant, such as the network address of the computer. For example, the remote terminal application telnet is a standard feature of most UNIX operating systems. Telnet communicates network addresses as part of its protocol. Users and groups in the usual system files are consulted during authentication. The telnet client is also part of NT. (However, *inbound* telnet is not a standard feature of NT 4.0 systems.)

In general, if you are forced to define new users and groups and enter access control rules using techniques different from the operating system, you are adding a new security model to your system. This new domain of subjects, objects, access control rules, and administrators is one more thing that you must diligently monitor for attacks.

For the operating system and applications delivered with it, the network security entities of interest are as follows:

- Users and groups
- Network nodes
- Network software applications

Network adapters are also part of network security because ultimately, network traffic must be marked for a specific physical address. However, these entities are treated as devices on the system itself and fall under the jurisdiction of the access control rules for files and directories.

## I&A for Users and Groups in a Network

You are already familiar with I&A for users and groups on stand-alone systems. In networked environments, the only additional concern is the *scope* of the definitions for these entities in the network. A stand-alone computer contains local repositories for identifying users and groups. Multiple independent stand-alone systems each control their own repositories of user and group information. The *namespaces* that define users and groups across systems can be disjointed or intersecting. Indeed, the namespaces that define any entities in a

### Security Models within Models

It's always amusing to remember, though, that the Notes clients, servers, and database files all exist as objects in the operating system, too. The Notes server is a process or thread running in the context of the operating system on which it is installed. The executable program that *is* the Notes server is stored on disk as an operating system file. Although the Notes server makes its own security relevant decisions about entities that it regulates, the server also has an operating system context, complete with UIDs and GIDs. This dual nature of independent reference monitors on systems is always interesting to think about because it shows how multiple security models can exist concurrently on a system and how a product that implements its own security model can be viewed as a subject or object within the context of a completely different reference monitor and security model. For the systems' administrator, these environments can be confusing and difficult to secure because so many entities and security mechanisms are crossing boundaries.

network can intersect or remain disjointed depending on how the site is configured.

In Chapter 2, "The Role of Identification and Authentication in Your Environment," you saw how a group of related nodes could share a single namespace for user and group information. Possible solutions included a central authentication server for many nodes based on NIS, Kerberos, or DCE. Hybrid configurations that permit local user definitions and definitions in a central server must define a *precedence* relation that claims whether the local repository or the global repository is searched first. NIS and NIS+ provide a configuration file for this purpose. Using local and global repositories for user definitions is tricky  because knowing precisely *who* the user is greatly affects what access rights a user has when connected to a system. Also, intrusion detection tools that try to assign accountability for actions across network nodes need to know the originator of a request.

Most operating systems permit complicated definitions, such as the same username with different UIDs—one on the local node and one in the central authentication server. When systems are configured this way, you must understand who (which UID) the system will reference when making access control decisions. Familiarize yourself with your system's documentation to understand how the user's identity is chosen at login time. NT generates a user's SID that does not have the same value as any user on another node. UNIX UIDs can be identical for different users on multiple nodes.

Higher layer protocols such as NFS assume a common namespace across systems. NFS also provides some basic security features such as transforming the root UID (zero) to that of nobody ($-2$) when root is accessing files across systems. The UIDs and GIDs stored in the usual operating system repositories, local or remote, are utilized by NFS as the basis for access control decisions. *Not all network traffic passes information about users and groups as part of the protocol data.* The mail protocol *Simple Mail Transfer Protocol* (SMTP) knows about network addresses only when it is forwarding mail from one system to another. The mail recipient's UID and GID  are not passed in the mail message itself. Instead, the username is extracted from the header by the mail server. The username is used to decide in which mail spool file to deposit the incoming message. As the mail is forwarded across systems, only the network address is important.

Many other network protocols exchange information between network nodes and do not require user or group information in the protocol. Examples include routing and gateway information protocols or low-level network messages that test whether a node is alive.

To summarize, users and groups are identified and authenticated in network security using one of the following techniques:

♦ The normal operating system login

♦ An authentication server

♦ Application-specific techniques

Also, when your identity has been verified, the network communication sessions need to pass your credentials around so that operations you request on remote systems can be evaluated according to that system's access control rules. When you want to run a command remotely on another system, at least one network message sent from your system to the remote node needs to carry your credentials. Otherwise, how would the remote system know how to run the operation securely on your behalf? The remote system will need to create a process context, just as a local login session does, to properly enforce the security policy.

If a user's access request is to an application object, then the access control rules are *evaluated in the context of that application* and not by the operating system. In other words, a *Database Management System* (DBMS) client-server access-control decision is (typically) based on the identity of the *user*, not on the identity of the computer on which the user is working.

## Network Node I&A

Even though users and groups are not always needed in network protocols, individual network nodes must be distinguishable from each other via some identifying information. Otherwise, the network would not know where to deliver messages. At a minimum, a *source* and a *destination* address for the network packet are required for uniquely designating the endpoints of the communication session. A network node can be a computer, a router, or even a printer attached directly to the network. When two computers communicate with each other, they must be able to establish their identities and authenticate each other.

The early days of the Internet were characterized by trusting souls. Although early critiques of Internet protocols identified weaknesses (Morris, 1985; Bellovin, 1989), defenses were not widely erected to thwart the threats. Many different types of network attacks exist today, but a frequent underlying theme is the capability to *impersonate* a network entity. If you are able to forge network traffic with the address of another entity, then a number of doors are opened. *Any authentication scheme based solely on the self-proclaimed identity of a network entity is flawed.* This practice is like letting users log in to a system by entering only their user names and completely discarding the requirement for a password. In other words, self-proclaimed I&A in networked environments only gives you the I without the A.

A node that claims to have a particular network address may not be telling the truth. Therefore, in network security, you cannot assume a trustworthy environment if you rely only on *address-based authentication.*

Recall from Chapter 2 that an authentication server is a useful facility for a network of systems. If an attacker can impersonate the authentication server, then havoc would reign in the network. In networks in which users can be trusted to refrain from network address impersonation attacks, applications and protocols may depend on address-based authentication. However, when network traffic must pass through an untrusted or hostile network, the communicating systems must *not* rely on cleartext addresses for authentication. Network address can be used for identity, but the values can be trusted only if they are somehow protected with cryptography.

Network nodes do not always use mutual authentication, but this guideline is a good one to follow, too.

## Software Can Be a Network Entity

With network computing comes the lure for peer-to-peer or client-server distributed applications. Software serving the role of a client or a server is also a network security entity. As in the case of Lotus Notes discussed previously, the application has an operating system security context. Sometimes, the operating system security context is sufficient for authentication between clients and servers. More frequently used is *application level authentication* in which the communicating processes are forced through a strong I&A exchange before sending messages.

Application level authentication is a subset of application level security, which also includes communication privacy and integrity. Cryptographic techniques are especially applicable here, and each communicating server is required to demonstrate knowledge of a shared secret.

Users can demonstrate knowledge of a secret via an interactive dialogue. However, client or server processes that are often started automatically by the system cannot wait for a user or administrator to enter a secret for each application. Instead, the secret is often stored on disk after undergoing a transform to prevent easy guessing. As part of its initialization steps, the server may read the secret from disk or from some other hardware device.

An interesting performance tradeoff occurs here. Good security programming dictates that passwords are not kept in memory for an extended period. Following this guideline, a software server process would read its server-specific password file each time the password is needed. This I/O can become a bottleneck if the server is very active and constantly initiating new connections. Reading the password once and storing it in volatile memory is one work around. However, sometimes this can backfire. A user might be able to force the system to dump core, and if the core file contains the server's address space, the password might be discovered.

As you can see with I&A in network security, plenty of stuff is available for the hacker to play with—impersonating the identity of a user, impersonating the identity of a network node, impersonating a remote software program, sniffing network packets, and locking out one of the nodes by flooding it with network messages. Even before you get to network access control, you can see why intrusion detection is needed beyond traditional network security.

## Network Access Control

Network communications also require some form of access control. *Explicit* access control, such as a feature that limits outbound network connections to only a specific set of users, is possible. *Implicit* access control also is possible through the use of cryptography in network communications. If a network layer receives a packet that cannot be cryptographically authenticated, the packet will be dropped. Any node or anyone not in possession of the appropriate cryptographic credentials, or key, will not be allowed to *access* the other node. Packets can be sent, but they will be ignored.

Network access control is most recognizable in the form of network packet filtering in firewalls or routers. Special network software or hardware is installed at a junction point between two networks to regulate the flow of packets across the networks. Routers provide access control by deciding whether packets are allowed to flow in a particular direction. Firewall packet filter modules compete with routers but claim more functionality, such as the capability to evaluate more complex access control rules. The defining feature of this level of access control is that decisions are made in the lower layers of the network stack. In most firewalls, this capability is provided by enhancing or replacing the operating system kernel level of the network.

### Network Application Access Controls

Network access control can occur at any layer of the network stack. Therefore, an application can introduce its own access control constraints in addition to whatever the operating system may be doing.

Worth repeating is that an access control rule can be stated only using the subjects, objects, and operations that the reference monitor understands. At the hardware device level of the network, access control is specified in terms of hardware IDs. At the next higher layer, rules are defined in terms of network addresses or

## The Importance of Naming

At the heart of network security is the requirement that each entity in the network, such as each computer, be *uniquely* identifiable. This process is no different from the way I&A worked for users and groups. Recall that some type of repository for user names is stored on the local computer or in a network-wide repository. The security officer responsible for adding users and groups to this repository determined the *universe* from which names and UIDs were assigned. The same requirement exists for network I&A. Some naming authority must be responsible for assigning network IDs to entities that need to communicate in the network.

When the network is entirely private, and no communications are needed beyond the company's boundaries, the network administrators can assign arbitrary, but related, network IDs. In practice, this is rarely the case and most companies are connected to the Internet in some fashion. Communicating with other entities on the Internet requires adherence to naming conventions regulated by the Internet Engineering Task Force. The *Domain Name System* (DNS) is the most widely used naming scheme on the Internet today. DNS supports a hierarchical namespace with different authorities responsible for various segments of the name tree. Obtaining assigned and preferred names is an out-of-band process regulated by the IAB for networks attached to the Internet. Naming of nodes in private networks is the responsibility of the site network administrators.

Before widespread connectivity to the Internet, some network administrators assigned arbitrary network addresses to internal nodes. Rather than reassigning a new number to hundreds or thousands of nodes, the addressing scheme was left unchanged. You could find your internal node had the same network address that was officially assigned to another company's public Web server. This practice led to some humorous situations.

A local user running inside a secure network relies on the routers and gateways to correctly delivery packets to their destination. If someone inside your private network tried to send you a message, your buddy could end up communicating with the gateway for another company if it had the same IP address. This accident might happen if your node is down or if someone misconfigured your company's routers or gateways.

host names. Any concept that is understood at a particular layer is fair game for appearing in an access control rule. For example, if network traffic contains timestamps, one can declare an access control rule that limits inbound network traffic from a range of network addresses only within a given time interval. This is only an example, though. Unless the incoming timestamp can be *trusted*, the rule is probably of little value.

Application level access control can be configured independently or in conjunction with network level limits. *Any subjects or objects that the application regulates could appear in the access control rule.* A packet filter rule might limit whether telnet traffic is permitted between two networks, but the telnet application itself can further control which users in the network are allowed to telnet between the networks. Packet filters work at a level of the network stack that does not know about users or groups. Only the application knows about these concepts.

Someone might want to make the packet filter access control layer smarter and try to imbed some of the application's intelligence into the packet layer. If this is possible, the packet filtering code can make more granular access control decisions. In practice this solution is not scaleable, and *both packet filtering and application level access control are needed in networks.* The packet filter operates at a lower network layer than the application. To make access control decisions that are as complex as an application, the lower packet layer would need to incorporate a good deal of the application's knowledge. You can see that this practice is impractical and that the proper solution is to keep application level access control decisions in the application itself.

## The Internet Protocol (IP)

The Internet is a collection of hundreds of thousands of computers and networks. A vital component of this infrastructure is the network software layer known as IP (Postel, 1981). The Internet has its roots in an open and trusting environment. During the early days, not many sites could afford computers or the network connections to the Internet. The first version of the Internet was the *Advanced Research Projects Agency Network* (ARPAnet), which was designed as a means for researchers to easily exchange research information. The various network nodes responsible for routing Internet traffic were tightly controlled and administered. However, the IP traffic itself was assumed to be trustworthy.

Morris (1985) and Bellovin (1989) were among the first to publicly identify shortcomings in the IP layer itself, although many weaknesses already were known in Internet layers above IP. Most of the attacks that these two authors described have occurred numerous times on the Internet. The weaknesses and how they are exploited will be described shortly. As a result of these problems and others in the IP protocol, a new set of standards for *IP security* (IPsec) have been defined and implemented. Most firewalls today provide a *virtual private network* (VPN) using IPsec. Before you can understand how IPsec improves upon weaknesses in IP, take a look at the original standard.

As Figure 4.3 shows, the IP layer sits on top of the network device drivers. Each entity in the network is identified by a 32-bit address. Thus, an IP connection specifies at least a 32-bit source address and a 32-bit destination address for the packet. IP Version 6 expands this original limited definition by providing for variable length IP addresses which require that the packet header include a length field for the address. Because the Internet was quickly running out of valid addresses, this new approach was needed. Regardless of the version of IP running, the important point is that the protocol uses a network address to uniquely identify communicating entities. As noted previously, in a private network,

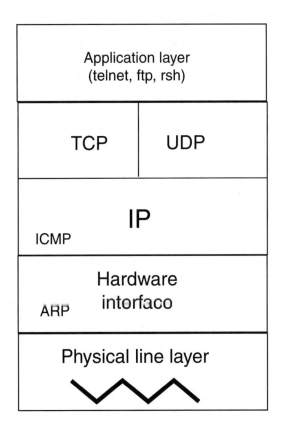

**Figure 4.3**   Layers in the IP standard.

addresses can be arbitrarily chosen. Addresses that are publicly visible on the Internet are controlled by a registration authority which governs the Internet.

Closely related to IP is the *Internet Control Message Protocol* (ICMP). More than two dozen different ICMP message types are available to assist with network communications. Examples include messages for testing whether a network address is *alive*, returning notifications of error conditions, and querying IP configuration settings at a particular node. From a security perspective, arbitrary ICMP messages should not be allowed through the firewall if they specify explicit destination network addresses found in your private network. One of the most important security guidelines for attaching your private network to the Internet is that any information about your private network is useful to a hacker. Therefore, you should practice information hiding as much as possible. Because ICMP messages can be used to explore your private network, be careful about what you allow into your private network. As you will see, a firewall can provide a solution for this and related problems.

Each IP packet contains a header portion and a data portion. The important values are the source and destination address. Other values include a *time to live* (TTL) that controls the lifetime of the packet. The IP layer itself does not guarantee delivery of a packet. Assurances for error-free delivery of packets also do not exist. No flow control is included in IP itself. Clogging a system by sending it many IP packets is not difficult, and thus launches a denial-of-service attack. Layers that sit on top of IP must implement techniques for handling errors, flow control, and the recovery of lost packets.

The 32-bit IP address is divided into different address *classes* by breaking the bits into groups. Addresses frequently are manipulated in dotted *decimal notation* consisting of four *octets*. Example addresses include 198.32.102.25, 127.0.0.1, and 9.34.10.1. The octets in the first address are 198, 32, 102, and 25. The addresses assigned and controlled by the *Internet Activities Board* (IAB) are organized into a hierarchy with each decimal representing a branch in the tree. The first three octets of an address usually represent different subnetworks (subnets), each with one or more network nodes attached. Depending on the address class and the number of bits allocated for the last octet, 256 or more nodes (0[nd]255) might appear on a subnet. No particular security problems are associated with the address classes, so more details are not given here but can be found in the references.

The Internet is divided into many subset networks that are connected by *gateways* and *routers*. Although technically different, both gateways and routers are responsible for correctly forwarding packets on through the Internet until the packets reach their destinations. Each packet that travels across the Internet moves one *hop* at a time. That is, a routing node, such as a gateway or router, moves the packet to the next routing node until the packet finally reaches its target.

## Probing Network Paths

At each hop, the TTL field is decremented once. If the TTL reaches the number 1, but the packet has not reached its destination, the last node holding the packet returns an ICMP message to the originating node indicating that the TTL has expired.

The *traceroute* application can be used to find the route that a packet will take across a network. By taking advantage of the TTL decrement and time-out relation, *traceroute* can find a network path. The algorithm sets TTL to 2, sends the packet to a target IP address, and receives the TTL expiration message and the IP address of the node that sent it. Because the last node to decrement the TTL and notice the expiration sends the ICMP time-out message, *traceroute* can map the path that the packet is *hopping* through to a destination IP address. By incrementing the TTL by one each time and keeping track of the IP address returned in the *timeout*, traceoute can construct the list of nodes in the path to the target address. When the destination node is finally reached, a different ICMP message is returned, thus completing the algorithm. The dynamic routing nature of the Internet may yield a different path each time. However, you should be able to see how *traceroute* helps a hacker discover interesting characteristics about your network, including its physical layout.

Flexibility in the addressing scheme of IP permits one to specify a *broadcast address* for the destination of a packet. Essentially, you are permitted to specify a wildcard for one of the octets that is interpreted to mean "send this packet to all nodes in this subnet." For example, sending the broadcast address 198.21.54.255 would send the packet to all nodes in the subnet with a prefix of 198.21.54. The value 255 symbolizes the wildcard. A packet with destination address of 198.21.255.255 would be delivered to even more nodes.

The *multicast backbone* (Mbone) is a special class of IP addresses that allows for encapsulation of many IP packets into a single packet. Standard IP unicast sends a message to a single target address. Broadcast sends the message to all addresses in a subnet. Multicast sends a message to a group of IP addresses. The Mbone can provide significant performance improvements for Internet traffic. Because the Mbone address represents several targets, it saves network overhead that would occur by sending a single unicast packet to each address individually. This advantage is not without security implications as you will see when you read about firewalls later in this chapter.

## Problems at the IP Layer

Before looking at some the network layers above IP, take a look at the common hacks against IP. Most of these attacks succeed because of the open nature of the Internet. If packets are sent unencrypted between systems, then an adversary somewhere along the path can  sniff the network and read information contained in the packets fairly easily. Two pieces of information that must always be in the clear are the source and destination IP addresses. Otherwise, intermediate gateways and routers on the Internet could not forward packets properly.

### Sniffing

The most frequent exploit is simple sniffing of network traffic. When some military and Internet sites were invaded in 1994, it was because users were sending passwords in the clear across untrusted networks. Poorly configured gateways or publicly visible servers would first be compromised by using a buffer overflow attack against an available network application or by guessing passwords. After a normal use account was hacked on the system, a root program vulnerability would give the intruder full access. Sometimes, the vulnerability required a carefully designed buffer overflow attack, but often privileged programs were buggy enough to allow nonprivileged users to execute any arbitrary command.

When full control was available, the attacker would plant Trojan Horse programs to hide any evidence. This plant would be followed by installing a network sniffer program for capturing other passwords as users would authenticate to or from remote connections.

### Address Impersonation

Identity in IP is based on the 32-bit source node network address. No authentication is provided in IP for these network addresses. A physical computer might have more than one network adapter installed, and as such, this system will have multiple IP addresses (one for each adapter). On multiuser systems, only a privileged user can change the IP addresses defined for the adapters. The operating system also provides programming interfaces that can be used to talk directly to the IP layer. However, only privileged users are allowed to create IP packets and place them directly on the IP stack for delivery.

If you have a personal computer or you are the superuser on a system, you can directly place packets on the IP layer. This means that you can set the source IP address field in the packet to any value you desire. The *ability to spoof or impersonate IP addresses* is one of the greatest threats to network communications. You do not need to be a network programmer to accomplish impersonation. Tools are readily available on the Internet for you to create arbitrary IP packets and send them out across the Internet.

## Impersonation Attacks

What kinds of mischief can you create if you can spoof IP addresses? The answers range from moderately annoying to very serious.

### Single Message Attacks

Because any user with a PC can send out an arbitrary IP packet, some denial-of-service attacks are launched by sending only a single packet. The attacker does not need to worry about receiving or handling responses from other nodes.

An old phone trick entails calling successive pizza delivery services and ordering pizzas to be delivered to another person. This attack is an example of impersonating the destination address. Caller ID, call backs, and customer log records appear in the arsenals of restaurants today to prevent this prank. However, in the days when it did succeed, this trick was nasty.

A similar attack increased in frequency on the Internet in early January, 1998. The older version of the attack was launched by faking a source address and sending numerous ICMP packets to different destination addresses. The common ICMP message to send is Echo Request, implemented at the application layer by the *ping* program. ICMP Echo Request and *ping* are patterned after the radar. A probe is sent out on the network to test the existence of a particular node by specifying a destination address. If you have access to the *ping* source code, it is easy to enhance it to cycle through several destination addresses or to ask for a source address. The result is an annoying hacker tool. The node that receives the Echo Request sends an ICMP Echo Reply to the source address that appears in the packet. Instead of getting a few dozen pizzas at the spoofed door, the victim of the attack receives the electronic equivalent—thousands of Echo Reply messages.

The denial-of-service threat caused by this prank reached a new level on the Internet when the ICMP Echo was sent with a broadcast address for the destination. The source address was spoofed as before. To flood a site with network traffic, send ICMP Echo to address 9.8.255.255. The gateway at subnet 9.8 would forward the request to subnets in its network and essentially to every node at the *site*. The poor node whose address had been impersonated would receive Echo Reply messages from many nodes and probably be unable to perform any useful functions. The network on which this source node was sitting also would experience performance degradation. Also, each of the networks receiving the Echo Request would be congested as all of the nodes tried to send Echo Reply messages. Quite a big mess can be created with relatively few messages. The defenses against this threat require configuration changes in the router or firewall gateway connecting the networks to the Internet. Blocking inbound ICMP requests at the firewall or router, particularly broadcast requests, will help defend against this problem.

Other ICMP messages are sent for flow control of a session, and these also can deny network services to network users. Single message attacks are not limited to ICMP, though.

The Internet and other IP networks are heavily dependent on other service protocols for routing, name resolution (DNS), and gateway configuration changes. Each of these services is provided on the Internet by many dedicated machines that exchange information for keeping the Internet available. Some of these protocols were originally designed to accept unidirectional messages for *push* updates of information such as routing tables. An attacker could inject a network packet instructing one of these nodes to modify a table entry to assist with future hacking. For example, a packet could tell a DNS nameserver to use the hacker's network address instead of the true authentication server. Passwords could be stolen for future use if this were to happen. The attack succeeds because early versions of these service protocols relied exclusively on address-based authentication.

Today, more secure versions of these network services employ cryptographic techniques for authentication. Also, careful configurations of controlled networks including routers and firewalls also help protect these sensitive public nodes from frequent attacks.

### Ping of Death

Not long ago a popular denial-of-service attack involved sending out an ICMP Echo Request packet also known as a *ping*. Most TCP/IP implementations ship with a built-in ping command, named after the sound radar makes in movies about submarines. An ICMP Echo Request packet checks to see whether the destination host is alive. When received, the target responds with an ICMP Echo Reply command. Only one message is needed to ping a system, although most versions allow for repetitive test packets. One of the ping options is to send an arbitrary text string along in the packet.

Many UNIX variants started from the same source code base, and consequently, a bug found in one version of UNIX has a better-than-average chance of appearing in other UNIX systems. The Ping of Death attack is not really a network problem but rather a buffer overflow problem. The IP stack on the receiving end of the ping did not perform adequate bounds checking on the input and would overflow if a message larger than 65,535 bytes was received. Some IP implementations choked on small packet sizes. The error-recovery procedures of the particular IP implementations by UNIX vendors varied, but most of them would hang. If the attacker was clever enough to encode the buffer just right, the receiving computer could be tricked into executing arbitrary commands.

Once again, poor programming practices lead to this weakness. By the way, you are not required to run the Ping of Death attack with an impersonated address,

## Are Your Mission-Critical Applications Safe from Attacks?

Information about Internet application weaknesses is readily found in books about firewalls. Each commonly known IP-based service is considered in turn and concerns about the protocols used are described. Based on these texts, firewall administrators get a good feel for what services to enable or deny at the firewall. *What is so amazing is that few people spend the time to interrogate the protocols in use by home-grown client-server applications running in the corporate network.*

The Internet applications that are critiqued in other texts have undergone years of public analysis and inspection. The same probably cannot be said for home-grown distributed applications. It is bad enough when these applications are running inside of private networks, but some people even put the client or server directly on the Internet. With some of these private protocols, the consequences of address impersonation are more serious than in the previous examples. Imagine the damage potential if your mission-critical applications are susceptible to address impersonation attacks. If you have an automated manufacturing facility, and the client-server communications depend only on IP address based authentication, a disgruntled employee or a paid saboteur can easily foul things up.

Sometimes, a weakness in the protocol between the client and server adds to the trouble. For example, you might have a private authentication protocol between the client and server, and it could even depend on cryptography for protection. Still, there could be flaws in the protocol design, which gives an edge to an attacker. Building robust client-server protocols is difficult. Designing secure authentication protocols is considerably harder. You should make an effort to review the security aspects of any client-server applications in use at your site. If any cryptographic authentication between the client and server exists, and you do not feel confident in your abilities, seek expert help in searching out weaknesses. Even very skilled programmers from prestigious companies have released commercial products with protocol problems.

but would you want to launch one from your own valid IP address? You might as well crank call everyone with a Caller-ID box.

### Impersonating One Half of a Session

If network traffic between two nodes flows in the clear and if you know the protocol that the nodes are using, you can disable one of the nodes and impersonate that node using IP address impersonation. Disabling a node is accomplished by physical sabotage or by flooding the target node with continual network traffic (so that it is unable to respond to the other half of the connection). This hack is different from the pizza trick because this attack assumes that a series of messages must be exchanged as part of the protocol.

Even if the protocol is not publicly available in source code form, or via a formal definition such as through an RFC, a determined adversary can piece together the protocol through packet sniffing. Security through obscurity provides no long-term protection. Assuming that a private protocol is safe because no one knows how the protocol works is a poor basis for security. If the protocol depends on IP addresses sent in the clear for authentication, someone eventually can impersonate at least one half of the connection.

### Session Hijacking

If you are an attacker and your node is in between two other nodes, you can hijack the session and impersonate two (or more) nodes. Even if the two nodes you are subverting have completed an initial strong authentication dialogue, it is possible to hijack the session if the remainder of their messages are sent in the clear. If the two nodes rely on cryptographic techniques for privacy, integrity, or authenticity, you will not be able to hijack the session unless you can discover the key or find a flaw in the protocol.

Session hijacking is conceptually simple. Two endpoint nodes of a communication session send traffic in the clear. Your location is such that all traffic between these two nodes must flow through a node that you control. On your node ,you sniff packets and create arbitrary IP traffic. You must handle both sides of the communication if you want to spoof both nodes into doing what you want.

### How Likely Is Impersonation?

Executing a successful address impersonation attack depends on several factors. First, the hacker must be able to drop packets with forged addresses onto the IP stack either by writing a program or using one of the readily available tools for doing so. Next, the location of the user's attacking station must be such that it is possible for the forged packet to be delivered. Some network routers and firewalls are configured to drop a packet unless the source address of the packet is within a range, fits a pattern, or matches an entry in a table. Therefore, the network on which the attacker is working may not deliver the packet beyond the attacker's network boundary. If such filters exist on the network, the hacker also needs to compromise the filter source (firewall or router). Because many ISPs do not bother to block outbound source address impersonation, attacks often originate from public Internet provider locations.

When the attacker's node is on the same subnet as the forged address, the impersonation attack is easier. The same is true if (as standard policy) the faked packets are routed to the subnet of the attacked node, such as the routing of packets between subnets of a university network.

What else is necessary if the goal is to *receive* traffic for a forged node and not just flood the victim with ICMP Reply messages? The simple answer is that the impersonated system must be unable to carry out its half of the communication session. The forged node must be unavailable. You can disable a node in a number of ways. The hacker with physical access can walk up to the node and turn it off. As a fallback, the node can be flooded with network packets, even from another dedicated node acting in cohort with the attacker's node.

### Open Networks and Denial-of-Service Attacks

Can you stop an unknown person from continually barraging your publicly published phone number with prank calls? Unfortunately, the answer is "No." A determined person can reprogram cell phone numbers, migrate from one public pay phone to another, enlist the help of numerous helpers to initiate calls from public phones all over the world, or choose from a variety of other techniques that hide true identity. This is the problem with anonymous source connections. Only if you forced all inbound calls to your house to provide strong authentication could you prevent this attack. Oh, you also can request an unlisted number, but that would hardly be useful if the phone number was for your business. *If the number must be public, you can do little to prevent denial-of-service attacks.*

The corollary in the Internet is true as well. If you have a publicly visible IP address, such as the one that identifies your business Web server to the world, you always will be open to some denial-of-service attacks. Some threats can be lessened by putting a filter, such as a router that blocks known denial-of-service attacks, between your node and the Internet. However, the attack has merely been shifted to the router, which will be burdened with analyzing and dropping the attack packets. Your Web server throughput will still be lessened if someone is launching denial-of-service packets in your direction.

### Impersonation and Tracking

Another unfortunate consequence of open networks is that tracing activities to a specific, prosecutable individual is very difficult. A serious hacker will obtain stolen credit cards, use these to obtain Internet access from ISPs, and launch attacks from these accounts even if address impersonation is not needed. Poor physical and configuration security at publicly available Internet terminals also offer nodes from which address impersonation attacks can be launched. As long as the network is open by design, and anonymous connections are permitted, true accountability for network behavior will remain illusive.

Address impersonation is a particularly threatening attack because it can lead to loss of confidentiality, integrity, and availability. A hacker, who can trick another node into sending information, might be able to gain access to confidential information such as passwords. The ability to fake an address and inject forged messages into the network can be used to trick another node into altering data and violating its integrity. Finally, the pizza attack shows how availability can be impacted. All of these concerns about IP can be summed up in one statement:

> Authentication based only on IP address is not secure unless cryptography is added to prove the authenticity of the addresses.

## IPsec

To improve upon the security of IP, the IPsec standard was introduced. The purpose of IPsec is to provide confidentiality, integrity, authentication, and nonrepudiation of IP packets in a network. The design of IPsec is flexible enough to support a variety of encryption and hashing algorithms to protect the packets. At the heart of IPsec is the notion of a *security association* between two endpoints. The security association contains various parameters about the communication exchange including cryptographic algorithm options and choices, as well as session status information. IPsec does not define how the keys used in the session are obtained.

IPsec provides two alternatives called *Authentication Header* (AH) and *Encapsulation Security Payload* (ESP).

### Authentication Header

If the environment is trying to prevent only tampering or impersonation of IP headers, and consequently of IP addresses, AH is sufficient. A cryptographic hash can be computed on the IP header and attached to the IP packet to provide authenticity and integrity. If public-key cryptography is exploited, nonrepudiation is also guaranteed. All values in the packet appear in the clear with AH because privacy is not a concern.

How does this prevent address impersonation? Each half of the session shares a secret key. The packets sent between the communication endpoints are protected with a digital signature or secure message hash. In the simplest case, a cryptographic checksum is added to each packet to ensure its authenticity and optionally its integrity. Without knowledge of the secret key, impersonation is impossible. IPsec also provides facilities to prevent replay attacks based on previously authenticated packets.

**Encapsulation Security Payload**

ESP can provide privacy, integrity, or both using one of two modes. If the entire IP packet is encrypted, and then concatenated to a cleartext version of the IP header before being sent on the network, this is known as *tunnel mode*. The receiving system uses the decryption key defined by the security association to decrypt the encrypted IP header and packet. Verification of the packet contents depends on successful decryption for privacy or successful hashing for integrity. Privacy for the datagram passed to the IP layer—the data portion of the IP packet—can be implemented separately in *transport mode*. Because only the datagram from the layer above undergoes cryptographic transformation, and not the IP packet header, performance is improved. Naturally, IPsec is slower than unprotected IP traffic because of the additional path lengths introduced for cryptographic computations and session parameter negotiation. Any packets that do not decrypt properly are dropped. This capability prevents address impersonation attempts.

## Supporting Protocols for IP

A number of other protocols are useful in the IP model. The three most important—ARP, DNS, and RIP—are briefly discussed in the following sections.

### Address Resolution Protocol (ARP)

Network communications ultimately occur at a layer below IP. The network adapters have unique physical addresses that are needed to deliver the packets between network nodes. A mapping is needed between the conceptual address of IP and the physical address of the adapter. When the Ethernet device driver receives an IP packet for delivery, it sends out a special broadcast packet containing the destination IP address of the IP packet. As part of the behavior of a correctly implemented device driver, a node whose IP address matches sends back a reply with the physical address of its Ethernet adapter. The original node now encapsulates the IP packet into an Ethernet packet and uses the newly found Ethernet address as the target. This is essentially how the ARP works. Different network device drivers might implement ARP using something other than a broadcast, but this is only a slight difference.

Most nodes cache results from ARP broadcasts for performance. Earlier ARP cache implementations would accept unsolicited ARP replies and update their caches. This form of address impersonation occurs at the physical instead of the IP layer. Indeed, nothing in the ARP protocol provides strong authentication. An impostor can respond with an ARP reply before the true owner and consequently spoof the requesting node. To be successful, the real owner of the IP address must be disabled or at least significantly hindered so that it cannot respond to network messages.

Note that address impersonation at this layer and at the IP layer has beneficial value, too. For cluster or high-availability environments, it is sometimes necessary for one node to impersonate the address of another to support a fail-over relationship. Controlled impersonation like this is unlikely to be configured across unsecure networks, though.

## Domain Name System (DNS)

Dotted decimal addresses are paired with more semantically meaningful names by pairing each octet with an alphanumeric string. The address 198.29.36.126 could be referred to as webserver1.boulder.ibm.com. The association between octets and string names is actually inverted, but this is not an important security issue. Like the decimal addresses, domain names are assigned by a registration authority. DNS is a protocol that is used to manage lookups for converting between dotted decimal and domain name versions of an address. Because the Internet depends heavily on this capability, a group of hierarchically related, tightly controlled *nameservers* populates the Internet. Each nameserver is responsible for names without a fixed domain but can request name resolution from other nameservers to which it is connected. DNS also defines a protocol for how nameservers communicate and receive updates to their universe of names, or *namespace*. Each nameserver is identified by one or more IP addresses.

Now that you know you can impersonate IP addresses, you can see that spoofing a nameserver can lead to serious consequences on the Internet. By feeding fake information to a nameserver or by impersonating the nameserver itself, you can intercept and forge traffic for arbitrary nodes. Frequent impersonation attacks against nameservers forced many changes to the programs used to implement DNS, most notably the *bind* program. Today, most nameservers on the Internet have been upgraded to avoid known attacks, but new threats are sure to arise. Luckily, the maintainer of *bind* is very responsive and has provided timely fixes to security problems. A good review of DNS is given in Bellovin (1995).

A proposed standard for secure, authenticated DNS has been implemented for some nameservers on the Internet. Trusted Information Systems is a leading vendor in this effort. Secure DNS is achieved by using cryptographic protocols for message exchanges between nameservers. Implementations can be found on the

Internet. More details on DNS and how to administer it are available in Link (1995).

### Routing Interchange Protocol (RIP)

Like ARP and DNS, RIP is used to provide message delivery information on the Internet or in private networks. Instead of helping to locate the target of a message, RIP is used to find the best route for a message to travel. RIP suffers from the same problems as insecure DNS in that RIP depends only on the source IP address for I&A of the message. A secure version of RIP is also available.

## User Datagram Protocol (UDP)

Sitting above the IP layer is a connectionless protocol known as UDP. Why does UDP exist? Programmers could write directly to the IP layer for network applications but that would not provide enough granularity and control. Several applications communicating simultaneously with the IP layer would need to coordinate in order to ensure the proper processing of incoming packets. To add another layer of abstraction, UDP was created.

A UDP packet contains a source and destination address like IP but also adds a new abstraction called the *port*. A port is a 16-bit number for a conceptual communication endpoint much like the ports on the back of your computer. Each port is uniquely addressable by the UDP layer. The port and IP address together form a *socket* address. The socket address can be used to uniquely communicate with a particular application running on the tip of UDP/IP.

Ports are integers that range from 0 to 65535. As a convention in UNIX, ports from 0[nd]1,024 are reserved for privileged processes. Most UNIX implementations honor this guideline, but ready access to network source code or PC computers means this assumption will not always be met. Reserved ports were used as a simple form of access control for network applications. A user communicating to a program running on a privileged or reserved port on another system might feel secure that the program was not a Trojan Horse planted by a nonprivileged user. However, this is no longer guaranteed to be true in today's world.

Because UDP is connectionless, it operates by dropping packets on the IP layer. UDP also lacks reliable message deliver, flow control, and error recovery. Applications running at layers above UDP must provide these services. Because UDP does not incur any overhead for setting up and tearing down a virtual connection, it is faster. Unfortunately, these same features make UDP easy to spoof.

## Port Security

As a convention port numbers 0[nd] 1,023 are reserved for privileged processes. In most operating systems, only privileged processes may open a connection to one of these reserved ports. As in the case of IP address impersonation, access to PCs with TCP/IP is sufficient for circumventing this tradition. The consequence is that no applications should assume the other half of a connection is trustworthy simply because the other port in use is in the reserved range. This practice is no different from trusting an IP address.

## UDP Security Concerns

The biggest security concern for UDP is address impersonation. Because all of the flow control and resiliency for UDP traffic must be supplied by the application running above UDP in the stack, it is fairly easy to spoof UDP-based applications. Few firewall administrators will permit UDP packets into the secure network when they arrive from the untrusted Internet.

# Transmission Control Protocol (TCP)

A connection oriented communications session layer is provided by TCP layered over IP. TCP provides for reliable message delivery and retransmits lost or damaged packets. Sequence numbers are included in the protocol to facilitate reassembly of fragmented packets. Thus, applications written to use TCP/IP do not need to worry about packets delivered out of order nor packets that are broken into fragments. TCP/IP handles these issues before delivering the datagram to the application layer.

The session between the communicating endpoints is maintained as a virtual connection. Although the network packets may take different routes depending on network congestion, the peer applications communicating over TCP/IP, are given the appearance of having a persistent network connection. The endpoints of the session are identified by socket addresses as in UDP. However, the TCP connection is uniquely recognized based on the 4-tuple formed by source IP address, source port, destination IP address, and destination port. This capability simplifies programming for servers that must handle multiple concurrent client-server sessions.

TCP guarantees *in order* delivery for packets. This type of delivery is accomplished through the use of sequence numbers in the packets. Both sides of the connection choose a separate, initial sequence number to be used during packet exchanges. Successive packets contain incremental values of the sequence number.

TCP differs from UDP in a fundamental way. A UDP packet is characterized by the *socket* upon which it communicates. A socket address consists of the combination of an IP address with a specific port number. The TCP connection is uniquely identified by a pair of socket addresses. The 4-tuple source address, source port, destination address, and address port uniquely identifies the TCP/IP session.

## TCP/IP Security Concerns

Because much of the Internet traffic runs on the TCP/IP layers, you need to understand security problems with TCP. The next few sections describe popular attacks.

### Address Impersonation

Like both IP and UDP, address impersonation is a threat to applications running on the TCP protocol. The TCP protocol is slightly more difficult to impersonate than UDP because TCP provides flow control and reliable delivery and consequently contains facilities in the protocol to detect anomalous conditions. TCP packets contain a sequence number that makes address impersonation a little harder.

### Sequence Number Guessing

Each side of the connection chooses an initial number and then transmits this value to the other half of the connection. The two sides of the connection depend on these sequence numbers for packet reassembly because some packets may be delivered out of order. To acknowledge receipt of the packet containing the sequence number, the recipient responds with the sequence number incremented by one and the ACK flag turned on in the packet.

A clever hacker can exploit a TCP connection during the initial handshake for the protocol if sequence numbers can be guessed. This attack was exploited frequently on the Internet in the last couple of years. Blind guessing of sequence numbers is possible but has a low probability of success. The favored choice is for the hacker to spend some time gathering information about sequence numbers chosen by the target for various connections. Network traffic sniffing is especially useful here, but not a necessity. How does someone gain information about sequence numbers without sniffing? If the victim is on a public network, you can send it as many TCP connection attempts as you like. Each packet you receive will contain a sequence number. If the algorithm for choosing sequence numbers is predictable, the game is over. Because a CERT advisory was issued for this attack, most vendors have chosen some pseudorandom method for selecting initial sequence numbers. If you like to dabble in statistics and discrete mathematics, you might be able to predict the period of the random number generator in use by a vendor.

It should be obvious that if the hacker's network location is between the communicating endpoints, network sniffing trivially provides the sequence numbers.

## Session Hijacking

If the socket addresses and sequence numbers are known, a node that is in between the endpoints of a TCP connection can hijack one or both halves of the session. Sometimes, this attack also is referred to as the *bucket brigade* attack. All the impostor must do is ensure that the two endpoints receive the appropriate protocol messages during the hijack. Because the attacking node is *in the middle*, intercepted packets can be easily altered, discarded, or substituted. Due to some protocol unique features of Token Ring networks, session hijacking is harder on these networks than it is on other networks such as Ethernet.

## Other TCP/IP Protocol Problems

Protocols are designed as state machines. Each side of the protocol starts in an initial state and transitions to other states depending on the type of input received. Designing a protocol that is resistant to attacks is a challenging task because of tradeoffs. TCP/IP was designed to be an open protocol. A node running TCP/IP or UDP/IP is listening for inbound network traffic from almost anywhere. Some initial trust was designed into the protocol to support this open behavior, but this choice has led to some bothersome attacks.

The SYN Flood attack is one example. TCP sessions begin with a three-way handshake between the two endpoints of the connection. Packet header fields are set to different values depending on the state of the connection (remember this is a state machine). One of the fields in the TCP connection requests an initial synchronization (SYN) by sending a message with the beginning sequence number as identified previously. To drag a machine's performance down, a well-known trick is to send the victim a large number of SYN requests. Not only does the attacked machine spend time sending back acknowledgment messages, but it also remains in a state that is waiting for the third part of the handshake. Depending on the machine's capabilities, a few hundred or few thousand outstanding connections can really slow things down.

Other similar attacks exist. If you can impersonate an IP address and see the traffic between two nodes, it's not difficult to cancel either half of the session by sending a properly formed packet with the FIN bit set. You also can reset either side of the session in the same way by setting the RST bit.

## TCP/IP Application Security

Because it is such a useful network service layer, TCP/IP is the basis for many popular Internet applications including HTTP and FTP. These applications have their own protocols that sit on top of TCP/IP and often provide their own additional security models. FTP allows files to be transferred between systems but requires a complete login process in order to gain access to the remote system. The login portion of FTP is almost always based on the same underlying mechanisms used for base operating system login.

HTTP, on the other hand, introduces its own security model. Web servers provide configuration files that are modified to define a virtual file tree whose meaning is only relevant to the Web server. Most Web servers can be set up to require an authentication dialogue before access is allowed to particular portions of the file tree. The users and passwords can be defined in a repository independent of that used by base operating system. Other settings enable the Web administrator to specify access control rules that are applicable only to the objects which exist in the virtual file tree. In reality, files from the operating system's file system populate the virtual Web file tree. However, the operating system permission bits are not interrogated by the Web server when an access request is evaluated. Instead, the Web server consults its own configuration files. The Web server is thus providing an application specific security layer above the security provided by the operating system.

### Trusted Hosts

UNIX networks have a convenience feature that simplifies distributed computing. Rather than requiring an authentication phase for every connection, some TCP/IP applications will honor a trust relationship if it has been defined by the administrator on a machine. UNIX systems support several configuration files with contents consisting of hostnames, IP addresses, and optionally usernames. These files are as follows:

- /etc/hosts.equiv
- A root .rhosts file
- Individual user .rhosts files
- /etc/hosts.lpd

The trust relationship is defined according to the IP addresses or hostnames of the communicating parties. Depending on the configuration file chosen from this list, the trust can apply only to specific users or to all users on a particular host. The hosts.lpd file is meaningful for the UNIX lpd remote printing protocol, so that some of these trust relationships are application specific.

Addressed-based authentication is the basis for these network authentication alternatives. However, because you have seen that address impersonation is a problem in networks, these weaker authentication facilities should not be deployed across untrusted networks.

## The Role of the Firewall in Traditional Security

Can anything be done to improve network security? Sure. First, think about the problem abstractly. Security is based on a security model. The model defines subjects, objects, and access control rules. Supporting facilities, such as auditing, assist in implementing security. The problems mentioned here can be put into three categories:

- I&A
- Access control
- Protocol design

Firewalls are the most widely known commercial tools for improving upon weaknesses due to the first two items (Chapman and Zwicky, 1995; Cheswick and Bellovin, 1994). Protocol design problems are not solved by off-the-shelf solution products. You cannot easily find a product that will safely design your client-server protocols to be resistant to attacks. Using cryptographic libraries that are commercially available or by relying on cryptographic services provided by firewalls, you *can* avoid security problems in your protocols.

### What Is a Firewall?

Firewalls are designed to provide a secure boundary between an untrusted network, such as the Internet, and a trusted network, such as your private corporate network. Other terms used are *unsecure* and *secure* network. Today, firewalls consist of one or more of the following:

- A packet filter
- A set of proxy servers
- Secure IP traffic or *virtual private network* (VPN)

Other software accompanies host firewalls to support these core functions. Examples include virus scanners, log reporting tools, strong authentication, and file system integrity checkers.

Firewalls are implemented using screening routers, bastion hosts, or both. A screening router can be configured to control network packet routing based on attributes of the packet, such as source address, destination address, port number, and direction. A bastion host is a hardened computer, with the operating system locked down to a minimum of services. The bastion host can run proxies *and* perform packet filtering.

## Packet Filters Provide Access Control Services

Packet filters improve upon the access control capabilities of network software delivered as part of operating systems. Access control rules are constraints or predicates that are evaluated to determine whether to permit an operation. Conceptually, the values held by a set of variables are compared against rules in the access control database. The variables are derived from state information representing attributes of the subjects and objects. For example, two important values in network traffic are the source and destination IP addresses. A packet filter rule can be configured to permit or deny IP traffic based on these values.

A packet filter is an access control mechanism for network traffic. Instead of processing or forwarding all packets that arrive on the node's network adapters, the packet filter consults its access control rules before handling each packet. Most packet filters are implemented as extensions or replacements for kernel components of operating systems because the lower layers of the network stack are running in the kernel. This practice is a very important because some firewalls completely replace part of the kernel, and others *hook in* and intercept function calls. What can a packet filter control?

Because the packet filter *is* the network stack, it can make access control decisions based on any of the fields that appear in the headers of network packets. If necessary, a packet filter also can inspect the contents of the data portion of packets to enforce a security policy or look for attacks. First generation packet filters passed or dropped packets by looking at fields such as:

♦ Source or destination IP address

♦ Port

♦ Protocol type (TCP, UDP, or other)

♦ Service type (FTP, telnet, DNS, RIP)

As protocol attacks became common, packet filters were enhanced to look at settings for SYN and ACK fields as well as other characteristics of the packet. When new protocol attacks are discovered, firewall vendors are quick to implement defenses. In other words, packet filtering access control capabilities are always being improved.

Packet filters are installed as *screening routers* or *bastion hosts*. Both routers and bastion hosts are *multihomed*, meaning that they have two or more network adapters. A router is a special-purpose computer that, in its simplest form, controls the flow of network packets between subnets. A bastion host is a general-purpose computer that has been *hardened* to remove unnecessary or security threatening software. A network node, such as a router or bastion host, with two communication adapters, can know the adapter on which a packet arrived. Notice that this knowledge is not explicitly encoded in the packet itself. A generic term meaning either a router or a bastion host is *gateway*.

The purpose of a gateway is to inspect packets and, based on the destination network addresses of the packets, send them to the appropriate subnet for delivery to the target hosts. If you want to block all incoming traffic from networks other than packets whose addresses begin with 1.22.333, you easily can configure a router to do so. In addition, most screening routers can detect attempts to impersonate IP addresses. A router or bastion host can look at inbound packets arriving on the network adapter connected to the untrusted Internet, and if the source IP address has a prefix of one of the private network subnets, then an address impersonation attempt is in progress. If a packet is received on the secure side adapter that means it's supposed to be delivered to the Internet, and the source IP address has a prefix that is *not* from one of the private subnets, one of the inside systems has been compromised. Both of these situations should be logged and flagged for the security administrator.

Besides blocking address impersonation attempts, firewalls are configured to reject inbound packets that have *source routing* defined for IP. An option of the IP protocol enables the sender to specify the precise route a packet should take. The route is declared as a list of IP addresses. Source routing can be used for a number of hacking purposes, including probing the network to determine its physical layout. Firewalls should be configured to block these packets.

*IP forwarding* is a feature in operating systems that automatically routes a packet between two network adapters in the same computer if necessary. This feature is undesirable in a firewall because the packet will have bypassed the packet filter rules. Therefore, IP forwarding is turned off in firewalls.

## Limitations of Packet Filtering

Reasons that packet filtering alone is not sufficient for network security include the following:

**Firewalls Are Complex to Configure.** Various public proclamations about penetration tests show that well over half of the firewalls regularly sampled are not properly configured. The ordering of packet filtering rules is particularly important.

**Filters Can Operate Only on the Fields That Appear in the Network Packets.** Some access control decisions require higher level knowledge that is only available after the data in the packets is assembled by the receiving application. It is unreasonable to presume that the same knowledge that exists in the application will be duplicated in the packet filtering code. Still, some firewall vendors provide general-purpose programming languages that can be used to strengthen the constraint capabilities of packet filters.

**When Much of the Network Traffic Is Augmented with Cryptography for Integrity, Authenticity, and Privacy, Packet Filters Provide Less Value.** If the traffic is cryptographically secured at the IP layer, packet filters can be applied on the receiving node after decryption. However, when application-level cryptography is applied, the packets are not decrypted until they reach the receiving application that is well past the packet filter in the IP stack.

**Packet Filters Do Not Contain Application Specific Knowledge.** For example, they cannot be used to limit who is allowed to log in to systems inside the network using telnet. Because *user* is an entity meaningful at the telnet application layer, the packet filter can limit only telnet connections at the granularity of the source IP address, rather than individual users on each IP address.

## Application Proxies Provide Access Control

In addition to packet filters, a firewall should include proxies. An application proxy is an application that acts as a gateway between the untrusted and trusted network but does so at higher layers in the network stack. The application proxy can make access control decisions that are expressed in terms of objects and attributes that the proxy understands. Examples of application proxies include FTP, telnet, gopher, and HTTP.

A circuit proxy (or gateway) is a generic proxy that does not know the specifics of the application but performs a more generic set of capabilities. SOCKS (Koblas and Koblas, 1992) is one of the more popular circuit gateways. The TIS Gauntlet firewall provides generic UDP and TCP circuit gateways, too.

In general, proxies improve upon the applications that they replace by supporting more granular access control. Many firewall texts prefer to distinguish between proxies based on whether they rely on the following:

- ◆ Modified user procedures
- ◆ Modified clients
- ◆ Transparency

Modified user procedures are rarely accepted and do not scale well. As an example, a user who needs to telnet from the trusted network to the untrusted network would be required to first log in to the proxy and then telnet from the proxy to the outside node. The second proxy type would avoid this inconvenience by requiring that each employee run a modified client program that would perform this additional step automatically. Concerns about this approach include scalability and cycle time. Supplying modified clients to thousands of users is difficult, and custom clients cost more to develop and may not be available.

*Transparent proxies*, best exemplified by the Gauntlet firewall from Trusted Information Systems, require neither modified procedures nor modified clients. Instead, the proxy runs on the firewall and transparently handles connections. A user on the inside initiates outbound connections just as if the firewall were not there. The application proxies running on the firewall intercept these outbound requests and deal with them according to configuration rules for the proxies. *Because security decisions are being made at the application level, a very rich access control language can be used to regulate network traffic with application proxies.* Any concepts or entities that are meaningful at the application level can appear in the access control rules. For example, one can limit FTP traffic so that only user Joe is allowed to GET files from IP address with a prefix of 7.88.99.

Generic proxies also exist for TCP and UDP; these proxies enable you to plug arbitrary client-server applications through the firewall. As with the specific proxies such as telnet, Lotus Notes, or Oracle SQL, access control rules can be defined to control which IP addresses, ports, or other packet values are allowed through these generic proxies.

Both packet filtering and proxies are needed in most environments to meet your security needs. Later, when you take a closer look at intrusion detection, you'll see some pros and cons of both approaches. The IBM Firewall provides packet filtering, application gateways, and circuit gateways. The Gauntlet firewall also supports all three approaches and transparent circuit proxies. To take advantage of SOCKS, you need to modify your applications and bind them to the SOCKS library when you recompile.

## Firewalls Provide IP Security

Almost every firewall today is equipped with a mechanism to provide secure IP traffic based on the IPsec standard. Interoperability tests are underway by various vendors to ensure that secure IP tunnels between vendors will work. Because the introduction of cryptography requires some notion of key management, unsurprisingly vendors distinguish themselves on whether they provide a useful key-management infrastructure. Support for X.509 certificates is mandatory because their use is increasing dramatically across the Internet. Firewall security policies based on the values in X.509 certificates are also appearing in products such as Gauntlet.

### IP Sec or Application Security

IP ESP and AH are applicable between two IP addresses. If you do not want to apply IPsec to all of the traffic running through your firewall, consider application-level cryptography. A number of alternatives are available. If your application runs on TCP/IP sockets, you can use SSL libraries available from Security Dynamics, Inc. Kerberos V5 and DCE both ship with Generic Security Services API (GSS-API), which is a set of library routines that provide application level security services including authentication, message integrity, and privacy. Finally, if you are writing applications on NT, the Microsoft Crypto API services are the best choice.

You should know that a number of vendors have signed up to support the *Common Data Security Architecture* (CDSA) initially proposed by Intel. The idea behind CDSA is to deliver a set of neutral security APIs that can be used for authentication, privacy, integrity, and nonrepudiation. The goal is to make available to vendors only one set of programming APIs that insulates developers from details of the underlying security implementation.

## How Complex Is Your Network Security?

In Chapter 1, "Intrusion Detection and the Classic Security Model," you were introduced to the idea that security models are implemented in software to provide services for enforcing a security policy. Regardless of how complex a particular solution might be, you eventually can identify the subjects and objects and how the reference monitor makes access control decisions. If multiple security models are in use at your site, each model is responsible for controlling security for a specific set of subjects and objects.

Network security is complex because so many different security models are in operation at any single moment. Traditional operating system network services work with familiar concepts such as users and groups. For example, the network applications FTP and Telnet use the operating system authentication subsystem before allowing access to a system. Not all popular network services follow this pattern. Web servers that run HTTP protocols over TCP/IP introduce their own notions of user, group, file system, and access control. Other client-server applications increase complexity by bringing along additional security models, including database management systems frequently used for critical business processes.

When you write a home-grown client-server application at your site, chances are that you will be crossing a number of security boundaries. Client and server programs have a security context meaningful to the operating system. They are associated with UIDs and GIDs, are stored as files in the file system, and are regulated by access control rules for IPC or sockets. As soon as you start worrying about how clients and servers communicate securely across a network, it's likely that another security context is introduced, such as the cryptographic framework you instrument your applications to use. The more back-end business systems the applications interface with, the higher the probability that a number of security models will be active.

A good example of this is the typical Web e-commerce application. To begin with, end users connecting to your site probably have an X.509 certificate signed by an authoritative source. The public key and private key associated with this certificate are used for secure connections to your site. The software products that generated the certificate constitute one security domain. On your end, the Web server is running on an operating system. That would be two new security contexts, one for the operating system and one for the Web server as described. The Web server probably has some client code that connects through a firewall to the back end business databases. Depending on how picky you want to be, that is either one or two new security models. The database manager definitely implements its own reference monitor, and the firewall also introduces a security model, although it overlaps some with the operating system's model.

When a hacker or a security expert looks at this kind of setup, they think "Wow, look at all the places someone can screw up security!" The first problem is that so many different models have to be administered. Users and groups must be managed, access control rules set up and modified, and client-server security established. To a hacker, this setup is just more opportunities for someone to configure the security policy incorrectly. Next, at each security model boundary, something interesting happens. Requests by subjects from one model are satisfied by subjects in another model acting with *on behalf of* semantics. If the mapping between the boundaries is well defined, no security leaks will exist. One frequently seen fiasco includes a database gateway application running on a Web server in which the gateway is given *unlimited* access to the back end database.

## Why Intrusion Detection Is Needed after Network Security

Simply put, firewalls are not enough either. Most firewall vendors have active intrusion detection strategies today. Why?

In order to be effective, all network traffic into the trusted network must pass through the firewall. Unfortunately, because many people use modems to connect to the outside world from the secure network, unwanted traffic can enter. This is only one of the reasons why firewalls alone are not enough to fulfill your security needs.

Firewalls are active security products. They run in real time and can even detect some kinds of hacker attacks, especially when the attack is a network probe. However, firewalls don't know what happens once someone gets through the firewall. Any insiders who are misusing systems will not be detected by firewalls, either. If you're still not convinced, you can always dig up your favorite two reasons:

◆ Someone doesn't configure the firewall properly.

◆ A hacker can exploit a bug that already exists in the firewall implementation.

In this chapter, you saw how access control and I&A are equally important for network security. The basic ideas of TCP/IP and UDP/IP were introduced so that you could understand how these network protocols are attacked. A number of network hacks then were described. The major suggestion was to add some type of firewall architecture to enforce stronger access control. Introducing cryptographic techniques at the network or application layers also was recommended to significantly improve network security. Despite these enhancements, there are still security weaknesses that must be addressed by additional products.

Given the complex nature of these networks, *monitoring is the only way* you can be sure that you have specified the right security policy *and* that the policy is being implemented properly. Stronger I&A, better access control tools, and improved network security with firewalls and cryptography go a long way toward securing your site. However, if you really want to worry less, turn to Part 2, "Intrusion Detection: Beyond Traditional Security," to see how monitoring and intrusion detection fill in the gaps left by other security tools.

# INTRUSION DETECTION: BEYOND TRADITIONAL SECURITY

Now that you've examined the roles and limitations of traditional security tools, it's time to take a closer look at intrusion detection. In this part of the book, you'll see how attackers can get through your existing defenses and how intrusion detection systems (IDSs) detect these events. This part includes four chapters that describe the following:

- ◆ What intrusion detection is, how this tool category differs from others, and the value that intrusion detection brings to your site
- ◆ How vulnerability scanner intrusion detection tools look for known program bugs or configuration errors to warn you of security holes
- ◆ How system-level intrusion detection catches activities that many other products miss
- ◆ How network-level intrusion detection sees hacker activities by inspecting network packets

As you learn about each of these IDSs, you also will be asked to think about the problems they do *not* solve. Your insights will help you understand the role that an IDS fulfills at your site. Also, thinking about how an IDS can be improved is necessary for evaluating future releases of IDSs.

# Chapter 5

# Intrusion Detection and Why You Need It

Within the last two to three years, many people thought that if they wanted to connect to the Internet, only a firewall was necessary to complete the security puzzle. In this chapter, you start by looking at how common scenarios you expect to be secure are really not. As you see why hackers can still get through, you will realize the value that an *Intrusion Detection System* (IDS) adds.

After going through these detailed examples, the central themes of an IDS are explained. In this chapter, you can read about the different type of IDSs, design tradeoffs in building an IDS, and learn the critical questions to ask about an IDS tool you might be considering. When you have finished this material, you will be ready to jump into the next few chapters, which describe specific IDS approaches in more detail.

## Do You Have Protection?

Figure 5.1 contains a diagram of an Internet configuration for a company with a public Web server. Notice that the Web server itself is encased in a perimeter network. At first, people tried to directly attach Web servers to the Internet without screening routers or firewalls to block attacks at the Internet entry point. This configuration was tried despite warnings from Morris (1986) and Bellovin (1988), which were discussed in Chapter 4, "Traditional Network Security Approaches." However, now it is rare to see a Web server connected directly to the Net without protection as shown in Figure 5.1. The question to ask is whether this Web server is safe from security breaches.

If the answer is "Yes," this chapter will certainly be short. As history has shown, almost no server is immune to penetration. The problem is that we can defend

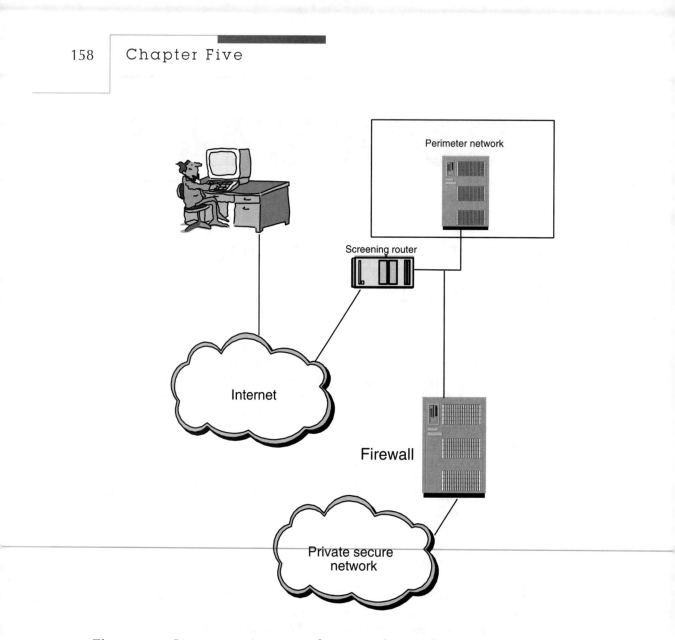

**Figure 5.1**  Common perimeter configuration for a Web server.

only against attacks known about today. Nothing *prevents* a publicly accessible system from being compromised by an attack that is newly discovered tomorrow.

The untrusted Internet and the perimeter network in Figure 5.1 are separated by a screening router. What is the role of the screening router in this configuration? TCP/IP packet level attacks that require address impersonation (or IP address spoofing) are eliminated by the router because it is configured to do the following:

- Block any inbound packet from the Internet to the perimeter that has a source IP address from the perimeter network
- Block any outbound packet from the perimeter to the Internet that has a source address from outside the perimeter network
- Block any inbound packet with source routing enabled

The screening router may be configured to block other attacks, such as Ping of Death or SYN Flood, which are targeted at the Web server. Other threats also may be addressed if the router is sophisticated enough. One thing that this screen will definitely *not* block is HTTP traffic. Otherwise, no one would be able to connect to the Web server.

Chances are that the router does not perform any application-specific checking of the network packets, such as looking at the URL being requested in incoming packets. Screening routers apply access control using network concepts, such as source address, destination address, port number, and TCP header field settings.

Several reasons why this common configuration alone is not enough for a secure defense are as follows:

- Vendor software on one of these systems contains a software bug that will result in a security problem. The bug could be in the operating system, in the Web server, or in the router implementation.
- Executable programs or scripts created at your site and called by the Web server can have flaws.
- One or more of the defense mechanisms will not be configured properly. Ample data supports this claim. When Dan Farmer ran a few scans against public Web servers in 1997, he found well over 80 percent to be open to some form of attack.

These items should be familiar by now because they are variations on the common reasons why hackers get through—software bugs or configuration errors.

In 1997, a rather nasty flaw in the *Microsoft Internet Information Server* (IIS) was discovered. With a little effort, it was possible to discover a URL of a particular length that would crash IIS. Anyone with a Web browser could send a URL of this size in HTTP. IIS would process the URL to open it, but a bounds checking problem caused IIS to hang or crash instead. Microsoft fixed the bug, but it serves as a good example of something that first-level defenses, such as screening routers, were not checking for at that time. The attack did not give the hacker access to the server, and therefore, Web site content remained safe. However, if a company had been depending on the Web site for revenue, the down time would have had a measurable impact. *The perimeter network shown in Figure 5.1 did not stop this attack because HTTP packets were allowed into the Web server.*

Microsoft was not the only vendor hit as a consequence of program errors. The Apache Web server also had a serious bug that impacted several sites. Writing error-free code is difficult, and as long as there is a possibility for bugs, a potential for security threatening consequences exists, as shown in Figure 5.1.

Most Web servers are populated with additional programs implemented using the *Common Gateway Interface* (CGI) or some other extensible environment, such as the Lotus Notes API. Two well-known Web hacks are the *test.cgi* hack and the *phf* hack. The details of these attacks are similar to those found during the early days of UNIX. Briefly, a programmer forgets to check for delimiter characters when accepting input from a user keying values or from another program. The input data values are to be used as parameters to another program. The programmer's code takes this input, concatenates the values with the command to be run, and passes this combination to the operating system for execution. Abstractly, this attack is shown in Figure 5.2.

In UNIX the semicolon can be used to separate multiple commands entered on a single line such as the following:

```
command-1 parameter-1; command-2 parameter-2;...;command-n parameter-n
```

NT relies on the & character for a similar capability. What happens if embedded in parameter-1 is the semicolon itself? For example, if parameter-1 is composed of the string "112 222 332; rm *," then the UNIX operating system will run the following:

```
command-1 112 222 332
rm *
command-2 parameter-2
```

This attack remains one of the most common attacks against Web servers, *even though the general problem has been known in the UNIX community for more than a decade.*

Both the *test.cgi* and *phf* hacks resulted from the way input data from HTML forms was processed by a CGI program. The user was asked to enter a name or some other text string. When the CGI script processed the data, it did not check for special delimiters. By appending a substring such as ";rm *" to the input field in the HTML form, the hacker could trick the CGI into removing all the files in the current working directory of the Web server.

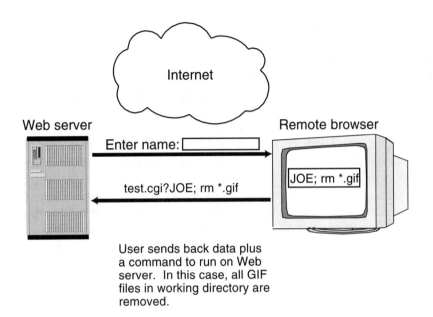

**Figure 5.2**   Command-driven attack enabled when delimiters are not filtered out.

Your Web server might be configured as securely as possible with all unnecessary network protocols disabled. There also could be a screening router in front of it blocking denial of service attacks as in the preceding figures. Yet, these defenses will not eliminate the *weak CGI threat*. If you have installed CGI scripts or other programs that have latent bugs, your site will get hacked. The amount of damage done depends on several factors.

If the Web server is running as root when this happens, all bets are off. For starters, the attacker can continue to execute one program at a time until the desired outcome is achieved. For example, the shadow password file can be changed so that a root password is not needed to log in. If the Web server daemon is running with some other credentials, the hacker will be able to access any resources that the Web server can access. In other words, the UID and GIDs identifying the Web server determine the consequences of the command executed with the CGI attack. Because the Web server's UID can access the Web site content, trashing is possible unless the entire Web site has been configured as read only for *all* users.

Programming errors are not limited to operating systems. Often vendor applications that you add to your systems introduce weaknesses, too. In UNIX these applications probably contain SUID or SGID programs. Even vendors who have a history of delivering quality software can make mistakes. In early 1998, a notice was posted in BUGTRAQ showing how a popular game, when played across a network, allowed remote users to penetrate participating nodes.

The list of potential configuration errors is extensive. UNIX and NT operating systems are delivered out-of-the-box with fairly open configurations today. The reasons for this are historical. Customers preferred easy to run, or load-and-go configurations. Security was not as important as ease of use to the marketplace. Now that more people are security conscious, this situation probably will change. At least there might be an option that allows someone to order the *locked down* version of a UNIX or NT system.

Like software errors, operating system configurations are not the sole source of problems. Configuration defaults in applications have been exploited to gain access to systems. The test.cgi bug affected a number of sites because it shipped as a default CGI for testing a popular Web server. By now almost everyone knows that Internet browsers also have endured their share of public humiliation for containing security bugs.

## The Role of Intrusion Detection

You should know that almost every day there is a new attack that shows up in a newsgroup or somewhere else on the Internet. Checking some of the links given in the Appendix will help you to stay abreast of the latest developments. Investing in an intrusion detection product, or perhaps a few products, will narrow the window of opportunity for someone trying to blast your systems. By now you should have a good idea of the relative value of traditional security products and how they are complemented by IDSs. The next few sections spell out the advantages in detail.

### Beyond I&A

What role does I&A play in your environment? I&A is needed in local and distributed systems because:

◆ I&A establishes your identity for subsequent activities on the system. Various reference monitors that decide what to do with your access requests need to know *who* you are to enforce access control.

◆ I&A blocks initial access to the computer until the requester has passed the authentication test. In addition to proving identity, this step is *preventative* because you cannot log in if you do not authenticate properly.

- I&A verifies the identity of noninteractive entities such as back-ground processes, daemons, and devices in order to regulate access control for these entities.
- I&A assigns *accountability* for activities that occur in the environ-ment. This is not important to everyone, but when accountability has consequences, knowing who did what is only possible with appropriate I&A.

In Chapter 2, "The Role of Identification and Authentication in Your Environ-ment," you saw ways to improve the security of I&A by using techniques or tools that defended against threats such as password cracking and network sniffing. It's clear that access control is needed beyond I&A for a complete security model, but why do you need intrusion detection in addition to I&A?

- Even improved authentication products, such as Kerberos, have been hacked. Weaknesses in the protocol have been described in Chapter 2 and elsewhere (Bellovin and Merritt, 1991; Dole, Lodin, and Spafford 1997; Mudge 1996).
- In 1997 the integrated Solaris-DCE login facility also had a serious flaw that rendered I&A untrustworthy. A similar flaw appeared in Silicon Graphics' IRIX operating system in 1998.
- Early versions of Security Dynamics ACE server also had problems that you saw in Chapter 2.
- A flaw in AIX rlogin allowed remote users to gain root access.

There are many other examples of failed I&A subsystems. Because bugs or loose adherence to corporate security guidelines will always exist, *I&A will not pre-vent all hacks*. You must at least monitor the activities of users, including sim-ple events such as failed login attempts, in order to detect problems. Preferably, you want to detect attacks in real time and have some automated responses to provide a scalable solution. Deploying an IDS that can detect attack patterns in I&A event data helps you get a handle on your security problems.

To reiterate a theme introduced in the opening chapter of this book:

*Good security requires prevention, detection, and responses.*

## Beyond Access Control

There are similar concerns about access control mechanisms that are responsi-ble for *preventing* unwanted actions. For nonnetwork resources, such as files, directories, devices, and IPC data structures, access control is designed to limit how subjects and objects interact. To effectively carry out its responsibilities, the reference monitor needs an access control database that is properly configured with the security policy to enforce. This database is the first place things can go wrong. As you saw earlier, either the vendor or your site administrator can improperly configure access control rules (or other aspects of your security policy) that lead to compromises. Remember, properly specifying access control rules for files and directories is an exceedingly complex task as the number of subjects and objects grows.

Next, if there are any bugs in the reference monitor itself, access control will not prevent violations of the policy. Although buffer overflows in privileged programs are not the fault of the reference monitor, these flaws are used to bypass the access control policy defined for the system. Perhaps the greatest latent threat is the large number of home-grown applications or custom programs that contain bugs or configuration errors which can lead to intrusions. As more enterprises connect these legacy back-end applications to front-end Web servers, the risk of penetrations increases.

When your system access control policy is violated, you also want to be able to detect the activity as soon as possible and have a scalable solution for responses. An IDS can add value here. An IDS is designed to detect and respond to attacks that get past your access control systems. The same is true for network access control.

## Beyond Network Security

How could it be possible that firewalls and encryption techniques are not enough? A few examples are worth walking through in detail.

In Figure 5.3, a packet-filtering firewall has been configured to allow HTTP traffic to travel in both directions. Two example hacks that can flow through this pipe are *test.cgi* and *phf*. Even if these two CGIs in particular are not running at your site, and hopefully they are not, there is always a risk that some internal CGI program has an exploitable weakness.

An increasingly common configuration is shown in Figure 5.4. Here, the perimeter network contains a Web server that must contact a business back-end server to complete the interaction with the customer. In these configurations a proprietary gateway program often communicates through the firewall with the back-end server inside the trusted network. The next few paragraphs describe some problems with this scenario.

Even if customers are using digital certificates to authenticate to the Web server, this same credential is not necessarily meaningful in the security context of the

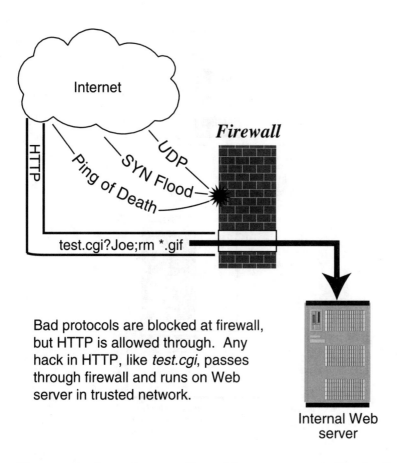

**Figure 5.3**  Intrusions unaffected by access control in the firewall.

database. The Web server and the database are separated by a security boundary with different subjects, objects, and ACLs. Some customer sites have granted the gateway program, running on the Web server, *unlimited* access to the database. In other words, when the gateway program connects to the database, it does so with the highest privileges when accessing the database. This programming choice alone should be enough of a reason to run an IDS on the database server.

The gateway program and the back-end server establish a client-server or peer-to-peer relationship. At a minimum, they communicate using a network protocol. Administrators know that certain Internet application protocols are not safe to punch through the firewall. However, these same conscientious employees often will allow proprietary protocols used by the gateway and back-end server

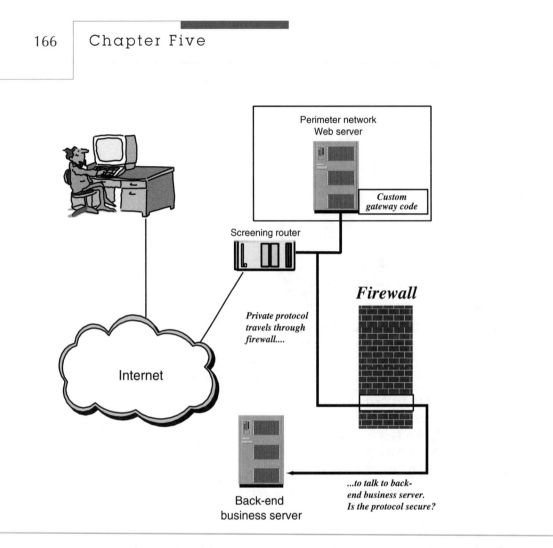

**Figure 5.4**  Gateways are paths for intruders.

to flow through the firewall. People realized weaknesses in some of the Internet application protocols because flaws were discovered by hackers or researchers over a period of years. These protocols are not allowed in the perimeter or through the firewall because they are flawed. The same type of introspection is warranted for private protocols that exist at your site, although private protocols are seldom given the same type of scrutiny. Private application protocols between the perimeter and the trusted network, or those run totally within the trusted network, are also potentially open to attack. Only by monitoring the activities of the participating nodes with an IDS can you be sure that your security policy is not weakened by proprietary application protocols deployed at your site. Although the IDS may not look at the protocol itself, it will detect improper activities on the system that result from weaknesses in private protocols.

Of course, you always can put your Web server into the trusted network, but all this placement does is move the target of the attack closer to the heart of the company. Any weak CGI script will still result in a compromise of some sort. You might *seriously* lock down the Web server with techniques such as read-only access, no logins except from a directly attached terminal, a hardened OS, and new Web pages installed only by a trustworthy individual. Unfortunately, none of these excellent ideas prevented the IIS attack noted previously. If a weak CGI is on your system, or a flaw is in a program called by a perfectly safe CGI, eventually someone will discover this opening. For some reason, there always seems to be a slot through which an attacker can slither.

By now you must have guessed that similar arguments apply to cryptography in network security. As distinguished and rich as the history of cryptography is, one lesson learned is that algorithms can be broken. Even if the cryptographic techniques are not weak, often secret keys are stored in encrypted form on local disk, and the key for the encryption is a user-chosen password. Secret-key cryptography is only as safe as the secrecy of the key. If someone can discover the key, the game is over (unless one-time keys are used). Even the secret-key component of a public-key pair is protected in local disk storage with a password. If people choose weak passwords, the benefits of cryptography will be lessened. Storing cryptographic keys in tamper-evident hardware devices is an alternative to keeping them on disk.

Look at the diagram in Figure 5.5. Both ends of the corporate network are protected by an IP tunnel that encrypts, signs, and authenticates all of the IP traffic between the sites. Threats to traffic as it passes through the untrusted network are neutralized, assuming that the keys are safe, and the cryptographic protocols are unbroken. What happens if an employee, visitor, or contract worker violates trust on either side of the IP tunnel? In this case, the tunnel functions properly except that it is being used to securely carry out improper behavior between sites.

If your Web site contains a weak CGI program that can be exploited like the test.cgi script, cryptography will not prevent the attack. When a customer connects to your Web site using a digital certificate or SSL, and your site contains a weak CGI, cryptography dutifully fulfills its role. Cryptography guarantees that the attack string flows with privacy and integrity, and that the string indeed came from the individual claiming to send it. What you get is an encrypted and authenticated hack that is guaranteed not to have been modified in transit by any intermediaries.

As you have seen with Kerberos attacks and random number cracking, it is the cryptosystem itself that becomes the focus of the attack. Once again, the solu-

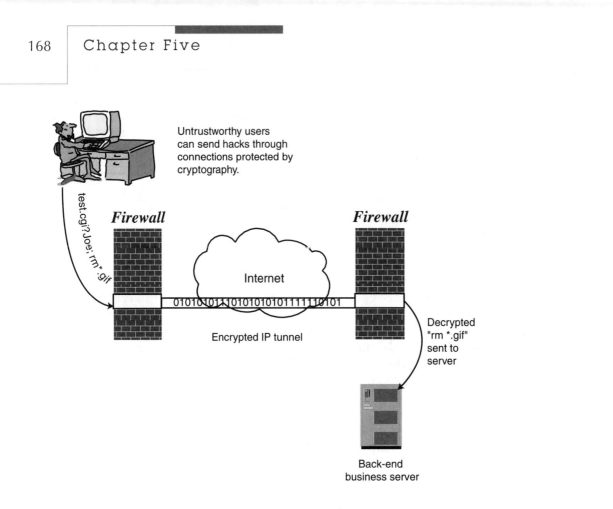

**Figure 5.5**   Encrypted tunnels can carry attacks.

tion is to *monitor* these network security products, which you certainly need to deploy, in order to detect problems as soon as possible. System or network level IDSs will catch problems that network security products and even cryptographic solutions miss.

If you want, you can substitute other firewall architectures for Figure 5.2. Custom proxies and SOCKS enabled proxies also are candidates for poor programming practices or improper configurations. Again, one notable feature of the TIS Gauntlet proxies is that the source is available for inspection. The proxies also are written with a minimalist view that limits the opportunities for mistakes.

Most firewall vendors today—including TIS, IBM, Checkpoint, and Axent-Raptor—all recognize the need for prevention, detection, *and* response. Though not a standard feature at the time this book was written, some type of IDS will be incorporated into firewalls as the need for product differentiation grows. Today, for example, IBM bundles the *Network Services Auditor* (NS Auditor) with its firewall offering.

Firewall packet filtering rules and application proxy access controls also are complicated to configure. Not every company can afford to hire experienced, well-paid network security specialists to perform these tasks. The dynamic nature of businesses adds to the complexity. Employees come and go, new applications are written to communicate across the firewall boundary, and revenue almost always takes precedence over security. Often, if the tradeoff is between more revenue and better security, it's not unusual to see people alter their definition of *acceptable risk.*

The general category of tools that are needed to further round out your security solution is collectively called *intrusion detection* even though different types of IDSs exist. Two different views of what an IDS is are offered: First are products that appear in the marketplace today. Some of these originated as research projects sponsored by the government during the last decade. Others were developed recently by individuals. For the research purist, though, an IDS is one of the currently active research projects at Stanford Research Institute (SRI) International or one of the handful of universities throughout the world focusing on intrusion detection. These projects usually have much loftier goals than commercial products. In this chapter and the next few, the focus is on commercial tools. See the References and Recommended Readings section at the end of the book for pointers to intrusion detection research papers.

## Intrusion Detection: Concepts and Definitions

A distinction is often made between *misuse detection* and *intrusion detection*. If the focus of analysis is on detecting problems from inside the trusted network by watching the activities of authorized users, the phrase misuse detection is more appropriate. When the interest turns to looking for attacks from outsiders or intruders, the latter applies. One difference is that misuse detection assumes that the perpetrator has at least one valid account on one of the systems in your network. An intruder (hopefully) has no legitimate account on your systems. Also, the distinctions between intrusion and misuse detection are fuzzy when an insider originates an attack from an inside node by hopping through an external node and coming back into the trusted network. In this chapter, the term *intrusion detection* is used to mean any misuse, intrusion, or misfeasance that is unwanted.

Distinguishing features of an IDS are the type of engine that makes decisions about intrusions, whether analysis occurs in real time as the events are received, and the source of data for events.

## IDS Engine Categories

*Statistical anomaly detection* is an IDS approach that looks for deviations from statistical measures to detect unusual behavior. A set of variables is defined for subjects and objects such as users, groups, workstations, servers, files, network adapters, and other resources. The baseline is established for each variable by looking at historical data or by declaring expected values. As system activities occur, a list of variables is maintained and updated for each subject or object of interest. For example, the IDS can keep track of the number of files read by an individual user over a given period of time. Variables often are combined mathematically with a weighting function to give a consolidated measure. In addition, the IDS watches for individual threshold conditions, such as three or more failed attempts to *su root*. An intrusion is defined as any unacceptable deviation from expected values.

*Pattern matching detection* compares activities against a collection of known attacks to find intrusions. The idea is to define, in advance, known problems and then to watch for event data that matches one of the patterns. Individual patterns can be composed of single events, sequences of events, thresholds of events, or general regular expressions in which AND and OR operators are allowed. Negation also is permitted when defining a pattern, although the computational complexity of looking for "everything but this event" can be staggering.

Some interesting implementation challenges are faced by IDS developers. Garbage collection is necessary when a pattern is partially matched but will never be completely satisfied. For example, if the pattern looks for actions only for the duration of a single program, and the program finishes without incident, active partial patterns waste precious memory unless discarded. Also, the efficiency of the pattern-matching engine is important for scalability. Finite-state machine models, well proven in compiler technology, seem to be suitable for filtering large numbers of events. Other pattern-matching engines include rule-based systems or decision trees. The computer science literature contains a tremendous number of pattern-matching techniques. Detecting computer intrusions is just one domain in which expert systems, neural nets, decision trees, fuzzy classification systems, or probabilistic reasoning models might be beneficial. Early IDSs were often based on expert systems. Therefore, you will find commercial tools that rely on rule-based inference engines for detecting intrusions, too.

Overlap with statistical techniques is unavoidable in pattern matchers because sequences such as "three failed logins in a row" represent patterns of interest. Thus, the division between a pattern-matching IDS and an anomaly detector IDS is not completely clean. One chief difference is that pattern-matching approaches have proportionally fewer statistical calculations than the anomaly detector systems.

The set of attack patterns that an IDS supports is compiled from various sources including CERT advisories, proprietary knowledge, and practical experiences. It is not always necessary to update the pattern database when a new hack attack is discovered. If the patterns are defined generally, and the new attack is really just a member of a *class* of problems, then an existing pattern will catch the intrusion. This capability is in contrast to virus detectors that must be continually updated as new viruses are discovered. A pattern-matching IDS does not necessarily need to be updated just because a new program experiences a buffer overflow attack. The challenge for the IDS vendor is to write the buffer overflow attack pattern in a general enough manner to truly detect the scenario, regardless of which program or system library exhibits the weakness. Vulnerability scanners are updated more often because they look for specific attacks rather than general patterns.

### Anomaly Detection versus Pattern Matching

To be accurate, many different types of anomaly detection and pattern matching IDS tools are available. Nonetheless, sticking with these two broad categories is enough for the moment. Both types have strengths and weaknesses.

The advantages of pattern matching tools include the following:

◆ The number and types of events to monitor are both constrained to only those data items needed to match a pattern. If you aren't worried about watching for Web server attacks because your system is a mail server, then you do not need to turn on all of the patterns in the database. Also, you probably can reduce the number and types of events you monitor.

◆ The pattern-matching engine tends to be more efficient due the absence of floating-point computations for statistical measures.

Disadvantages of pattern-matching approaches include the following:

◆ Scalability and performance is a function of the size and architecture of the pattern database or rule base.

◆ Extensibility is often difficult because no general-purpose pattern specification language exists. Adding your own attack signatures is complicated.

◆ Additions to the pattern database are required as new classes of attacks are found. Although patterns are flexible and do not need to be updated as often as virus scanners, some new attacks may not be caught by existing patterns.

◆ Learning is not generally designed into the model, although nothing precludes the addition of a learning component into pattern-matching models. None of the commercial IDSs exhibit any type of artificial intelligence learning capabilities today. This feature would be one way to automatically update the pattern-matching database as new attacks are *learned*.

◆ Converting a natural language description of a hack into a pattern can be difficult. Hence, the task can require substantial manual encoding efforts. If the pattern is not specified correctly, it won't catch the hack. Therefore, IDS vendors who build patterns are required to run extensive test cases to guarantee that attacks are caught. Reporting an intrusion when one did not occur also is to be avoided by the pattern creator.

The chief advantages of the statistical anomaly approach include the following:

◆ Well-understood statistical techniques can be used, provided that the underlying assumptions about the data are valid.

◆ The set of variables that track behavior does not require a significant amount of memory storage.

◆ Statistical techniques also can be used for dealing with time. Moving averages, smoothing techniques, weighting, and interval multipliers all provide refinement methods for improving the accuracy of what the system detects.

◆ Simple thresholds of behaviors, such as failed logins, are easily understood by operators.

Concerns about statistical anomaly approaches include the following:

◆ The underlying assumptions about the data may not be statistically sound.

◆ Combining values from different variables also might be statistically incorrect.

◆ Establishing the baseline is often a challenge. How do you know what is *normal* for all of the users, networks, applications, and other entities at your site?

◆ Not all users exhibit consistent behavior. Some employees may log in at different times each day, execute different commands somewhat randomly, and access resources in unpredictable ways. Experienced users are the usual example for variable behaviors.

♦ A hacker who knows that intrusions are being determined based on statistical behavior is able to circumvent detection by avoiding activities that are measured and by choosing an alternative attack instead.

♦ An attacker who uses multiple accounts can spread abusive behavior among the accounts without exceeding thresholds.

♦ No provisions have been made for the order of events. A pattern-matching engine will detect a race condition attack, but a statistical engine will not.

♦ Understanding when intrusive behavior begins to be *averaged out* over time is not easy. Alternative days of heavy and light use of a resource tends to be averaged out over time. Therefore, more complex statistical techniques may be required if user's behaviors vary widely. Complicated statistical models make it harder to interpret the results.

♦ Setting thresholds for indicating intrusive events requires experience. How do you know when someone has read too many files?

Statistical approaches have been applied to pattern-matching problems, too. Successful projects have been developed for fingerprint systems, robotics, manufacturing, and voice recognition systems. Additional research is ongoing to find the best fit for statistical techniques in intrusion detection.

Do you need both types of IDS engines? At this time, it appears that both anomaly detection and pattern matching are incommensurate, meaning that you can certainly benefit more by having both tools rather than a single type. Most current research IDS projects rely on both statistical techniques and pattern-matching tests to catch intruders. See www.csl.sri.com/emerald or www.csl.sri.com/nides for examples.

## Real Time or Interval Based

*Vulnerability scanners,* which look for weaknesses in your environment, normally are run on an interval basis. The idea is to occasionally inspect your network and systems for weaknesses. The problem with interval scanning is that you might discover a problem only after an intruder has damaged your data.

You also can run anomaly detectors and pattern matchers in batch or interval mode, although the more useful approach is to run a real-time version of these monitors. Running a product in real time naturally has performance and resource-consumption consequences. A real-time IDS that exhibits *adaptive* behavior is not commercially available yet but should appear in the future. The idea is to monitor a subset of the total range of events and increase the number of events you want to monitor only when something interesting happens on the system. The challenge is to define the minimum initial set of events to monitor and to know when to start logging other events. Picking the wrong initial set of events might cause you to miss some intrusions.

As it turns out, both real-time and interval scanning IDSs are needed. When risk of an event is low, checking for problems on an interval basis is recommended. When the threat is high or the consequences are serious, watching for intrusions in real time is required. Deciding which events to monitor in real time as opposed to which events to scan for occasionally should be configurable by the customer. In this way, you can decide what is important in *your* environment.

## Data Source

The two main categories of information that an IDS examines are network data and system data. Network traffic is usually obtained by activating a network adapter in promiscuous mode. Most network IDS vendors recommend that you dedicate a system on the network to sniffing and analyzing traffic. Note that this data source *comes for free*. That is, you do not need to turn on any special auditing or logging features in your products to capture network traffic.

The traditional source of system information is the audit trails emitted by the kernel. With a few exceptions, audit logs contain sufficient detail to track activities to individual users. RACF and similar mainframe security products have long been praised for their auditing capabilities. Even though auditing can generate significant amounts of information, no other facility is available for gathering a comprehensive picture of system activities.

IDS vendors are under increasing pressure to examine application logs. Indeed, one can argue that all the interesting subject-object interactions will be occurring at the application level rather than the OS level in the future. If you look at the /etc/passwd file or NT Registry in the near term and find no significant user accounts, it's probably because all of the users and groups are defined in application-specific data stores. Databases are the obvious example, but other examples are not hard to find. Because the majority of interesting transactions will be occurring at the application level, IDS vendors will need to apply their expertise to developing additional models and patterns specifically for individual applications. Because many IDS tools are being deployed with firewalls, you can expect future IDS releases to analyze firewall logs for intrusions. Axent's

ITA already supports analysis for a number of firewall logs. The Computer Misuse Detection System from SAIC also monitors log files from Raptor, Interlock, and CyberShield.

One way vendors enter a market is by showing product differentiation. Although each IDS may have unique characteristics that provide value beyond other tools at a site, the net impact on the customer is that many products are needed rather than one. Some IDS builders focus on network intrusions; others focus on system intrusions; some provide real-time analysis; and others concentrate on periodic assessments. *Having all of these options in a single tool suite would be beneficial to the marketplace.* The consolidation of IDS vendors into larger security companies appears to be the way to achieve this goal.

An important issue to consider with respect to the data source chosen by an IDS product is whether this information is already being captured at your site. If you are not currently running the audit subsystems of UNIX or NT systems, adding this overhead will have to be considered if the IDS product you choose requires this as a data source. On the other hand, if you truly want to assign accountability and know details of system activities, auditing is the best way to get this information.

Network data sources are less problematic because the traffic is already available for analyzing. A network IDS does not introduce a new data source, nor does it alter any existing data sources. *One problem you will have is trying to analyze encrypted network traffic.* If two sites are protected by an IP tunnel, the network IDS must be placed at the point in the network where the traffic is decrypted. Unfortunately, if applications at your site have employed application-level encryption, a network IDS cannot examine these packets because they are not decrypted until they reach the application layer.

If you adhere to the belief that much of the network traffic in the future will be application specific and encrypted for each application, you should wonder about the long-term role of the network IDS. The services provided by network IDSs will still be needed; it's just that they might be embedded in other components of the system, such as in the application decryption routines in which the packets finally appear in the clear.

The choice of data source also affects *what* the IDS can discover. Recall from the discussion on firewalls that access control in network traffic is affected by the type of firewall. Network packet filters operate on packet concepts such as IP address and port numbers. Application gateway firewalls can form access control rules that contain application-specific information such as specific URLs for a Web proxy. The same arguments apply to intrusion detection data sources.

Information about failed logins, failed file accesses, planted Trojan Horses, and other system events can be found easily in the audit logs. However, system audit logs contain limited information about network activities. Attacks such as Ping of Death and SYN Flood are not surfaced in the audit trail. Instead, these attacks must be detected at the IP layer itself by the operating system, a firewall, or a separately attached network IDS. Conversely, information about buffer overflow attacks and higher level system abstractions (UID, GID, file, and printer) *does* appear in the audit trail. This same information is not readily available when you are sniffing network packets.

*Therefore, a system-level IDS can detect intrusions that a network-level IDS cannot and vice versa.*

Needless to say, any application-level abstractions are meaningful only to the application itself. For a network sniffer to be able to watch packets and detect application-specific attacks, the sniffer must contain at least enough of the application knowledge to be able to extract meaning out of the packets. In a trivial sense, this practice would require that the sniffer have the capability to combine various packets destined for the application into meaningful groups, which is precisely what a good deal of the application code itself does. Another way to phrase this is to say that the network IDS must have a substantial portion of the application knowledge to catch application-level attacks.

RealSecure from ISS detects some application attacks by sniffing network packets. For example, it detects the *rlogin -froot* AIX bug, and rlogin is certainly an application. The right architecture in the long run is for the applications to invoke IDS service routines in order to make their *own* decisions about intrusive behaviors. Another argument for this architecture is the increasing use of application-level encryption. Only the application itself ever sees the data in the clear.

## A Generic IDS Model

Dorothy Denning (1987) introduced a generic intrusion detection model that is shown in Figure 5.6. The model is widely applicable to intrusion detection systems today. The three main components are the Event Generator, the Activity Profile, and the Rule Set. Early intrusion-detection systems often relied on expert system techniques and consequently the idea of a rule base appears in the generic model.

In order to make decisions about whether security problems exist, some form of *instrumentation* must be provided by the system(s) being monitored. The Event Generator is the component of the model that provides information about system activities. Events are derived from system audit trails, from network traffic, or from application-specific subsystems such as firewalls or authentication servers. Sometimes in the literature, an *event* is defined as a higher level abstraction than a primitive such as *this file was opened*. In other words, a series of audit records from the operating system might be combined into a single notable event.

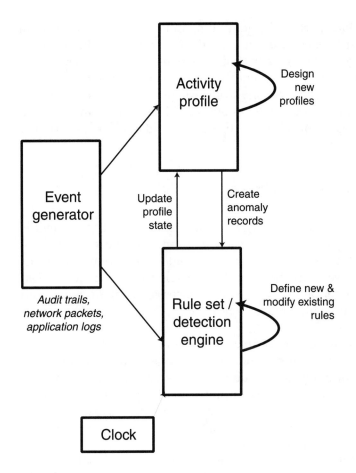

**Figure 5.6**  A generic intrusion detection model.

The Rule Set is best thought of as the inference engine that decides whether an intrusion has occurred. Rule-based expert systems frequently were the preferred inferencing tool for early IDSs. However, Denning's model allows for statistical approaches as well. The best way to think of the Rule Set is as a generic detector engine examining events and state data using models, rules, patterns, and statistics to flag intrusive behavior.

The Activity Profile maintains the state of the system or network being monitored. As events appear from the data source, variables in the Activity Profile are updated. New variables might be created as well depending on the actions dictated by the Rule Set.

Feedback is an important part of the generic model. The presence of some event might trigger the rule base to *learn* and add a new rule. If the Rule Set detects a threshold change in the Activity Profile, one response could be to alter the types, frequency, or details of events emitted from the Event Generator. Note that there is no architectural limitation on the generic model that restricts it to a single system. Each of the three main subsystems could be running on different nodes in a network, and each individual subsystem could itself be partitioned further across multiple nodes.

## Getting Ready to Look for Hacker Trade

The introduction of *intrusion detection systems* (IDS) into your environment is targeted at filling in the gaps left by other security products. In previous chapters, system and network weaknesses were identified, and recommendations were made for improving security. Despite the possible improvements, weaknesses still exist. This chapter described how I&A, access control, firewalls, and cryptography are still not enough for complete security, and why an IDS rounds out the solution.

Differences in intrusion detection products were described, and the pros and cons of different approaches were briefly mentioned. Vulnerability scanners were the focus of this chapter, although subsequent chapters will deal with network and system-intrusion detection products in more detail. System and network scanners were shown to play a vital role in securing your site because they look for evidence of hacker behavior, examine configuration weaknesses, probe for well-known security problems, and provide useful reports.

If you want to dig a bit deeper into intrusion-detection research before heading into the next few chapters, here are some pointers. Excellent papers and links for intrusion detection can be found at the COAST and UC Davis Web sites. COAST is spearheaded by Gene Spafford and cranks out some papers on intrusion detection. Some of the documents are limited to sponsors, but many have been posted electronically on the site and have been published in journals and conference proceedings. Check it out at www.coast.purdue.edu. A particularly useful page with one of the most comprehensive collections of security links is maintained there at www.coast.purdue.edu/security-links.html.

UC Davis has several IDS researchers and graduate students. Much of the original work on intrusion detection funded by DARPA involved collaboration between UC Davis and other sites such as Livermore Labs, Los Alamos, and DoD teams. Browse the pages at www.ucd.edu/security for good background and current readings. Be sure to pay a visit to the cryptography pages maintained there as well.

Visit the SRI Web site at www.csl.sri.com to see active research from some of the founding members of the IDS field. Peter Neumann and his colleagues are working on the EMERALD project there and are seeing promising results. As a final note, get your hands on conference proceedings from NISSC. Numerous papers on intrusion detection and computer security in these collections.

# Chapter 6

# Detecting Intruders on Your System Is Fun and Easy

Well, perhaps the title of this chapter is a *slightly* misleading. Supposedly, *becoming* an intruder is fun and easy, too. If you want to detect intruders, you should know what type of system resources can be depended on for providing evidence. Should you want to become an intruder, you ought to know how commercial IDSs look for traces of your activity.

Scanners are designed to take a look at your system and to let you know whether you have configuration problems or holes that can be used for attacks. If your system was previously set up in a secure fashion, and an intruder has altered this configuration, a scanner will detect this change (when you run the scan) and notify you of the problem.

System-level intrusion detection tools differ from scanners in a couple of ways. If the IDS runs in real time, it can let you know the instant a compromise has occurred. Also, if the monitor gathers its data by reading an activity stream on the system, it can detect a range of features that a single scanner cannot. For example, scanners will not tell you that someone just entered three bad passwords and exceeded the failed login threshold.

By the time you finish this chapter, you will understand the following:

- ◆ How to classify attacks according to how they originate and the threat they pose
- ◆ The pros and cons of different data sources that a system monitor can use for decisions
- ◆ What system monitors can and cannot detect
- ◆ The tradeoffs you may need to make for monitoring your systems in real time
- ◆ What it takes to really track someone through a network

As you will soon see, you need to consider a number of issues when trying to build a system-level IDS.

## Classes of Attacks

Table 6.1 provides a convenient way of looking at attack categories. You can see that threats generally are divided between *internal* and *external* points of origin. Along the other axis, you see increasingly more severe attacks. Inside the table are relative indications of the seriousness of the consequences. If an internal user obtains privileges belonging to other users, you usually can rectify the situation and perhaps take legal action. When someone outside your network is able to gain superuser access into one of your nodes, you have a catastrophic breakdown in security somewhere. Also, because so many ways to hide one's identity from the outside exist, the chances of catching the intruder are slim.

### Internal Attacks

Statistics from the FBI Crime Lab consistently show that the majority of computer crime occurs from the inside. True, as more people connect to the Internet, the threats from outside increase. Today, most crimes still are committed by insiders, or at least outside criminals are assisted by insiders. The theft of millions of dollars from a major U.S. bank was launched from Russia, but collusion from an insider made the task easier. Most of the money was returned. Although some companies do not like to think of their employees, contractors, or business partners as potential criminals, historical data encourages them to do so. What are some of the threats that an insider poses to internal systems?

#### Internal Denial-of-Service Attack

Recently, a number of NT systems at the University of Texas were hounded by a denial-of-service attack against the IP stack delivered with NT. The attack was a

**Table 6.1**  Categorizing Attacks in Two Dimensions

|  | Point of Origin | |
| --- | --- | --- |
|  | Internal User | External User |
| Denial of Service | Annoying | Annoying |
| Increased privilege | Moderately serious | Serious risk |
| Superuser privilege | Very serious | Disaster |

variant of the *Teardrop* UDP attack that was possible because of a bug in NT. By sending certain types of UDP datagrams, an adversary could cause the system to crash. Because UDP packets often are blocked by screening routers or firewalls, this threat was unlikely from outside sources. Someone with access to one of the UT labs launched the attack internally.

Users with accounts on various company servers or on university systems pose threats because they already have access to the system. When you are able to establish a login session on a computer, a number of denial-of-service attacks rare possible:

♦ Consume all of the disk space in the /tmp directory of UNIX systems to slow or crash the system (depending on how that particular version of UNIX handles this condition)

♦ Write a program to consume all available resources such as all of the memory buffers allocated for sockets

♦ Fill up the printer queue directory

♦ Create a number of concurrent I/O bound processes that thrash the disk repeatedly

You really don't even need an account on a system to cause problems. As shown in Chapter 2, "The Role of Identification and Authentication in Your Environment," physical or network access is sufficient for locking all accounts with failed login attempts until the lockout threshold is hit for each account. If the system permits remote logins from other nodes inside the enterprise, failed login attacks are possible even when physical access is not granted.

Most environments run a large number of client-server applications. The telnet program is a well-known example. However, numerous proprietary client-server protocols are running throughout the enterprise, and each of these also is susceptible to denial-of-service attacks. For example, it is unlikely that many legacy applications are performing adequate authentication of packets received. Forged IP addresses and packets can find their way into listening servers and cause denial-of-service attacks. If the servers are designed to accept connections from any internal node, it's easy enough to create packets, flood the server with them, and thus render the server useless.

> In general, the closer you can get to running on the system directly, the more damage you can potentially do.

Most UNIX systems now contain user limits to prevent some of these attacks. The Berkeley quota system is designed to prevent someone from consuming too much free disk space. If the quota is large, and the amount of free disk space in /tmp is small, you can still launch a denial-of-service attack. Other limits include those for memory, the number of simultaneously opened files, the number of concurrent processes, and similar constraints for commonly used resources. Unfortunately, these checks are made against the *effective UID* (EUID), and a user can bypass checking by running SUID or SGID programs that can cause resource exhaustion.

## Internal Privilege Escalation

UNIX and NT systems both provide ways for users to gain increased privileges through program execution. NT uses its access rights mechanism, and UNIX relies on the now familiar SUID or SGID concepts. Even if the privileged program does not give the user access to *everything* on the system, even a little privilege boost can help. For one thing, if the average UNIX user can gain privileges of the mail group by exploiting a SGID mail program, then that user will have access to the mail spool directory. Denial-of-service attacks, or worse, are then possible.

Privileged programs are compromised in a number of ways:

◆ The program does not check buffer limits and is subject to a buffer overflow attack.

◆ The program does not check input parameters and is tricked into executing one of the parameters as a command (test.cgi hack).

◆ The program makes invalid assumptions about its environment.

◆ The program is tricked into operating on a different resource because of poor programming practices.

The first two attacks have been discussed previously. A program that makes invalid environment assumptions is poorly written. The classic example is a program that does not set its own PATH environment variable or does not use fully qualified path names for the programs it calls. If a privileged program contains an instruction that tells it to run another program, such as the following, the hacker will install a program with the desired behavior into a writable directory and then invoke the privileged program:

```
system ("ls -l");
```

Instead of running /bin/ls, the privileged program runs the bogus version planted. This problem is so  well known that you would expect it to be rare. However, if you were to spend some time digging in commercial operating systems, you might be surprised at how often this poor programming practice still occurs.

UNIX programs also are impacted by inheritance. When a child process is created, it inherits the environment of its parent. If a user's UMASK setting results in the creation of world writable files, and the user runs a SUID or SGID program that does not reset UMASK, files created by the program will be world writable. If the program treats the file as a cache, writing values into it and reading values from it, then any user will be able to supply chosen data values to the program.

This last type of compromise of privileged programs is especially fun. The idea is really simple. A program reads a parameter, such as a file name, that tells the program which resource to access. The program has a *handle* to the resource. Before the program accesses the resource, an adversary is somehow able to replace the resource with a different target. Here is a practical example.

The first line of a shell script in UNIX tells the system which shell interpreter to use. A race condition exists in that the kernel looks at this first line and picks out the shell interpreter. The kernel then starts the interpreter with UID and GID according to the SUID and SGID permission bit settings for the file. Before the kernel feeds the script's statements to the interpreter, the file's contents can be replaced. This is a well-known race condition. You might think this last step is impossible unless you have write access to the shell script file. However, you can create a symbolic link from the SUID or SGID shell script in your current directory, start the script, and replace the file in your current directory with anything of your choosing before the commands are fed to the interpreter. You can use other tricks to broaden the window of opportunity for exploiting the race condition. If the shell script is not privileged, this hack does nothing exciting. For shell scripts with SUID or SGID bits set, the result is that the hacker will be able to run any shell commands with the EUID and EGID of the owner of the symbolic link. As a general rule, you should not have SUID or SGID shell scripts on your systems.

## Internal Superuser Privileges

The biggest threat to a system is when a user gains superuser or complete administrative privileges. The same kinds of attacks and problems mentioned previously apply for root or administrator privileged programs. Buffer overflow attacks, data-driven attacks, spoofed resources, and spoofed network packets have all been exploited by normal users to gain privileged access to a system.

Will a firewall prevent these privilege escalations from happening? Well, if the network attack is like the test.cgi attack, and the Web server is running as root or Administrator, then the firewall will not help. Do people actually run Web servers as root?

Many systems now support HTML interfaces for system administrator tasks. The HTML pages launch CGI programs that *must* run with root privileges because they do things the root user normally would do from the command line. The only way to accomplish this is by running the httpd daemon as root so that it can spawn CGI processes with these same privileges. If a user on the internal network is able to send in an HTTP packet to the Web server running as root, the server can be tricked into executing arbitrary commands.

If you have seen any of these privileged Web servers, you know that as a first step, the person connecting to the server must authenticate using a user ID and password. The Web pages are protected with standard Web server access control rules. When authentication is complete, the httpd daemon will respond to requests without requiring additional authentication. An attacker can spoof the IP address of the administrator's station and send arbitrary HTTP commands to the privileged Web server. This attack is hopefully not possible from the outside because a properly configured network will not permit external access to a Web server running as root. However, because this same node might be an internal data server, most users will have access to it, meaning that the threat of forged packets is real. To avoid attacks against Web servers running as root, use SSL or IPsec to prevent network node impersonation.

## External Threats

When you have publicly visible systems, as almost everyone does today, there is a always a threat that someone can find a way into your systems. In the preceding chapter you saw how properly configured firewalls could allow HTTP attacks from the outside into internal systems. Systems in the perimeter network are usually the first ones to be hit. When someone attacks your system, the result could be denial of service. For example, your Web server can be slowed considerably if it is hit with a denial-of-service network attack. If someone manages to gain a login shell as a normal user, this represents the next level of severity in threats. Naturally, if someone obtains complete control over a system by gaining root or superuser privileges, and this adversary is a remote user unaffiliated with your enterprise, this represents the worst threat.

### External Denial-of-Service Threats

In Chapter 5, "Intrusion Detection and Why You Need It," you saw that publicly visible network addresses are nearly impossible to defend from *all* denial-of-service attacks. If your Web server allows arbitrary users to connect, someone can write a program to generate a large number of HTTP transactions with your server as the target. The net result is a flooded Web server. Most Web servers are not designed to detect or defend against these attacks, although this is precisely the only place to adequately defend against such as threat.

A firewall or screening router is also not going to be of much help here because it is difficult to state a packet filtering rule for this condition. For example, a large number of HTTP packets with bad data from a single source address are hard to distinguish from a large number of well-formed HTTP packets unless your filter is smart enough to know the details of the HTTP protocol and partially assembled packets. To really solve the problem, the component that has the highest semantic view of the packets, in other words the Web server program itself, must implement this form of application-level security. If the Web server detects a series of bogus packets or even good packets from the same address in a fixed interval of time, the server could notify the firewall to block incoming traffic from that address. Of course, the clever denial-of-service hacker would just forge a series of IP addresses to avoid detection.

## External Privilege Escalations

Hopefully, this class of attacks is becoming less frequent as knowledge of security problems spreads. A remote user can escalate privileges in two different ways:

♦ A program that does not permit logins is running on the target node but is accepting network connections (such as a Web server).

♦ The remote user is able to gain access to the system via a login, or in other words, a network login program is listening for external connections.

An example of the former is, of course, the Web server daemon. Poor CGI programming practices can permit remote users to execute arbitrary commands on the system, albeit only with the privileges of the Web server daemon. A rather nasty example surfaced in 1997 with some implementations of FTP.

An FTP client can issue a command to the FTP server that requests multiple files at once. The client issuing the *mget \** command is asking the server to send all files in the current directory of the server. Unfortunately, some FTP client implementations did not bother to check that the files sent by the server were only those included in the current directory. A user in a home directory who then FTPs to a malicious server and executes the *mget \** command could find many other files being added to the home directory. The server could push viruses or Trojan Horses to the receiving client because of this bug. If a root user on a UNIX system happened to be executing one of these FTP clients from the root file system directory, the malicious FTP server could replace the password file.

Cases in which remote users gain login access to servers were discussed in Chapter 2, "The Role of Identification and Authentication in Your Environment."

Even if strong authentication is used for login proof of identity, sessions can be hijacked unless other precautions are taken. If a root or Administrator user connects remotely via a protocol that is not protecting against packet injection or session hijacking, the adversary has the opportunity to effectively have root access. The amount of damage done is dependent on what operations the protocol supports. Again, think of the Web server running as root and subject to a CGI hack to understand the consequences.

## Layers of Information Sources

To understand the role of various intrusion detection products, take a look at the simplified diagram shown in Figure 6.1. Here, the distinction is made between three different levels of analysis for a computing environment.

### Warning: Opportunities for Hackers!

The Internet is often used as a replacement for private leased lines. Proprietary client-server protocols that have been operating across private leased lines or LAN connections are sometimes being deployed across the Internet. Unfortunately, the implementers of these solutions don't always understand the limitations of their protocols.

Why do firewalls block packets? The decision to block a particular type of network traffic is based on the history of that protocol. If the protocol has been hacked in the past, or if it divulges too much information about the private network, the packets are blocked. Examples include source-routing options on IP packets, RPC, most UDP (although this is changing to some degree), finger, Berkeley r-cmds, and NFS. These protocols are not allowed through the firewall because they are deemed to be unsafe. Years of pounding on these protocols by thousands of users have contributed to the decision to avoid running these protocols across untrusted networks. Sometimes, the protocol is sound, but the programs have bugs (sendmail is a good example) in the way in which the data sent in the protocol is processed.

Do you think the same rigorous, robust analysis has been applied to the private protocols that are now being pushed across the Internet? It's unlikely. Still, the risk seems to be worth the reward. Previously unconnected sites now can share data by transferring data through a socket opened across the Internet. The glamor is too alluring to wait for detailed protocol reviews by

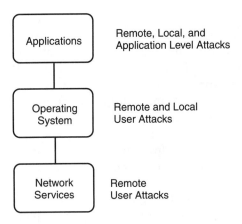

**Figure 6.1**   Layers of information in the operating system.

security experts. Yet, each of these private protocols presents an opportunity for an attacker to enter your private network, hijack a session, or launch data-driven attacks against the endpoints of the socket.

Many customers do not want to open additional ports through the firewall. Sites may allow HTTP and SMTP through the firewall, but nothing else. Other sites depend on proxy servers for outbound sessions such as FTP, telnet, and Gopher. Some application programmers know about these limitations and are afraid to ask the firewall administrators to open a new port for a proprietary protocol between two enterprise sites. One trick is to write the application so that the endpoints communicate on port 80 (the HTTP port). Ouch! Essentially, the developers are using port 80 as a general-purpose hole through which to punch private protocols.

The problem with this style of thinking is that the fundamental purpose of the packet filter is not understood. The security of the network traffic is not determined by the port number but rather by the protocol that flows through that port on the firewall or by the receiving applications. HTTP can be set up to run on any port, and the security of the protocol is unaffected by this configuration change. To take this reasoning to an extreme, wouldn't it be just as reasonable to take an unsafe protocol such as rsh and run it through port 80, too? It's hard to believe someone would answer, "Yes," to this question.

At the bottom is the network layer, which can be further subdivided into many different layered components itself. For the purposes of this discussion, think of the network layer as a single entity in which all of the TCP/IP or SMB traffic is handled. At the next layer is the OS. Technically, the OS includes the network stack, but think of this OS layer as containing all of the components that are not directly responsible for processing network information. Example components at this second layer include commands, libraries, backup routines, login routines, and other core subsystems that would be in operation even if the computer were not attached to a network. (This distinction is still fuzzy because a computer can open a socket to itself even if it is not directly connected to the network. Don't think too hard about these divisions.)

At the highest layer are the applications. Think of this layer as containing all of the products that are not normally delivered as part of the operating system. As the last few years have shown, the set of products in this upper level has changed drastically as OS vendors rush to include "for free" add-ons for product differentiation. Still, think of Lotus Notes, Oracle, DB/2, add-on mail programs, manufacturing or CAD software, and a payroll application as examples from this layer. The main idea to drive home here is that these applications typically bring along additional security models with subjects and objects beyond those that are part of the operating system.

This layered view, though simplistic, is important because at each level you are able to discern security activities not apparent at other levels. Each of these three layers can provide data or instrumentation that describes activities which the other layers cannot detect or understand easily. For example, the operating system knows when someone fails to enter a password correctly. This event is recorded in at least one place, perhaps in more than one place, depending on the amount of logging you have initiated. On the other hand, the network deals primarily with the task of receiving or sending network packets.

When packets are received, the network layer is responsible for routing the packets to the appropriate listening programs. When packets are sent to the network layer by a program, the packets are sent down onto the physical network layer for delivery to the target. The network layer itself is not responsible for controlling whether someone enters a correct password.

Similarly, an application with its own database of user IDs knows whether one of its application-specific users has failed an authentication step. In the ideal case, the application can reuse the repository of users and groups found in the operating system, including the possibility of relying on the operating system's authentication programs. The trend is for this to occur more frequently on NT systems than UNIX systems, although this is just an opinion. Such tight integration between an application and the OS is rare, and the more common approach is for the application to introduce its own repository for users and groups. When this happens, the OS itself has no knowledge of successful or failed login activities completely under the control of the application.

## Commercial IDS Layering

In the commercial IDS marketplace, it is common to find a particular product focusing primarily on network or system monitoring, with modest support for application-level monitoring. Often, this product differentiation strategy is made for competitive reasons. That is, vendors have historically chosen to focus on monitoring system activities or network activities to ensure a positive business case for the company. Like much of the computer security industry, this practice is changing, too, as the need for complete solutions drives requirements. IDSs that process network data, system data, and application data are found in research systems such as EMERALD and NIDES (www.sri.com/csl).

Over time this situation is bound to change. Commercial vendors will combine or cooperate. A strong need exists for a cohesive network and system-level intrusion detection product.

Intrusion detection on a system cannot be solved at a single layer of that system. Here, the layers are simply the network, the operating system above the network, and then the application layer as shown in Figure 6.1. A general rule of thumb is that the component with the most knowledge about the data being attacked is best suited for housing the intrusion detection logic. IP address spoofing, SYN Flood, and Teardrop attacks are detected by the network software layer because these attacks exploit data with meaning at that level of the stack. Buffer overflow attacks executed by users with an active login session are detected by the operating system-level intrusion detection monitor because these events are not generated at the network level. You might argue that if the users are connected over the network, then *any* keystrokes are visible at the network layer. A network IDS could analyze keystrokes looking for buffer overflow attacks. In research and practice, this approach has not been feasible, and it especially is impossible when the network traffic is encrypted.

Finally, attacks that operate on data at the application level can reasonably be detected only by the application. True, some application-level attacks will leave a residue in the operating system logs, and an OS level IDS could detect them. An example is someone who uses the test.cgi attack to trick the Web server into deleting some of the GIF images on the system. A system-level monitor would detect this activity because the subject and object (the Web server daemon and the file) have *meaning* within the OS level.

An application with its own notions of subjects and objects will not leave any activity residue that the OS can understand. Databases are the best example of this. The database files are divided into logical areas for records, fields, and metadata. Only the DBMS knows about access control to these various subdivisions of the file. When several database users read and write database content, the OS sees only that the database daemon was repeatedly accessing the file in which the database is stored. The OS does not *see* into the file in the way that the database manager does. If a database application program can be hacked, the OS will still not know what is going on. Only the DBMS will be able to detect the intrusion because it understands the actions performed by the hack.

In the same way that various security tools were needed to solve different problems, IDSs are also needed at different levels of the stack—network, system, and application. Until a single IDS can combine all of these capabilities, you will need to pick up a different tool for each layer.

At the network layer, the interesting data to look for includes any information that might appear in the headers of network packets:

- IP addresses
- Port numbers
- Sequence numbers
- Protocol type
- Names of network entities, such as server names in SMB
- Checksums
- Option settings, like source routing for IP

These fields are the ones that network monitors inspect when looking for attacks such as address spoofing and session hijacking. At this level, a number of events cannot be easily detected such as failed logins or file deletions. Assuming that the network IDS relies on network traffic only, the only way to know that a telnet login failed is by knowing as much about the packets as telnet does. In other words, just to detect a telnet failure, one would need to know the telnet protocol and watch it through the packets. The same would be needed for FTP failed logins. Detecting failed authentication in third party products such as SecurID would be next to impossible, particularly if the network traffic is encrypted.

You can see that the more types of attacks an IDS wants to glean from data, the more details it must know about the data. At the network data, the most easily extracted information comes from the list shown here, such as IP addresses.

Inspecting the packets can be trivial for some types of attacks, but general-purpose packet data scanning requires code that approaches the complexity of the application itself, which processes the packets. This is really not practical.

Types of network threats that can be detected are those which are arguably network or system attacks. One example is the AIX vulnerability known as *rlogin - froot*, which exploited a programming bug in rlogind. The bug permitted a remote user to gain root shell access (ouch!) without specifying a password. Because rlogin is really a network application for TCP/IP, you might call this a network attack. Given that the result is a root login shell, it is also a system attack. So much for clear definitions in intrusion detection.

## How Does One Get the Data?

In order to monitor a system, the data must be obtained somehow. To get the most realistic view of events occurring in real time, the best approach is to go directly to the source. Replacing or intercepting system calls in the bowels of the software, the kernel of the OS for example, is the most reliable way to gather data for a single event.

If you are an IDS vendor and you choose to intercept an OS routine, performance consequences will occur. You cannot avoid these consequences if the original routine has $M$ instructions, and you intercept and require $N$ additional instructions, the total path length will be at least $M+N$. Because the OS incurs penalties when loading and unloading your subroutines, the price is more than just $M+N$ instructions. This simple principle can be stated as follows:

> *Interception of routines will tradeoff performance for accessibility to the data.*

Sometimes this tradeoff is unavoidable. Firewalls provide a good example. Without the additional packet filtering code in the IP stack, the network packets would travel faster. However, to make intelligent security policy decisions, the packets are intercepted and fed through additional code paths that implement the firewall software. As you saw in Chapter 3, "The Role of Access Control in Your Environment," Memco's SeOS is another product that intercepts system calls to expand the security policy capabilities of the base OS and applications running on top of it. Recall, however, that SeOS and firewalls are designed to be preventative products, although both product types provide ample logging from which one can deduce intrusive behaviors.

### Intrusion Detection Inside a Firewall

Is a firewall an IDS? Today, the answer is "No." Commercial firewalls are not marketed as IDSs, although many probably will include scanners if not already doing so. The purpose of the scanner is to check the firewall for problems, but add-ons make the scanner useful for checking other systems.

Could a firewall be an IDS? Sure. Checkpoint's firewall provides for abitrary user-exits on received packets. The language the firewall demands is INSPECT, a proprietary language that people can use to add other *filtering* capabilities to received packets. If INSPECT is general enough to support stored data values and the main programming statements (sequence, selection, and iteration), then it can be used to write intrusion detection code. Axent-Raptor Eagle also checks for some application level attacks in its proxy servers.

Also, no reason exists to prevent the routines that make up products such as RealSecure and NetRanger to be embedded in the firewall logic. Sure, all of these products drag along their own systems management frameworks for configuration and event reporting. The core IDS logic could be easily combined with a firewall to add network IDS capabilities. Whether this is practical is another question altogether. Would you rather pay the performance penalty of adding IDS code to the firewall packet filters, or would you rather put an IDS sniffer inside the secure network immediately after the firewall? Different sites would prefer one approach over the other.

In the previous chapter you saw that network monitors can intercept data without affecting performance. As long as the network sniffer is running on an independent node and merely passing packets through, no performance penalty should occur. If the sniffer is also making decisions about whether to route the packet, because it is being inspected for decisions, performance implications will occur. Network IDSs that sniff packets and report events after the fact are nonintrusive.

### Relying on Others for Data

If your IDS philosophy is to rely on data sources provided by others, you do not pay performance penalties for intercept or replacing calls. Depending on another software component for data has its drawbacks, though:

◆ The data is emitted by the component after the event has occurred.

◆ The amount of data provided may not be sufficient for the IDS model. You might not get the UID of the offending process, for example.

◆ The events you are interested might not be reported by the system.

◆ At some point, the net value of generating data decreases as the amount of resources a system consumes emitting the data increases. In other words, if the system is spending most of its time reporting events instead of running the payroll, you should question the value of your approach.

◆ The component emitting the data can change the format of log records. This change happens often enough so that IDS vendors are required to modify their software to keep up with OS or application changes.

◆ The data may not be regularly reported for that system.

This last point is particularly important. System, application, and network logging can be an expensive operation. If a customer already is accustomed to storing large log files, rolling an IDS into the environment is not going to add additional requirements. If a customer does not regularly run the auditing subsystem, some convincing is necessary if the IDS relies on the audit trails. OS auditing can generate a fairly large number of records, although all of these records do not need to be stored if the IDS runs in real time, or if the environment does not require post investigative analysis of system audit logs.

## System Data Sources

For monitoring systems, the two main sources of information about OS activity are *syslog* and the *audit trail*. In NT, the audit trail is called the *event log*. Audit log and audit trail are used interchangeably.

### syslog

UNIX provides a common service for logging events called *syslog*. The syslogd daemon supports logging across systems, relying on IP address authentication for accepting remote log entries. By far, the more common approach is for processes to create syslog record entries and call the OS interfaces to log the event to the local syslogd daemon. The syslog configuration file controls whether events are reported to the console, a file, or both. Events from syslog also can be piped to other processes.

No commonly agreed upon standards exist for the format of messages logged to syslog. The record format consists of some header fields including the following:

- name of the logging program
- priority
- facility generating the message
- text of the message itself

The priorities for syslog in decreasing order of severity are as follows:

- emer(gency)
- alert
- crit(ical)
- err(or)
- warning
- notice
- info
- debug

Facilities provide a convenient way of indicating that the message came from a particular component of the OS. Common facility definitions include the following:

- kern(el)
- user (user processes)
- mail
- lpr (line printer)
- auth(orization subsystem)
- daemon (a system daemon)
- news
- uucp
- local*0..n*

The syslog configuration file contains entries of the following form with wildcards supported in each of the two fields of the first parameter:

```
facility.priority     [TAB]     action
```

One or more tab characters must separate the first parameter from the action. Possible actions are as follow:

◆ A destination log filename

◆ A user name, list of names to which the message is mailed (* means to all logged in users)

◆ The form @hostname that identifies the remote syslogd to which the message should be sent

◆ The pipe character " | " followed by a program name

The syslog daemon listens on UDP port 514 by default and accepts unauthenticated datagrams from any system. Therefore, the syslog daemon is not to be run across an untrusted network. Also, syslogd will accept messages from any program. It's possible for a user program to emit *any* message onto the console.

Quite a bit of useful information about system behavior is available from syslog. Important information that an IDS looks for includes the following:

◆ Failed and successful login events

◆ Failed and successful su events

◆ Password changes

◆ System reboots

For many people, the amount of information provided by syslog is sufficient for watching their systems. However, activities are logged into other files. The UNIX OS also emits other useful logs including the following:

◆ *sulog* that shows the use of the su command

◆ *utmp* recording each current login session

◆ *wtmp* in which login, logout, shutdown, and restart events are written

◆ *lastlog* in which the most recent successful and unsuccessful login events are recorded for each user

◆ A log file, dependent on the OS, in which bad login attempts are kept (/etc/security/failedlogin for AIX)

◆ Accounting files

ITA also looks at accounting files for evidence of intrusions. Accounting files are designed for charge back systems. Therefore, their entries include information such as which command a user ran, how much CPU time the command consumed, whether the user was a privileged user, whether the command ran as the result of a fork() operation, and the time the process executed. Important information you do *not* get from accounting logs is as follows:

♦ The full path name of the program executed
♦ The arguments passed to the program

Detecting whether the root user ran /home/Joe/ls instead of /bin/ls is difficult to do from the accounting files. Information about any resources accessed by the user's program are sketchy.

Axent's Intruder Alert also watches syslog and other system logs for intrusive behaviors. ITA depends on a rule-based approach to look for problems on the system. The rule base is extensible for third-party applications. One useful benefit of this capability is that vendors who write messages to syslog can build rules for plugging into ITA. Because ITA also includes a distributed, heterogeneous, client-server event reporting framework, other vendors can develop rules that indicate intrusive behavior and watch the events get reported to the ITA console.

Unfortunately, syslog does not include all of the information necessary to detect a number of intrusive and misused behaviors. The OS audit logs are needed for a more detailed analysis. Which is better—syslog or audit logs? There is no simple answer.

If you are content to know about failed su events, failed logins, bad password changes, and other events reported by syslog, then this is a sufficient source of instrumentation. The question you must consider is whether other events, such as those described in the following sections, which you want to detect. Also, you must decide whether you can afford the price of auditing. When you turn on the auditing subsystem, performance implications will occur. On the other hand, if your site security policy *requires* auditing already, adding an IDS that processes this data further is probably acceptable.

## Audit Trails

The OS audit trails contain a significant amount of data about system activities. Each OS reports on a different number of events, but almost *any* OS system activity is reported. For example, Solaris reports more than 240 audit events, AIX almost 100, and HP-UX around 125. Microsoft NT emits about 100 different events as well.

Unlike syslog and the accounting logs, audit records include important, security-relevant data values in each record. Figure 6.2 shows the audit header fields for AIX. Note that today AIX does not report the EUID or EGID of a process, which makes detection of buffer overflow attacks difficult.

Among other values, the audit records contain the following:

- Details about the object being accessed, such as the parameters passed to the program
- Fully qualified path names of executables

When a user completes the login process, the kernel assigns as *audit ID* (AUID), which is the prefix for each audit record written for that user. Even if the user runs a SUID root program, the AUID remains the same. This means that a user cannot *hide* an activity by pretending to be someone else, whether root or another user. The AUID is what proves accountability for activities and identifies the user responsible for the event.

How reliable is the AUID? The answer depends on your environment. If most of your users log in using the normal mechanism, run various programs, execute commands, and then log out, the AUID will be a reliable indicator for accountability. However, in a couple of cases the AUID is not particularly helpful.

A number of daemon programs started automatically by the system will run with AUID=0. Any audit records cut for those programs will show that root initiated the activity, even though it did not happen from a login shell. If these programs are listening for interprocess communication from other programs run by normal users, assigning accountability gets a little more complicated. When your program sends a message to one of these daemons and asks it to perform an

---

**Figure 6.2    Audit record header fields for AIX.**

---

```
ushort_t  arb_length;              /* length of tail of this record */
char      arb_event[16];           /* event name with null terminator */
unsigned  int arb_result;          /* the audit status - see auditlog for values */
uid_t     arb_ruid;                /* real user id */
char      arb_name[MAXCOMLEN];     /* program name with null terminator */
pid_t     arb_pid;                 /* process id */
pid_t     arb_ppid;                /* process id of parent */
tid_t     arb_tid;                 /* thread id */
time_t    arb_time;                /* time in secs */
time_t    arb_ntime;               /* nanosecs offset from ah_time */
};
```

activity on your behalf, it is the root AUID that will appear as the prefix for the daemon's audit records, not your UID.

A more complicated problem exists for Web servers and systems without login sessions. Systems of this type are usually running server programs that are listening for network connections from other nodes. The only AUID in the audit records might be the that of the root user. Even if you have created a special user ID under which you run your Web server, the AUID probably will be zero (root's UID) because of the way in which the Web server is started by the system. If the server is started by an rc script or via the init program, the root AUID will be the prefix for the audit records.

The AUID can be changed by a privileged process, which is good because it provides a facility for programs to set the appropriate AUID value. However, this feature also means that an intruder who gains root access will be able to change the AUID. While this may seem nasty at first glance, this event itself will be logged with an audit record.

Can an attacker stop the audit subsystem from running? Yes. This process, too, will generate an audit record before the subsystem shuts down. The attacker then would either need to delete the entire audit log or try to modify it. Changing the audit log by editing portions of it is nontrivial, and there have been no public reports of this occurring successfully. Still, it is possible if the attacker understands the auditing subsystem.

If you look at security tool Web sites such as COAST, you will find a program called *zap*. It was written to hide intruder tracks and is likely to be the first program installed when your system is compromised. Specifically, it doctors the utmp, wtmp, and lastlog files so that they do not show evidence of the intruder's logins. A second set of tools available as *rootkit* contains hacked versions of *ps* and other status tools that are designed to hide activities, too. So far, none of these treasure chests include tools for tricking the auditing subsystem. Chances are it's just a matter of time.

## Tracing the Path of Activity Can Be Difficult

An IDS traces the path of activity so that an operation can be traced back to a specific user. In other words, the IDS will look at more than one event to make a policy decision. This process is much different from an OS that relies on the credentials of the running process at the instant an access control decision is made. Consider the policy violation that occurs when a user is able to read a file for which that user is not granted explicit read access (see "Monitoring Policies").

### Monitoring Policies

One unresolved issue is the difference between the *preventative security policy* you define and the need for a separate *monitoring policy*. When you configure an IDS, you can decide which events to monitor and how to respond to them. Unfortunately, you cannot make broad statements such as the following:

> P1: Alert me anytime someone reads a file that they should not be accessing.

The monitoring policy needs to be more specific, such as the following:

> P2: Alert me anytime someone reads a file for which they do not have explicit read access.

Huh? How can someone read a file if they are not explicitly given read permission? The answer lies in that recurring them *on behalf of* semantics. A user with UID=231 can access a file by running a program that has enough privileges to read the file on behalf of the user. In UNIX this is accomplished via the SUID and SGID bit settings. In NT escalating privileges to SYSTEM or Administrator accomplishes a similar goal.

No good mechanism exists today for specifying a single security policy that different products will read and enforce or monitor. One reason is that no particular vendor provides both a comprehensive preventative tool and an equally strong monitoring tool. If this mechanism were available today, the vendor would immediately realize how much trouble it is to define both a prevention policy *and* a monitoring policy. Stated somewhat differently, defining a series of access control rules in one product and then configuring events to monitor in another is a problem that only the enduser faces today. Having a single tool in which to enter a comprehensive policy would be useful, even if the prevention and monitoring policies are not identical.

The path through which an activity occurs could be very elaborate, and not all IDSs can detect the full range of conditions. For example, you might log in under your normal user ID and run a program that opens a socket to background daemon. When you send commands to the daemon through the socket, one consequence could be that the daemon reads a file that you could not normally access and then sends data about the file to you through the socket. The OS is happy because the access control decision for the read operation succeeded because the daemon had sufficient authority to access the file. In this case, if the security policy is violated, it is because the daemon did not perform enough checking to verify that your program had the necessary privileges. Hopefully, weak security programming such as this does not exist at your site.

What would an IDS need to track to detect the policy violation? Here is a partial list of what the IDS must know about *you*:

- The login event generated by you
- The process or thread create event emitted when you ran your program
- The socket events for your program— create, read, write, and possibly bind

For the daemon process, the IDS would need to know the following:

- The identity of the process—its UIDs, GIDs, and other privileges
- Socket events
- Resource accesses, such as files created, deleted, read, or written

Knowing these two sets of events is useful but not sufficient. What else is missing? Assume for the moment that your program is the only one communicating with this daemon. How would the system know that you were somehow given access to data in a file that is normally unavailable to you? The IDS might watch for a sequence such as the following:

- A write socket event from your program
- A read socket event from the daemon
- A read file event from the daemon, of which the file is one that your UID or GIDs cannot access
- A write socket event from the daemon
- A read socket event from the daemon

Not only would these individual events need to be monitored, but the IDS would need to somehow correlate the events into a higher abstraction such as a *session*. Correlating events is not difficult when they share data values. In this case, its the socket endpoints that define the relation between the event records in the audit trail or system log. Because the session is defined as the 4-tuple <source address, source

port, destination address, destination port>, and your program and the daemon share these four values, events on these sockets can be clumped together logically.

Still, this sequence of events is not proof of a problem. Many background daemons and programs regularly access privileged files on your behalf without disclosing information in the files. The only way to know for sure that you were allowed to read data that you should not have access to is to monitor some lower level operations, such as the following:

1. The daemon program reads from a file into a buffer.
2. Your UID and GIDs do not have access to this file.
3. The buffer is written to the socket by the daemon.
4. You read the socket.

Aha! Now we're getting somewhere. Here is clear proof that the daemon read some data and dumped it into the socket that you read. What happens if the buffer is manipulated by the program? Can that be tracked, too?

1. The daemon reads from a file into a buffer.
2. Your UID and GIDs do not have access to this file.
3. The buffer is copied into $N$ different smaller buffers.
4. The secondary buffers are written to the socket by the daemon.
5. You read the socket.

OK. This most likely can be tracked, too, but the IDS probably is getting a bit tired and frustrated. More complications are on the way:

1. The daemon reads from a file into a buffer.
2. Your UID and GIDs do not have access to this file.
3. The buffer is transformed though any number of operations into $N$ other buffers.
4. These secondary memory buffers are further convoluted and transformed.
5. The secondary buffers are written to the socket by the daemon.
6. You read the socket.

Still, this seems to be something that an IDS can track. As long as a *path* can be found from the source buffer to the final memory storage location written to the socket, the IDS will be able to detect that data has been compromised. Before you get another cup of coffee or tea, consider a more complex scenario. The daemon's first two steps are the same as before. Instead of transforming or copying the buffer as the next step, the daemon follows an algorithm:

1. Grab the first byte of the buffer and store it as an integer in temporary variable $X$.
2. Compute the $X^{th}$ Fibonacci number and write it to the socket.
3. Your program reads the socket and computes Fibonacci numbers until you find the same result, and now you know $X$.

This is really getting hard. Of course, you could have picked a more efficient algorithm. The point is that the path is getting harder to follow. The compromised data is becoming more *obscured*. Now instead of the path being based on memory copies and elementary transformations, all we know is that part of the buffer was used in computing some function $f(x)$. The result of the function then was written to the buffer. There is more to consider before drawing some conclusions:

1. Grab the first *bit* of the buffer and store it in temporary variable $X$.
2. If X=1, write an odd number to the socket, else write an even number to the socket.
3. Your program reads the socket and inverts the previous step.

In this case, the *action* the daemon took by inspecting the buffer indicates a problem, and not the fact that the buffer itself or some derivative of it was communicated to your program. This is a simple case of a *covert channel*. Anytime one program can *leak* at least one bit of information to another program, there is a threat that a read constraint will be violated. Any number of operations not related to the socket could have been performed to leak the bit of information contained in X:

- The daemon could create a file in directory A that is readable by your program when X=1, and create a file in directory B otherwise (where B also is readable by you).
- The daemon could write data into a file that you are allowed to read. Then the daemon reads data back from this file into a buffer. The buffer then is written to the socket for you to read. The IDS would not know, without detailed knowledge of the file's history, whether the data sent to you was allowed or not. Note that an MLS OS will

not permit this operation because it does not allow write down when the operation violates sensitivity labels.

◆ If X=1, the daemon runs the /bin/true program, else it runs /bin/ls.

In other words, the daemon can perform a number of different sets of two different actions to leak information to your program.

You're not done with extending this line of reasoning yet. What happens if the daemon is listening to any number of sockets simultaneously? The daemon reads data values $Y$ from $N$ different sockets, reads $X$ from the privileged file, and then it computes some function $f(X, Y_1, Y_2, ..., Y_N)$. After this, the daemon returns this value to your socket. Beforehand, you and the daemon signed a pact agreeing on the algorithm so that you can invert the data received on the socket. All of the $Y$ values are meaningless except for yours.

The problem here is that the leaked data is getting more obscure. To make it worse, assume that there are some legitimate $f(X, Y_1, Y_2, ..., Y_N)$ computations that the daemon sends to you, those which do not leak information about the privileged file. With this slight twist, the IDS will really have a difficult time distinguishing between legitimate and intrusive behavior. Some theory-minded people would look at this last case and start mumbling terms like *intractable*. In practical terms, the examples indicate that the more indirection an attacker can introduce into the intrusion, the harder it is to find the path that identifies the events as intrusive.

Taking a few steps back, what happens if your program and the daemon are running on different systems? In this case, the IDS needs information from *two* systems to keep a path of identity and activities. If the path you took to obtain a login shell traversed several intermediate nodes, then each of these also would need to report activities to a central IDS monitor in order to maintain the path. Tracking activities across multiple systems is challenging. The Distributed Intrusion Detection System (Snapp et al., 1991) was a research system that tried to solve this problem. When you log in into a system, your UID represents who you are. To preserve your activities across UID transitions, the OS assigns an AUID to you. If you run a SUID root program, your AUID does not change. Therefore, auditing can assign accountability for behaviors.

The same type of immutable ID is needed for tracking activities across a network of nodes. DIDS assigned a network ID to the user when the first login event for that user occurred in the network. This assignment was actually made in a batch fashion when the audit logs were processed, but it easily could have been accomplished in real time. DIDS tracked users as they jumped across systems using remote commands. However, it did not track communications activities, such as socket data contents, to find complex attacks such as the scenarios just discussed. No commercial products can detect interprocess hacks in a general way, although some specific attacks are monitored. For example, Ping of Death is an a example of a client-server socket data flow that launches an attack. No commercial product claims an attack signature for detecting when a remote user accesses a local process via a socket and then reads privileged information through that socket.

Is this series of examples really intrusion detection? Well, if the file being read happens to be the shadow password file, the end result is no different from when a user manages to read encrypted passwords via a buffer overflow attack. As hackers get more sophisticated, complicated threats like the ones discussed will increase. The key to success for an IDS is to determine that a *path* exists. The path must reflect knowledge about *data* and *actions* to be useful for detecting intrusions. Success requires tracing this path through a variety of activities on the system.

If you are an intruder who gains privilege in order to read privileged files, you can bet that most IDSs will report that as an event. The more complicated scenarios in this chapter are not handled by commercial products today. The reason is that enough data is not available to the IDS. To detect sequences, such as those presented in this chapter, the IDS needs access to memory locations used by the program as well as very detailed information on instructions executed by the CPU for that program. Not only is the level of detail minute, but for the OS to provide this much information, it would need to emit an auditable event for almost every CPU instruction. If one were really paranoid about covert channel leaks, every CPU instruction and its parameters would need to be logged. This means that each CPU instruction requires several other instructions for writing the audit log. It doesn't take a genius to see that in this degenerate case, intrusion detection dominates the system's resources.

Note that in these examples the daemon is essentially an application running on top of the OS, although it has not introduced its own security model (its own subjects and objects). Interprocess communication between programs on the same system is one place where a boundary occurs—between the two endpoints of the session. At a given moment in time, either half of the session is performing services for the other half. When this happens, it is imperative that appropriate security be enforced. As you have seen in previous sections, lax programming practices can lead to problems.

## Simple or Complex Attacks

By far the largest number of attacks detected by IDSs involve a single event. Examples include the following:

◆ A nonprivileged user changes a privileged program by writing to its location on disk.

- A nonprivileged user reads a privileged file.
- A program deletes *too many* files in successive operations.
- Someone creates a filename with special characters.
- A privileged user runs a program whose full path name is incorrect, such as /home/joe/ls instead of /bin/ls.
- A spoofed IP address packet.

After this initial category are thresholds of events:

- *N* failed login attempts
- Port scanning from the same source IP address
- Resource flooding, such as sending too many ping packets

Sequences of events form the next level of difficulty in detecting an intruder:

- A normal user executing a privileged program, which in turn forks a root shell on a UNIX system (likely evidence of a buffer overflow attack)
- Three failed attempts to su to root followed by success (evidence of a guessed password)

If you take the set of attacks defined by a single event and you combine them with each event separated by an OR, you have one large IDS pattern. If you take some single events, like failed login, then combine them with an AND, you have sequences and thresholds. Taking single events and joining them into graphs with many AND and OR operators leads to the next category. Activities represented as complex graphs, possibly requiring metadata, constitute the most difficult category of attacks. An example in this category would be failed login thresholds successively exceeded for each user, with events in the same order as the users listed in the password file or registry. The metadata used in the pattern is knowledge about the order of entries in the password file. The sequence of events is a series of failed logins. If the sequence is followed by a successful login, an intrusion definitely occurred.

## Prepare to Scan for Weaknesses

In this chapter you have seen how some intruder events are detected easily, and how others are more complicated to uncover. The focus of a particular IDS can be at the network level, system level, or application level. As the IDS industry matures, products are beginning to look for problems at all three levels.

Regardless of the focus of a product, some data source must be relied upon for catching intruders. The choice of datastream, a technique for capturing data, and the method of analysis all impact the types of problems that the IDS can find. Also affected by IDS design choices are whether the event is captured in real time, detected after the fact, and assigned to the appropriate UID if possible. Tracking hackers across multiple systems was shown to present special challenges, particularly for accountability.

In the next chapter, you will learn about specific attacks against your systems and how you can deploy a vulnerability scanner to start looking for holes before they are exploited.

# Chapter 7

# Vulnerability Scanners

A scanner is an IDS that performs a periodic assessment of risks on your system. An IDS looks for vulnerabilities that might open up your system to threats. Intrusion detection scanners look for potential problems with your system that might result from the following:

- The back level of a software program that is known to have an exploit
- A configuration error resulting from an out-of-the-box installation with known holes
- An administrative error that places the system in an unsafe state, with the problem residing in either an operating system configuration *or* an application configuration
- Known rogue programs that someone may have planted on your system

In this chapter, you will learn about some vulnerability scanners that look for weaknesses in UNIX systems. (NT scanners are discussed in Chapter 10, which deals exclusively with NT IDSs.) When you complete the chapter, you should be able to identify the role of vulnerability scanners in your environment. You will see the types of problems that scanners can detect, how they can be spoofed, and why they are an important security product to have in your arsenal.

## What Is a Scanner?

First, you should know that scanning intrusion detection products are *not* the same as network sniffers. Vulnerability scanners do not look at network traffic in real time. Instead, they are run periodically against *systems* to look for problems.

A product that looks at intrusions as they occur in real time is really dealing with *threats*, not with *vulnerabilities*. Real-time IDSs catch hackers while they are on your system. Scanners examine your systems for cracks that someone can sneak through or for evidence of intrusions after they have occurred.

Two main types of scanners are available:

♦ A local scan is run on a node by a software program that resides on the node itself. This operation is introspective because the node is examining itself.

♦ A remote scan is run over the network *against* the target node by probing it for vulnerabilities. The IDS software is actually running on an administrative system and scanning the target across the network.

A scanner might be probing multiple systems in the network. In doing so, network attacks are attempted against the target node to look for potential holes in the target. Although network packets are sent from the scanning system to the target, the scanner itself is not actively sniffing all network packets to look for problems.

## Characteristics of Scanners

Local and remote scanners share common characteristics. Rather than looking for events as they occur in real time, *scanners examine the state of a system periodically*. One potential advantage of interval scanning is that *resource utilization is less* on the average than that required for real-time monitoring. Intuitively, this is easy to see because you are consuming resources only when the scanner is active rather than constantly watching events as they occur.

Scanners make a sweep of the system's configuration to look for vulnerabilities. Scanning the system for problems will reveal weaknesses or holes that lead to cracks. A real-time monitor will miss configuration problems because it is primarily designed to catch hackers *in the act*, rather than to look for vulnerabilities that can be exploited later. For example, a real-time detector is not much help in finding problems with a fresh, out-of-the-box configuration. Thus, scanners and real-time IDSs are complementary.

Because the scanners are run periodically, they will not be able to detect events as they occur. Vulnerability scanners try to prevent problems by alerting you to flaws in advance. If a hacker manages to bypass your security defenses and introduce a vulnerability in your system, the scanner should detect the exposure the next time it is activated. For example, if the scanner looks for root equivalent accounts on a system, it will detect that a hacker has created a root account on the system the next time a scan is performed. How do scanners improve your security?

◆ Scanners prevent intrusions and misuses by alerting you to vulnerabilities in advance, even if they result from accidental configuration errors.

◆ Scanners detect vulnerabilities that arise in your system as a consequence of an intrusion or misuse.

Of course, the hacker's challenge is to know what the scanner looks for and to cover tracks to avoid detection. Because many vendors publish the list of problems they look for, a wise cracker can use this information to avoid activities that will be flagged.

When you look at scanning products, it's important to know that some types of weaknesses can be found only by running the scan locally on the node of interest. If the system is locked down so that no network attacks are possible, local file system permission problems or SUID programs may still lead to system compromise. Even if you have a system that is not connected to a network and has only directly attached terminals, you can have vulnerabilities.

One desirable feature of scanners is that they do not introduce new data sources. System-level IDSs require that you turn on auditing or syslog if you are not already doing so. Scanners discover vulnerabilities by looking at configuration data or by attempting to carry out an attack.

## Local Scanners

Local scanners can plow through the contents of files looking for configuration problems. Many real-time network and system IDSs look at individual events, such as the moment that a file is modified, without knowing *what changes* were made to the file. A system scanner can look into the file to discover configuration errors or unwanted changes made by a hacker. A very useful hybrid approach would combine the best of both real-time IDSs and scanners. When the file change event is detected by the real-time IDS, part of the scanner is invoked as a response to inspect the file's contents.

Many times in this book, we have mentioned that a difficult administrative task is configuration of owners, groups, and permissions for files and directories. Scanners can help ensure that these aspects of your security policy are properly implemented. For example, even if you add SeOS to your systems, scanning the SeOS configurations and the OS resources you may have not included in

SeOS will improve security. As a security officer or administrator, you are paid to be paranoid. Worrying about whether you have initially configured your systems properly or whether your original secure configurations have been changed is part of the ongoing assessment necessary for a secure site.

Because the local scanner is actually a process running on the target node, you can look for problems that cannot be detected by remote scans. For example, in order to run programs and look for buffer overflow attacks, you must be able to create processes on the system. A remote scanner cannot create *arbitrary* processes on a system unless it is able to crack into the system.

Local scanners also can inspect patch levels to ensure that you have the latest security fixes installed. As in looking for buffer overflow attacks, this process requires the capability to query the system's software product inventory. A remote scan is unable to do this unless some type of systems management application is running to provide this information in a client-server manner.

Network configuration errors for a node also can be inspected locally by looking at files such as /etc/services, /etc/inetd.conf, and /etc/rc.tcpip. A remote scanner is unable to peer into individual files (again, unless it is able to crack the system).

## Remote Scanning

Remote scanners examine the network and distributed computing vulnerabilities in your system. If your system allows anonymous FTP users to write into the public download directory, hackers can use your site as a distribution center for stolen software. Network services that give away information or allow a hacker to gain access into your system should not be running. The remote scanner will look for these scenarios.

Local scanners look for buffer overflow attacks in programs by running them. Remote scanners look for buffer overflow attacks in network services by sending them bogus packets. To make something happen on a local system, you either run a program or send a program a command. The corollary in network computing is to send a packet to a listening process or software server. Remote scanners primarily probe your system by sending network packets.

Sometimes a remote probe sends random packets to look for any exposure in the system. More intelligent poking also occurs when scanners look for trust relationships to exploit. A root .rhosts file, which is spoofable by IP address impersonation, is one trust weakness that a remote scanner tries.

Many of the exposures a system will exhibit are independent of how the system is being used, such as running network services that you should not. A remote scanner also looks for specific weaknesses in your firewall configuration, your

Web server configuration, and possibly application configurations. Intrusion detection products are continually moving higher up the OS stack, and application-specific scans already are creeping into products such as ISS SAFESuite. A local scanner will peek into the contents of a Web server and firewall configuration files to uncover mistakes.

A scan run locally on a node will look to see whether there is a root /.rhosts file and report this finding in its results. The /.rhosts file can be used to exploit a system from a remote node, so it is really a network security vulnerability opened by the local system configuration. A remote scanning engine will look for this same problem by attempting to gain system access via programs that rely on /.rhosts for authentication. Both types of scans are discovering (a) a configuration problem in the target system and (2) a network security vulnerability.

As you can see from the discussion so far, combining local and remote scans is necessary in your environment because they complement each other. Sometimes, they detect the same problem in different ways, but this is also useful because it implements security in layers.

## How a Scanner Works

A scanner probes for weaknesses in your system or network by comparing its database of known vulnerabilities against data about your configurations. Most scanners enable you to configure *what* you want to scan and *when* you want to scan for it. Extensibility is another important feature to look for in a scanner. You want to be able to add your own scanning routines to look for site-specific application weaknesses that concern you.

Under the general category of systems management, your scanner should provide for optional centralized reporting. If you have two or three systems, running a local scan on each node and reading the reports on each node may be tolerable. Sites with dozens of systems or more want consolidated reports on a central server. Other capabilities such as the grouping of nodes into scan groups, flexible output report formats, and customized scan options are valuable for large environments.

Using a scanner is actually simple. If you don't require any customization, by default the scanner will look for a preconfigured list of vulnerabilities and report the results to you. Usually, the results are saved in a file so that you can come back later to review the findings. The scanner works by either examining attributes of objects, such as owner and permissions for files or by emulating the hacker. To act as a hacker, the scanner runs a variety of scripts that try to exploit weaknesses in the target node. To keep the systems and networks from being overloaded, you should give careful thought to what you want to scan and when you want to scan for it. Otherwise, you might find that your entire site becomes sluggish because the mission-critical servers are busy responding to a simulated SYN Flood attack.

Scanning is not limited to computers. Routers and other switching devices also can be scanned, because they, too, have been exposed in the public news forums for containing security flaws.

## Improving Your Security with Scanners

Dan Farmer introduced COPS while working with Gene Spafford at Purdue University. The popularity of this public domain tool is hard to estimate. Literally thousands of people use COPS today to periodically examine their systems for security weaknesses. Commercial derivatives have appeared over the last several years. This section focuses on the ISS SAFESuite scanners, which are positioned as *vulnerability assessment* tools.

When Chris Klaus was a graduate student, he put together the Internet Security Scanner and gave it away for free on the Internet. After seeing how much interest the product generated, he decided to start the company with Tom Noonan now known as Internet Security Systems or ISS for short. In addition to delivering security products, ISS sponsors a number of newsgroups (www.iss.net/vd/maillist.html), provides useful Web site links, and backs security research at universities. Sitting on the fence between target and perpetrator, ISS also provides funding for DEFCON and maintains a good rapport with the underground.

### ISS SAFESuite

Currently ISS scanners come in two main flavors. You can get the *System Security Scanner* (S3) or the Internet Scanner. Inside the Internet Scanner, you will find separately charged features for a Web scanner, a firewall scanner, and an intranet scanner. Before looking at the features of the product you might be interested in the following details:

- The ISS scanners are not invasive—they do not intercept or replace operating system calls.
- Scans are run on an *interval* basis. This means that they look for problems at the time of the scan. If you also are interested in detecting intrusions *when they occur*, think about adding a real-time intrusion detection product.

♦ Both system and network problems are analyzed. For example, checking for weak user passwords is a system probe, while IP port scanning looks for network configuration weaknesses.

♦ No additional security model is layered into the environment. ISS has not added complexity by introducing its own subjects, objects, ACLs, and reference monitor.

The product family supports a client-server and heterogeneous configuration. By now you should automatically wonder how secure communications are handled between nodes. ISS provides shared-secret, challenge-response authentication between nodes. When messages are exchanged between nodes, the traffic is encrypted as well.

## System Security Scanner

The important features of S3 to examine are its alternative configurations, its reporting capabilities, and the set of vulnerabilities it handles. The initial screen for S3 is shown in Figure 7.1.

### Local and Remote Scan Configurations

S3 can be run on a single node to scan for and report on security weaknesses on that node. Each system in the network that requires scanning must be installed with a separate copy of S3. If the number of scanned nodes is small, this might be a preferred configuration because network traffic is minimized during scanning and reporting. This design tradeoff is desirable.

If the administrative model at the site is centralized, one or more scanning *engine* workstations can be configured to control distributed target nodes. Each target requires the sssd daemon. Luckily, ISS also does not introduce

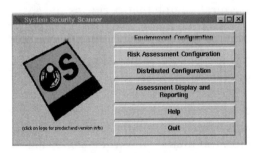

**Figure 7.1**  Initial S3 screen.

its own software distribution framework for propagating these daemons. Note that S3 does not scan the node remotely. Instead, the distributed configuration enables you to manage S3 configuration files remotely and to receive scan results from other nodes. The engine on the central node processes the results files.

Target nodes can be combined into groups, and a node can belong to more than one group. Groups can be scanned at different times, and variations in the vulnerabilities inspected may be specified for each group. This process enables you to scan some nodes *deeper* than others. If you have many users on some systems, you can look for user configuration weaknesses on those nodes. However, if you have servers with no user accounts, you can configure the scans for that group to omit looking for most user vulnerabilities. Scan options for each node or group are managed through configuration files.

One efficient feature is *caching*. For example, when password brute force attacks are run, S3 optionally will omit trying passwords that have previously failed. You also can customize the cracking dictionary.

Whether scans are local or remote, activities are controlled via a GUI or CLI. Some of the scans accept parameters, and these values can be entered in the GUI or by editing configuration files directly. Examples of parameters include permission bits for application files that ISS would not know by default.

### Detect and Respond

When a system is scanned by S3, a *fix script* is incrementally composed with recommended corrective actions. You can customize this script or run it as is to eliminate the vulnerabilities identified by the scan. S3 also creates an unfix script that enables you to *undo* the fix script.

### Internode Authentication in S3

In distributed mode, S3 is installed on a central engine that performs the scan, and a separate daemon (sssd) is configured on each target node. To establish trust for remote communications between the engine and the target, a shared authentication secret is defined. The secret also is used as a key for encrypting results transmitted back to the engine for reporting.

An authentication file on the engine declares the shared secret and host name association. A different shared secret can be configured for each host. The recommendation is to pick a pass phrase rather than a simple password. On each target node, a corresponding authentication file must contain the same shared secret entered on the engine. Because the same secret controls information flowing in both directions, the authentication protocol could be open to replay attacks and reflection attacks assuming IP address impersonation is possible (see Chapter 4, "Traditional Network Security Approaches").

### File Integrity Checker

Like many other security products, S3 includes a facility for computing cryptographic signatures for selected files. The database of signature-file pairs is stored and examined at future intervals to detect possible Trojan Horses. An MD5 signature is computed from various file attributes. Stored in the database with the file name are its MD5 signature, permissions, owner, group, and size. If any of these parameters change, the next file integrity scan will generate an alert. Shipped with each installation is an OS-specific baseline file containing a predefined set of file names to monitor with the integrity checker.

### Results and Reporting

Scan outcomes are stored on the local node if the scan is local and in separate per-node subdirectories on the central engine for distributed scans. Results files are not in human readable format and must be analyzed with either the GUI, CLI, or an HTML browser. The first level detail output indicates the number of high-, medium- and low-risk vulnerabilities found along with informational and error messages. Failing to complete a scan due to network faults would generate an error condition.

In the GUI, results can be examined by node, by group, or by vulnerability type. Users familiar with file system browsers such as NT Explorer easily will adapt to the hierarchical reporting user interface shown in Figure 7.2. In addition to sending output to the screen, S3 optionally generates ASCII, comma-separated, and HTML reports.

### Vulnerabilities Scanned

S3 organizes its vulnerability database hierarchically within several different categories, including:

- Files
- Users
- Groups
- Passwords
- Hacker signatures

The entire set of scanned items is too long to list and describe in detail here. A summary of scanned weaknesses is given in Table 7.1. You should consult the ISS Web site www.iss.net for the most current list.

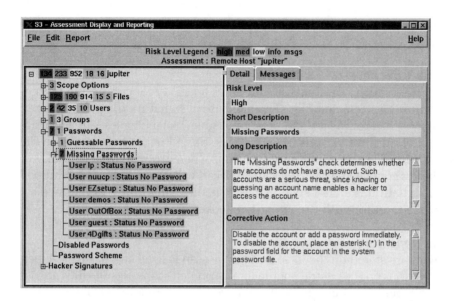

**Figure 7.2**    Example output from an S3 scan.

## Internet Scanner

The ISS Internet Scanner looks for a number of system and network weaknesses in your nodes. The model is remote scan from a central node, and all results are centrally captured because the scan is only running on one node. Depending on the options purchased, Internet Scanner will look for Web, firewall, common, and system weaknesses. The possibilities are controlled by an electronic license key. The initial Internet Scanner screen is displayed in Figure 7.3.

### Vulnerabilities Checked by Internet Scanner

Some of the same problems that S3 reports also are discovered by Internet Scanner, although in a different way. For example, a world-writable NFS exported file system is a potential security vulnerability (depending on the security policy at your site). S3 detects this vulnerability by looking at the currently exported file systems or by examining the NFS exports configuration file in case the file is not currently exported for mounting. Internet Scanner checks for this same vulnerability by either attempting to mount exported file systems with read-write access or by querying the list of exported file systems on a node using the showmount command.

**Table 7.1**   Vulnerabilities Scanned by S3

| Vulnerability Scanned | Description |
| --- | --- |
| Password File | Blank lines in password file; Improper characters in password file |
| Trusted hosts | hosts.equiv and .rhosts for system or users; .shosts files for ssh, and .netrc files |
| RC files, crontab, user-owned files, and printcap | Improper ownership and permissions for files; Bogus path names in entries; Improper settings for programs invoked by cron, RC scripts, printcap, and user profiles; Improper symbolic links |
| External and local file system | World-readable and world-writable file system exports; Wrong owner or permissions on critical system files and programs; SUID and SGID programs; Unusual file names; Hidden files and directories; |
| Internet services | HTTP daemon user and group account security (no root or Administrator access); Incorrect permissions on directories in the Web virtual file tree; Unrestricted FTP access; Unsecure services enabled—tftp, chargen, fingerd, FSP, and others; Ownership and permission problems for programs; Bogus path names in configuration files |
| Sendmail | Old version checks; VRFY and EXPN enabled; Mail aliased programs; Authentication warnings; Permissions and ownership of mail spool directories |
| Software bugs | Checks for known vulnerable programs to see whether patches have been applied; extensive checks for buffer overflow attacks |
| Users and groups | Invalid UIDs and GIDs; Accounts with root privileges; Duplicate UIDs and GIDs; Invalid home directories or initial programs; Dormant accounts; Unused accounts; Weak, missing, or easily cracked passwords; |
| Netscape browser settings | Java and JavaScript enabled; POP mail password |
| Network adapter enabled for promiscuous mode | Checks for sniffer activated |

Telling Internet Scanner which vulnerabilities to probe is straightforward. Figure 7.4 shows a screen image for IP spoofing scan options for the Internet Scanner. As you can see, the interface is slightly different from S3. Choices are indicated by setting radio buttons and entering optional data in fields. In Figure 7.5 you see some of the possibilities when the target of the scan is a Web server. Note the inclusion of the phf.cgi attack. The List CGI button causes ISS to check

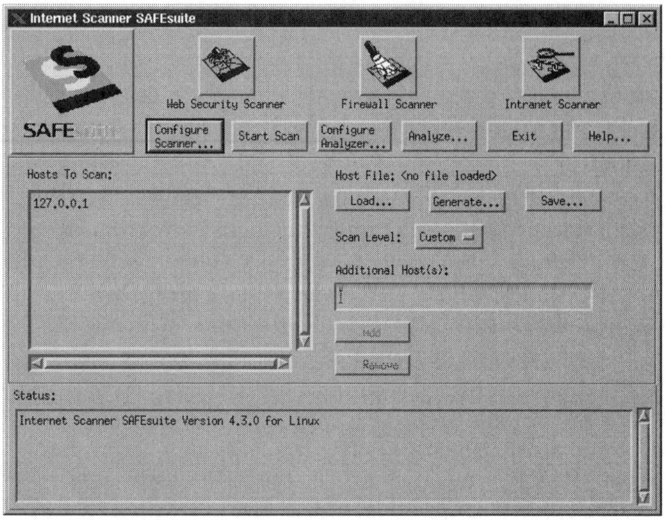

**Figure 7.3**  Main screen for Internet Scanner.

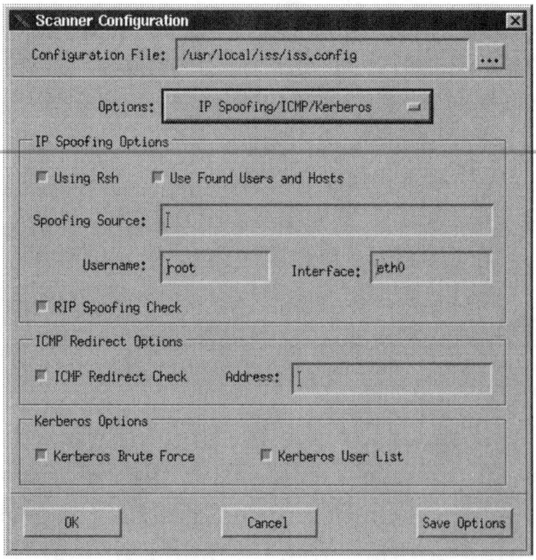

**Figure 7.4**  Configuring IP spoofing options in Internet Scanner.

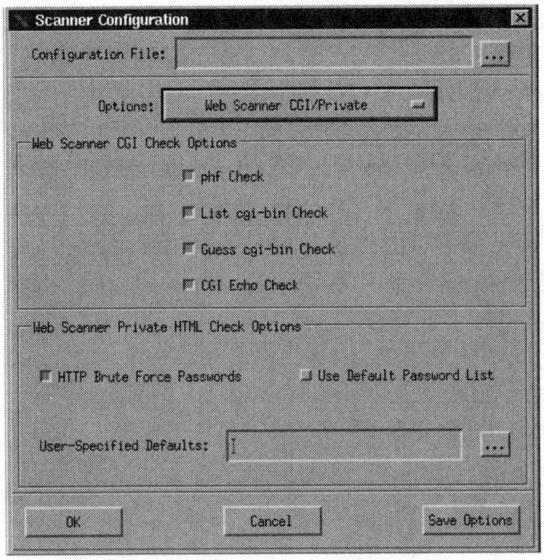

**Figure 7.5**  Web server scan options in Internet Scanner.

for the test.cgi hack. You can select different scan intensities-full, heavy, medium, and lite. A custom configuration is easily defined as shown.

Following is a list of the vulnerabilities that are potentially scanned. Not all options are always available. Firewall and Web specific items are supported only if you have purchased the appropriate license. See the ISS Web site for the most current list.

### Vulnerabilities Remotely Scanned by ISS

Admind

Alerter and Messenger Services

All Access NetBIOS share— Everyone

All Access NetBIOS share— Guest

All Access NetBIOS share

Anonymous FTP

Bootparam

Brute-Force

Brute-Force Netware FTP

Brute-Force Cisco

CGI Exec

Check Share Passwords

Data Flood

Echo, Chargen, Time, and Daytime Services

Files Obtained

Finger

Finger Bomb

Finger Names

Finger Output

FTP CD ~root Bug

FTP Site Exec

**Vulnerabilities Remotely Scanned by ISS (continued)**

| | |
|---|---|
| FTP Writable | PCNFSD |
| Guess cgi-bin | Ping Bomb |
| IIS ".bat" and ".cmd" Bug | Ping 'O Death |
| IP Spoofing | Popd/Imapd |
| Kerberos IV Brute Force | Proxy Scan |
| Korberos IV User Peek | Rexd |
| Lan Manager Security | Rexec Service |
| Linux Time Bomb | RIP Spoofing |
| List cgi-bin | Rlogin froot |
| Microsoft "cd .." Bug | Root Dot Dot |
| Microsoft Network Client Password Cache | Routed |
| | RPC/NIS Update |
| NetBIOS Null Session | RPC Pcnfsd |
| NetBIOS Share | RPC Statd |
| Netstat Check | Rsh |
| NFS | Rsh Null Account |
| NFS Access Files | Rstat |
| NFS CD .. Bug | Rstat Output |
| NFS Cache | Ruser |
| NFS Export | Rwhod |
| NFS mknod | Selection Service |
| NFS Portmapper Export | Sendmail Debug Mode |
| NFS Sun File Handle Guess | Sendmail EXPN |
| NFS UID | Ident Service Test |
| NFS Write | Sendmail Identd Bug |
| NIS | Sendmail Remote Execution |
| Open/Close Flood | Sendmail Syslog |
| Open NetBIOS Share | Sendmail VRFY |
| Out of Band Crash | Sendmail Wizard Backdoor |
| Password Permutations | SNMP |
| phf Check | SOCKS Scan |

SYN Storm

Sysstat

System Log Flood

Telnetd Linker

TFTP (Trivial File Transfer Protocol)

Traceroute

Trusted Hosts

UDP Bomb

Ultrix NFS Remount Bug

Unresolved HTTP Link

UUCP

Vulnerable HTTP Servers

Vulnerable NNTP Server

Window NT Active Server Page Bug

Windows NT DNS Server

Windows NT 4.0 beta

Writable NetBIOS share— Everyone

Writable NetBIOS share— Guest

Wall

Writable NetBIOS Share

WWW Directories without an index

WWW Proxy Penetrated

X25

X Window System

Earlier we mentioned that most remote scanners cannot peer into your system like local scanners do. Actually, some protocols, such as RPC and NIS, can be used by remote scanners to peek inside your system much like local processes. For example, in older implementations of NIS, you could get a copy of the password file by running ypcat on remote nodes in the NIS domain. Remote vulnerability scanners use some of these protocol techniques to look for weaknesses in your systems, too.

### Where Is ISS Headed?

By the time this book is published, you can expect to find ISS rounding out its offerings with a system-level IDS as well. Other vendors are acquiring or developing complementary technologies, too, to offer scanners, network, and system IDSs individually or as part of a suite. When this occurs, you will benefit from common configuration files, similar user interfaces, and a common management framework (or console).

## Other Scanners

A number of other scanners are in the market today. Two others are mentioned here. The list of competitors is growing almost daily. Ballista, developed by Secure Networks, Inc., is now owned and marketed by Network Associates. The IBM Network Security Auditor (NS Auditor) is another alternative primarily for UNIX systems.

## Ballista

Developed under the leadership of Alfred Huger, Ballista boasts the largest list of vulnerabilities detected for UNIX systems. Although systems management and scalability features are clearly important to many customers, there seems to be a laundry-list factor in how purchase decisions are made. Whether the list of attacks scanned becomes the distinguishing feature for the market leader in scanners remains to be seen.

Ballista is a remote scanner that provides informative graphical reporting on results. The list of attacks is too long to include here, but you can find it at www.secnet.com or at www.neta.com (the Network Associates site). Not only does Ballista have an impressive list of recognized vulnerabilities, but the IDS is based on an extensible architecture known as CAPE. This leads to some very interesting possibilities. You can build your own attack patterns to scan or plug Ballista into other products.

## IBM Network Security Auditor

The IBM Firewall is packaged with the Network Security Auditor remote scanner as an added bonus. The NS Auditor has its roots in the days of the Internet Worm incident. Two scientists at IBM Research were nose down in graduate school at Texas A&M University when the Worm hit. Not long after that incident, several other attacks were launched on the Internet. Dave Safford and Doug Schales were involved in discovering, monitoring, and repairing the damage caused by these attacks. The results of their efforts are widely distributed as the TAMU Tiger package. These two are also the initial authors of NS Auditor.

The NS Auditor is unique in that it uses heuristics (AI techniques) to make some decisions during its scanning phase. A wide range of options also can be specified for controlling the scan, including the following:

- ◆ Time-out limits for open port connections
- ◆ Whether to walk anonymous ftp trees looking for writable directories
- ◆ Factors affecting the speed of the scan

At this time, IBM does not offer NS Auditor as a separate product, although the tool is used by IBM consultants. The version of NS Auditor that ships with the firewall is limited to scanning an individual subnet of addresses rather than being wide open to scanning *any* addresses. Other scanners impose the same limitations using a license-key mechanism. The reason is simple—the differ-

## Keeping the Scanners Current

Most scanners rely on knowledge of historical problems rather than on predictive capabilities. Because a new exploit is discovered at least every week, keeping the scanning database up to date is necessary. Companies that aggressively market intrusion detection products often maintain a skilled set of researchers who monitor newsgroups, communicate with the underground, and generate original results to find new hacks to add to the products. The X-Force team is one good example (www.iss.net/xforce). Others include the squads at Secure Networks Inc. (SNI, now part of Network Associates) and the WheelGroup (now part of Cisco). L0pht Heavy Industries is particularly skilled and has reported many important findings.

ence between a network assessment and a network penetration attempt depends on the person running the scanner. A scanner with no limitations on network addresses for targets could be used to probe systems throughout the Internet.

## Are You Done Yet?

Nope. In this chapter, you saw how scanners can look for vulnerabilities either locally on a node or by remote testing for weaknesses. Recall that the two primary ways a hacker gains access are through the following:

- ◆ A configuration error by the vendor supplying a product or by the administrator running the system (or in some cases via user mistakes)
- ◆ A software bug

Scanners look for these types of weaknesses in your systems by examining configuration data or by attempting to exploit a vulnerability. Relative to other IDSs, the distinguishing feature of vulnerability scanners is that they run occasionally, rather than constantly.

Before you get too excited about scanners, you should remind yourself that they are software products, too. Security vendors are generally more attentive to good programming practices, so hopefully the likelihood of a buffer overflow attack *against your scanner* is small. However, the vulnerability assessment will detect only the things it is configured to scan. If the administrator does not set up and configure the scanner properly, hackers will continue to operate undetected.

Although scanners are a necessary tool in your environment, they are not sufficient for a complete security solution. The missing feature is real-time detection of attacks as they occur. In the next chapter, you'll see how system-level IDSs supplement scanners at your sites.

# Chapter 8

# UNIX System-Level IDSs

In the last chapter, you saw how scanning a system for flaws can reveal security weaknesses. The scanner periodically runs directly on the target to look at the contents of configuration files, for back-level programs with security holes, for known rogue programs, or for hacker tracks. Alternatively, you can run a network scan against a target node looking for vulnerabilities. In this chapter, you'll examine IDSs that run at the system level. These tools run directly on the target system and look for evidence of misuse or intrusions.

Stalker is traditionally a tool that runs on an interval basis from one minute to daily. However, by the time this book is published, Stalker should be available as a real-time monitor to catch intrusions or misuses *as they happen*. The Computer Misuse Detection System runs in real time, and, thus, also catches intruders in the act. Real-time detection and response are valuable features beyond those provided by scanners.

Stalker and CMDS differ because Stalker is marketed as a pattern-matching tool, and the strength of CMDS is in its statistical capabilities. After reading this chapter, you will see that both pattern matching and statistical anomaly detection have advantages. You will be glad to know that neither CMDS nor Stalker introduce new security models. That is, no new subjects, objects, reference monitors, or access control lists are added to your environment when you install CMDS or Stalker. Also, both of these tools are known for analyzing audit logs, although their core architectures support analysis of other data sources, such as firewall or Web server log files.

To truly understand the strengths and limitations of system-level IDSs, you begin by learning example UNIX hacks that they can detect. After this, several sections describe Stalker and CMDS. After you know what system level tools are capable of finding, you will explore their shortcomings.

## Detecting Hacks with Stalker

Stalker is a client-server, heterogeneous IDS for UNIX systems. In addition to providing intrusion and misuse detection, Stalker also can be used for *audit reduction* to whittle down a collection of audit records into meaningful information.

Stalker employs a client-server model for distributed, heterogeneous UNIX systems. The Stalker Manager software is installed on a central server from which clients are administered and monitored. Each node in the network watched by the Manager is called an Agent. The purpose of the agent code is to format the audit logs generated by the operating system into a common form. The intrusion detection engine thus is insulated as much as possible from subtle differences in the audit record layouts from different systems. From the Manager station, an administrator can configure the audit subsystems or analyze different client nodes. Today, only one node at a time can be the target of an operation, whether the operation involves configuration or analysis.

Stalker was originally intended for misuse and intrusion detection through reporting. Analysis would be scheduled by the administrator to run during the evening so that reports would be available in the morning. If an alert appeared in one of the reports, the administrator would see who did it, what happened, and how the perpetrator committed the crime. Because the audit logs show the AUID for the event, and the path to an event can be tracked by Stalker's engine, the sequence of events leading up to the problem would be shown in the report.

Several variations of Stalker have appeared in the marketplace including WebStalker, RT Stalker, and ProxyStalker for NT. These products use the same intrusion detection engine but run in real time and provide automated responses. Combining one of these real-time IDSs with the traditional investigative capabilities of Stalker gives you a powerful suite for monitoring your security policy.

The four main components in Stalker include the following:

♦ Audit Management
♦ Trace/Browser (TB)
♦ Misuse Detector (MD)
♦ Storage Manager

The Storage Manager is a set of shell scripts that can be used to migrate audit logs through a storage hierarchy. Many companies rely on home-grown or commercial storage management products to perform this task today. Therefore, this component is not discussed in detail here.

## Audit Management

Configuring and maintaining audit logs on UNIX systems is no trivial matter. A number of different parameters need to be properly set. Expertise in UNIX audit administration is not a widely available skill. Furthermore, the management concepts and tasks across different UNIX systems differ widely. For example, the AIX audit subsystem provides a *panic* capability. Paranoid administrators can panic the system if there is not enough space to write audit records. There *are* people who would prefer to see the system go down rather than have an incomplete audit trail. The Audit Management subsystem of Stalker provides a GUI that attempts to hide the complexities of audit administration for several versions of UNIX. Because the concepts and tasks are not identical on all platforms, you will fill in different screens depending on the OS running on the Agent.

In the audit configuration screen, some of the items you can control include the following:

◆ When to close the current audit log and start another
◆ What events to record in the audit log
◆ Whether to turn auditing on or off
◆ Where to store audit records

Most UNIX systems support two modes for storing audit records. In *bin* mode, the audit subsystem writes records into the first bin (file) until it is full. The audit subsystem then switches and writes into the second bin, until it, too, becomes full, and the first bin is used again. In *stream* mode, output from the audit trail is passed in real time to system-defined processes. For example, Stalker intercepts the audit events in real time in stream mode and writes, formats the output into a common format, and then writes the data into files.

Processing records in bin mode can result in the loss of records. Stream mode records are lost only if the file system space fills up. Stalker configures UNIX systems to run in stream mode. The Stalker agent code then attaches to the stream and captures audit records as they are generated. When the records are reformatted into a common form, they are written into ASCII files that the detection engine analyzes. You can choose whether to keep the original audit records generated by the system as part of Audit Management.

On Solaris systems, you can choose to monitor more than 240 different types of audit events. Other operating systems monitor 100 event types or more. Therefore, deciding which events to monitor is your responsibility as an administrator. By default, Stalker configures Agents to monitor only a subset of events. For performance reasons, not all file opens are monitored. AIX provides per-file auditing, so it is possible to watch opens for only certain files, such as /etc/security/passwd. Unfortunately, there will be many legitimate accesses to this file as part of the normal operating system behavior, particularly if there are many logins and logouts during the day at your site. On the other hand, if you don't watch people writing to /etc/security/passwd, you can miss attacks.

### Tracer/Browser

Auditing subsystems generate substantially large files. Haystack Labs would suggest that customers plan for 10–50 MB of data per user per day. Your mileage might vary.

The *Tracer/Browser* (TB) is a query tool for filtering through these large amounts of audit data. To look for *specific* entries in the audit logs, you select a client from the GUI, click on the TB icon, and fill in the next few screens. Note that the TB is designed to search through audit logs for events that match your search parameters. It does not look for sequences or complex patterns of events.

The TB enables you to filter on many different fields:

♦ AUID, RUID, EUID, RGID, and EGID
♦ Object name (such as individual file names or regular expressions)
♦ Success or failure of the audit event
♦ Audit event class or type
♦ Source IP address if the event is for network activity
♦ TTY or terminal from which the user is connected

You can form very complex queries in the GUI. For each field, you may define inclusion and exclusion qualifiers, such as asking for all AUIDs not equal to zero or all file names that match a particular regular expression. Predefined lists of values for a search field are also allowed. That is, the GUI will let you create a list of critical file names to monitor, assign a name to this list, and reuse the list in different queries over time. You then can search through the audit logs looking for audit events showing attempted accesses for only those files.

The output from the query can be displayed, printed, mailed, or saved to a file. When saved to a file, the format can be either a text report or an audit event file that can be *further reduced* with a query. Queries may be formulated in advance and then stored as *templates*. Scheduled TB queries are then run via cron jobs to reduce the audit data into regularly delivered reports.

When would you use the TB? When you want to keep records of important security events, such as when users are added or removed, a convenient report can be created in the TB. Thus, you can use TB reports for documenting your security activities. Stalker is shipped with a number of default TB queries and reports. One example is a report with both successful and failed logins. Notice that this report is not an intrusion detection signature. It's just a useful report showing you who connected and who had trouble connecting. An attack signature happens to use the same data to look for someone trying to break into the system. You might also want to know anytime someone runs the su command or executes a SUID program. All of these types of queries are supported by the TB.

You also can use the TB to look for trouble. A second built-in report that Stalker provides is the mail-policy-violation-report. A simple query looks for typical UNIX mail files and finds audit events that show that someone other than the file's owner tried to access the file. If you think of the audit logs as a relational database table and envision the TB as a query interface into this database, you see that there are a number of important uses.

Stalker looks for attacks against UNIX systems. If you install application software for which Stalker does not include predefined reports or queries, you can design your own queries or reports to track activities against these files. If the application introduces its own subjects, objects, and access control events, Stalker will not report on those activities *unless* they are added to the audit trail by the application vendor.

Today, Stalker provides only batch or interactive queries. The capability to filter for specific queries in real time would be an added advantage. This feature would introduce some interesting tradeoffs for you as well. Each real-time filter would add load on the network and on a centralized monitor. Configuring a feature like this in a distributed environment would require a few tries to perfect, particularly if you have a very large site. The capability to organize analysis engines into a hierarchy also would be beneficial for *any* real-time distributed monitoring tool.

## Misuse Detector

The patented component of Stalker that is most interesting is the collection of intrusion detection patterns along with the engine that analyzes them. In simplistic terms, audit records are dropped into the engine, which maintains a series of state transition diagrams representing intrusions and misuses. When a particular pattern reaches a terminal state, a misuse or intrusion event is indicated.

This analysis component of Stalker is called the Misuse Detector (MD) for historical reasons. Technically, it is both a misuse detector and an intrusion detector. Recall from earlier discussions that misuse detection looks for abuses by internal users, and intrusion detection is focused on attacks from outsiders. Today, these terms are often used interchangeably.

Like the TB, the MD can be run interactively or scheduled to operate in batch mode. Stalker detects roughly 80–90 different attacks depending on the version of UNIX running on the client. Not all patterns are supported on each OS. From the MD GUI, you can choose which attack signatures you want to monitor.

## Attacks Detected by Stalker

Stalker conveniently groups patterns into classes, such as Trojan Horse. Space does not permit an exhaustive list and description of attacks detected by Stalker. Table 8.1 summarizes this information.

The MD was developed over several years and has a good foundation in intrusion detection research. IDSs use different engines for analyzing attacks. Some,

**Table 8.1** Stalker's Misuse Detector Signatures

| Attack Signature Category | Types of Attacks Detected |
| --- | --- |
| Covering Tracks | Detects when a user tries to modify audit configurations, delete entries in system log files, or run known rogue programs like *zap* to cover tracks. |
| Gaining Privilege | Detects a number of different ways that user gains privilege on the system. |
| | These signatures can be configured to permit or deny specific privilege transitions, such as when the RUID changes to zero. |
| Known Attack Programs | Looks for instances of a user running one or more known rogue programs. |
| | A preconfigured list is provided but can be modified. |
| Misuse Outcomes | Looks for evidence of attacks that have a known outcome, such as password guessing attempts matching the order of names in /etc/passwd (indicating the user file has been stolen). Another example is reading someone else's data or bypassing ACLs by gaining privilege. |
| Self Defense | Watches the Stalker directories for evidence of tampering. |
| System Access | Detects when critical systems files have been altered, or attempted to be altered. This category includes Trojan Horse signatures. |
| Vulnerabilities | Looks for evidence of someone trying to exploit a known security advisory. |
| Masquerading | A user switches to another user and then attacks the system. |
| Tagged Events | Tagged files or programs that a user accesses (planted by the administrator as bait) or a tagged user account being accessed. |

such as CMDS, rely on rule-based expert systems. Stalker employs a *finite state machine* (FSM) for recognizing attacks. As you probably know, finite state machines are the underlying technology for compilers. Recognizing patterns with the utmost speed is one of the reasons FSMs are used in compilers. This reason was also one of the reasons it was chosen for Stalker.

You also can buy a Misuse Detector Toolkit to add signatures to Stalker. This toolkit is not particularly easy to use and requires skill in C++. Over time you can expect Stalker and other IDSs to provide a scripting language for writing new patterns.

## Is Stalker Right for You?

At the time this chapter was written, the real-time, client-server, heterogeneous Stalker product was not available. Naturally, you should check the Network Associates Web site for the latest information. Many enhancements to Stalker have been planned and will roll out over time. You want to remember that batch reports are an important part of security monitoring. Monitoring *everything* in real time is probably not the best approach. Also, Stalker's capability to go query and search through past audit logs is valuable. If you find that you have been hacked, it's good to know that you easily can filter for specifics through large amounts of historical audit data using Stalker.

Stalker will be a good match for your environment if you consider the following:

◆ Real-time analysis is *not* necessary.

◆ Identifying the accountable user is *very* important.

◆ Audit trails already are captured at your site, or you do not mind logging audit records.

◆ You need a tool to perform audit reduction.

◆ You need a tool that detects a wide range of UNIX system attacks.

◆ Detection of privilege escalation problems is *very* important at your site.

◆ You want the capability to scan for custom-defined events in large volumes of data.

◆ You audit several different UNIX systems.

Stalker has a large set of attack patterns for UNIX system-level monitoring. If the set of attack patterns is useful to you, which it probably is, deploying Stalker on critical systems is a good way to get started.

Unlike accounting files, the audit trail can detect privilege transitions. The Morris worm, which overlaid itself with a fork() and then an exec(), would not have been detected in the accounting files, although it does show up in audit logs. When a user runs a similar attack, the AUID remains unchanged, and thus accountability is preserved. The AUID also persists when a user runs the *su* command, even though the RUID changes. Other transitions in privilege also are surfaced in the audit log. With Stalker's TB and MD capabilities, you can catch these type of security events on your systems.

Depending on your needs, Stalker may not be the best tool for your environment. For example, if you want real-time consolidation of audit logs from the clients to the Stalker server, the tool does not provide this feature today. Your requirements might cause you to see the following as limitations of Stalker:

◆ Batch analysis of audit logs.
◆ Only one client at a time can be interactively administered or configured *interactively*, although initial definitions for clients can be input via a batch file. (You can run several simultaneous reports in batch mode.)

Given the number of valuable reports that Stalker can generate for you, these problems are not particularly difficult.

### Some Alternative Stalker Configurations

As noted in other chapters, many tradeoffs can be made in system monitoring. The two most important variables you can tradeoff are CPU and network performance. If you run Stalker Manager and Agent software on each node, you can analyze the data on the systems where it is created. You will spend CPU cycles on each node performing the analysis, but you will not be sending large audit logs across the network. If you get clever, you can use the Stalker Manager code on the Agent systems to reduce the audit logs before sending them to a central server for storage. Unfortunately, the pricing model of Stalker does not make this configuration too attractive at this time.

On the other hand, if you do not want your agent nodes wasting CPU cycles doing intrusion detection, you can eat up some network bandwidth and send the audit logs to the server using NFS, FTP, or your favorite distributed file system tool. By the way, a Stalker Agent is not necessarily a puny little workstation. Agent is a *role* that a system plays in the Stalker environment. An agent could be a big megaserver with loads of storage, memory, and plenty of parallel processors. Similarly, the Stalker Manager could be run on the oldest single user

UNIX workstation you have at your site, although this would not be a good choice for something that needs to analyze quite a bit of data.

A special version of Stalker is modified to monitor the IBM Firewall. The product includes some custom reports to monitor configuration and executable files that make up the firewall. This feature is complementary to the Tripwire type of file checking that the firewall already does. Stalker will report on who is changing firewall executables or configuration files and describe the audit events that led up to that behavior. Although it would be a useful extension, Stalker does not read or monitor the log files emitted by the firewall. Special attack patterns also have not been developed explicitly for firewalls. Now that Haystack has subsumed into Network Associates who owns the Gauntlet Firewall, a closer fit between IDSs and firewalls is likely.

### Stalker V3

A new version of Stalker is planned for 1998. One notable enhancement is real-time processing of MD signatures, so that you can look for attacks as they occur. Information exchanges between Stalker Agents and the Manager will be accomplished in real time using a secure communications protocol.

In Chapter 2, "The Role of Identification and Authentication in Your Environment," emphasis was placed on the following triad:

>   Prevention + Detection + Response

Stalker V3 also provides capabilities for different real-time responses when attack patterns are matched. Possibilities include e-mail, paging, custom scripts, killing processes, disabling logins, blocking logins for an interval, and SNMP traps. The design is flexible enough to enable you to respond in unique ways to different intrusions and to vary your responses by time of day.

Before moving to the next section, it is worth mentioning again that Stalker also provides *threshold* detection for a few events, such as failed logins or failed su events. Thus, Stalker shares characteristics with anomaly detectors such as CMDS. Exceeding a threshold of a specific event is the simplest form of statistical anomaly detection. Conversely, CMDS includes a few pattern matching rules, too. You can even find a few sites that run *both* CMDS and Stalker.

## Detecting Hacks with the Computer Misuse Detection System

Like Stalker, CMDS is an audit trail analysis tool. CMDS performs audit reduction from heterogeneous and distributed *target* nodes. CMDS development at

*Science Applications International Corporation* (SAIC) was led by Paul Proctor (Proctor, 1994). The CMDS *server* analyzes the data provided to it by monitored targets. Analysis occurs in real time unless CMDS is configured otherwise. Historical audit logs can be saved and interrogated later as in Stalker.

Because the audit logs are the primary source of information for CMDS, accountability can be attributed to users via the AUID or to remote systems by gathering all activities for a particular IP address. Statistical profiles for a given network address can be thus be created and tracked historically.

Often, potential IDS customers ask for "useful management reports" to pass up the chain of command. Summary statistical reporting is another CMDS strength. The original sponsors were looking for a system that could provide good summaries of suspicious activities. This requirement helped drive the development of good reporting in the core CMDS offering.

When a survey of existing IDSs was done as part of the CMDS background research, it was discovered that many existing tools were tailored to the data source and other characteristics of the environment. At that time, Stalker was just beginning to emerge to provide a general-purpose framework adaptable to audit sources from multiple systems. CMDS arose concurrently with the same architecture goals. To prove its easy adaptability, CMDS was modified to support a multilevel secure OS audit trail from B1 DG/UX in a mere two weeks.

## How CMDS Works

CMDS is best known for its statistical anomaly-detection approach, although CMDS also includes an expert system with pattern-matching signatures. Many early IDSs were written using rule-based expert systems, although this programming paradigm is not widely used today.

### Analysis Modes

CMDS can analyze target node data in real time, batch, or on-demand modes. Each target runs a daemon that preprocesses the audit data, converts the data into a normal format, encrypts the data, and then sends the data to the CMDS Server. Optionally, the audit logs can be stored on the target and sent to the central server on a scheduled basis.

Most installations run in real time and perform on-demand analysis when an alert is generated to fine tune monitoring activities. When an alert occurs, it is indicated via one of the following responses:

♦ A pop-up alert screen on the server
♦ E-mail

- ◆ Pager notification
- ◆ User defined

Administrators who do not need real-time analysis can run reports in batch mode, perhaps during off hours so that the analysis will be available to the security officers in the morning.

## Statistical Measures

CMDS computes means and confidence intervals for several different usage measures. In simple terms, the system tracks what a user does in real time by counting the occurrences of different events. The *categories* that CMDS monitors include the following:

- ◆ Failed logins
- ◆ Failed reads
- ◆ Execution or programs and system calls, whether interactive or batch
- ◆ Networking audit records such as socket events
- ◆ Browsing activities, such as reading files and changing directories
- ◆ su attempts
- ◆ Access to devices

Customers can define new categories by associating specific audit events with a category. When an audit record of that event type is detected, the category count is incremented. Category statistics can be tracked by user or by IP address. This differentiator is important because it enables you to know that a particular user was busy copying files or that one odd system saw a spike in the total number of file deletes.

## Reporting Anomalies

CMDS enables you to report statistics by user and node. An example report is shown in Figure 8.1.

These reports are available in addition to real-time detection and response for threshold exceptions. Notice that both upper and lower boundaries are defined for a category. If a user's measure remains within the boundaries, all is well. Any time an activity crosses the upper limit or falls below the lower limit an anomaly is reported.

A user's statistical *profile* is composed of a collection of category measures. The profile is computed from the last 90 days of activities. In addition to com-

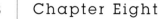

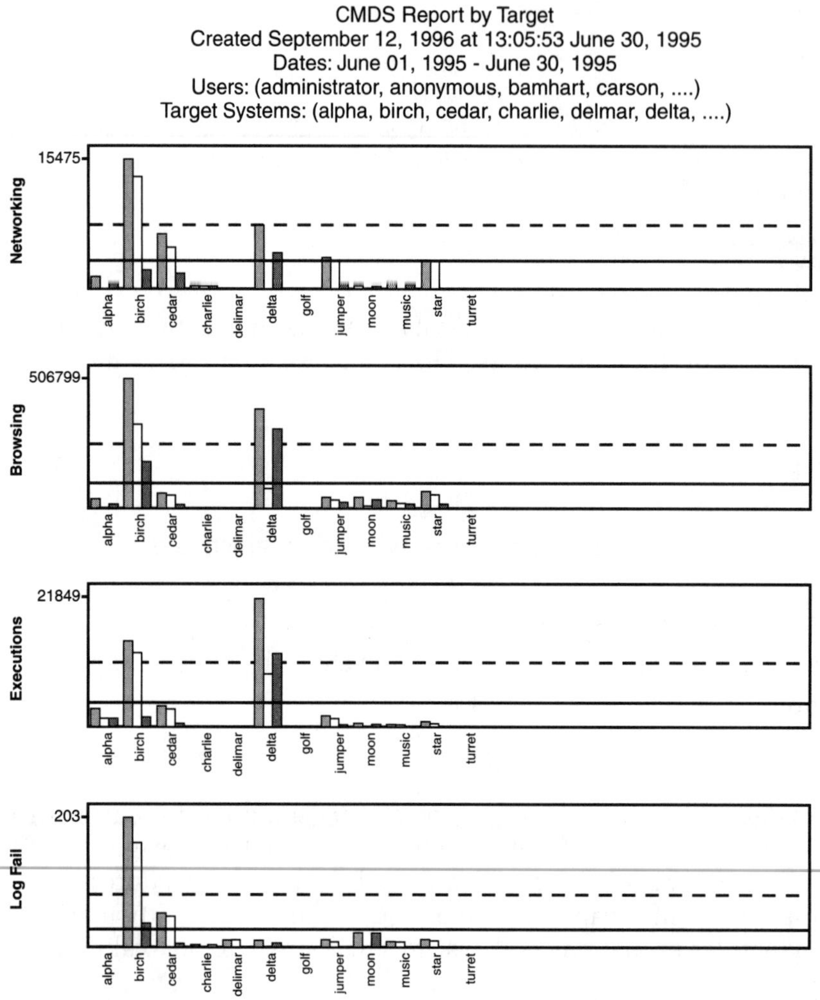

CMDS Report by Target
Created September 12, 1996 at 13:05:53 June 30, 1995
Dates: June 01, 1995 - June 30, 1995
Users: (administrator, anonymous, bamhart, carson, ....)
Target Systems: (alpha, birch, cedar, charlie, delmar, delta, ....)
Networking
15475
Browsing
506799
Executions
21849
Log Fail
203
alpha
birch
cedar
charlie
delimar
delta
golf
jumper
moon
music
star
turret


**Figure 8.1** Example report from CMDS.

puting frequency values and means, a total category count is maintained. Thus, you can know whether a user ran 90 percent of the file delete commands for the day. Reported also is the total number of records per category relative to the total number of audit records. You can know whether file deletes accounted for 50 percent of the day's activities for the system. CMDS tracks both the AUID and the EUID for an activity to assign accountability.

The daily profile for a user or IP address is broken down by hour. These values are presented in the graphical reports that can be printed on-demand or on a batch schedule. In case you are wondering, the thresholds are computed by calculating the mean for a category and then computing confidence intervals that you can define. The confidence intervals define the upper and lower threshold values.

Alerts can be generated from a single threshold violation from a combined measure from different categories. You can configure these options in the GUI provided with CMDS. Statistical measures can be treated independently or combined. The count from one audit category can be combined with another statistic to invent a third category. The number of combined categories is practically unlimited. Monitoring of thresholds in real time can happen sequentially or in parallel. This feature enables you to prioritize what the engine monitors.

## Pattern-Matching Signatures

CMDS uses the publicly available *Common Language Integrated Production System* (CLIPS) expert system developed at NASA. CLIPS is a forward-chaining, rule-based expert system. Backward chaining can be implemented in CLIPS, but CMDS uses the forward-chaining model. In forward-chaining systems, the expert systems reason from facts to goals. An oversimplification is to think of this as the process of elimination for goals known in advance. Backward-chaining systems, should you be curious, assume a goal and then try to prove or disprove it as facts arrive for processing. If you want to know more about all of the gory details of commercial expert system building tools, plenty of sources are available (Waterman, 1988; Harmon, 1990).

CMDS detects roughly 20 attack signatures including the following:

- Setting the SUID bit on a file
- Browsing attacks, such as unauthorized reads
- Known weakness exploits, such as the Sun load module buffer overflow attack
- Successful and unsuccessful remote break in events
- Changes to system accounting configuration
- Trojan Horse planting or execution
- Password attacks
- Masquerade attempts
- Tagged user login

- ◆ Tagged file lists which can be customized by the CMDS administrator
- ◆ System events such as shutdown, halt, or reboot

To create a signature you must know how to add new rules to a CLIPS knowledge base.

## Role of Statistical Anomaly Detection

Anomaly detectors look for statistical differences in *behavior*. They assume intrusions are rare and thus will show up as exceptions to *normal* behavior. An anomaly detector will trigger when an upper or lower threshold is passed by one of the statistics being calculated.

Often, skilled users pose problems for statistical models because they might use a wider range of commands or occasionally rely on a rarely used command (Smaha and Winslow, 1994). Configuring the event monitor so that it does not report false alarms for skilled users can be difficult. Another way to describe this limitation is to say that statistical techniques are most effective when applied to homogeneous data, such as credit card activities, securities trading, or loan processing.

Not all anomalies are intrusions. If you are a programmer or researcher and decide to run a program a number of times although you do not normally do this, the event could trigger an alert if this activity is one of the statistics in your profile. A system that relies on statistical profiles only may not assign accountability correctly. For example, if one statistic is cumulative evidence of running rogue programs from an account, it is also important to know whether the login user is performing these tasks or whether someone has switched to that user ID from another. Remember that CMDS does *not* have this problem because it tracks both the AUID and the EUID to assign accountability for actions.

## Other IDS Features to Consider

So far you've seen that Stalker and CMDS are complementary system-level IDSs that catch a number of attacks which scanners and network sniffers cannot. The next few sections summarize some other important issues to consider about system intrusion detection.

### Ease of Set Up

Both Stalker and CMDS are distributed, client-server products. Depending on your network configuration, the installation and setup can be simple or complex. The usual rule of "your mileage may vary" is a good one to keep in mind.

Agent code must be installed on each CMDS target or Stalker agent. Although some autodiscovery is provided, the Server or Manager will need to be made aware of which nodes to monitor. The time it takes to configure nodes is a small constant value in most cases, but you need to multiply this value by the number of nodes you have.

As with most systems that rely on host names and IP addresses for identification, the use of *dynamic host configuration protocol* (DHCP) or regular changes to host identifiers will require additional administration. If you treat all monitored nodes uniformly, administration is simpler. However, if you want to analyze different statistics or attack patterns on each node, your administrative workload also will increase. Any variability in your monitoring requirements per node naturally will drive configuration changes on either agents or servers/managers.

## Distributed Intrusion Detection

Neither Stalker nor CMDS track the activities of a given user across multiple systems unless the assumption is that a person will have the same UID across all systems in the enterprise. Because this assumption is highly unlikely—even though the login name might be the same, the UIDs across systems may not be equivalent—tracking the activities of a single user throughout the enterprise is not straightforward.

One solution would be to add to each audit record, when consolidated on the server, with the originating host IP address. Unfortunately, this solution does not work for systems with multiple network adapters because the node will have several IP addresses. Also, in sites where IP addresses are assigned dynamically with DHCP, relying on an IP address to be meaningful would be a mistake because it could be reassigned at a future time. The host's name would probably be more reliable. When consolidating activities across systems, CMDS relies on the host's name and UID paired together to uniquely identify a user.

Distributed systems management framework vendors, such as Tivoli, are all too aware of this identity problem in networked environments. The favored approach is to assign a framework-specific host identifier that is persistent across changes in IP addresses or other system parameters, such as the planar ROM ID. Assigning a network user name that is independent of the system on which a user operates also would be useful. However, such an extension would require changes in core parts of the OS, such as the login process and the generation of audit records, in order to track user activities across multiple systems. One research project prototyped this approach for intrusion detection across systems (Snapp et al., 1991).

## Monitoring and Privacy

Keystroke monitoring has not been a fruitful approach to intrusion detection. As with many other computer science endeavors, context-sensitive analysis of data is one of the most difficult reasoning challenges for a program. Therefore, no commercial IDSs rely on keystrokes for determining misuses or intrusions. If such a tool were to exist, how would you handle privacy issues?

Most companies own the intellectual property of employees and also legally restrict computer activities to only those approved by management. A common practice is to present this warning to all computers users as part of the normal login message. This does not mean that *all* managers in a company own *all* of the correspondence of *all* of the employees. Especially unclear is how to handle the conflict that arises between privacy and monitoring. For example, if your IDS *does* monitor keystrokes, then someone is capable of reading the e-mail of employees. Sure, the company owns the content of these messages anyway. But, what if the message is from an employee to a superior complaining about harassment on the job. Is this something from which an IDS might generate alerts or message excerpts?

Unfortunately, you should be worried about privacy and IDSs even though they do not perform keystroke analysis. What if someone is filling out a medical form online and enters words such as "attack," "weakness," and "confidential?" Many network sniffers would look for these as part of a standard set of watch words. Ideally, you could configure the sniffer to ignore these words when the user was in the *context* of a medical application online, but it's unlikely the tool supports this because it is a difficult algorithm to generalize.

System monitoring tools also require caution. Audit trail reports contain the full command and its parameters in most cases. Knowing that an employee is suddenly sending several mail messages to someone in personnel could be confidential. This situation particularly becomes a problem if the manager is receiving IDS usage reports (to look for misuse problems), and the employee is documenting improper behavior by that manager. In this particular case, the best advice is to document the problem on a home computer rather than risk discovery by unauthorized sniffers being used at your site.

By the way, these privacy problems are not limited to intrusion detection. In plenty of cases, developers use network sniffers to capture packets that are needed to debug a problem. Separating confidential information from test environments is the right approach for solving this dilemma. An interesting legend has gone around about how some user IDs and passwords from a reputable company found their way into one distribution of Crack when the software was tested in a production environment.

If you run a scanner and configure it to mail reports, verify your configuration so that you are not mailing the list of easily guessed passwords to everyone at your site, or even worse to your favorite newsgroup on the Internet. In some instances, someone mailed the output of a scan to a personal account *outside* the company, and the mail message flowed in the clear across the Internet. Remember, without encryption the Internet is like one big party line that many people share.

## Finding New Attacks

Companies that build IDSs know the importance of keeping up with new attacks. Companies do this in several ways.

ISS recently has put together a talented team called the X-Force. This group spends a great deal of time uncovering their own exploits, as well as maintaining contacts in the hacker community. Secure Networks, Inc., also has a dedicated team of researchers that look for exploits, as did the WheelGroup (now folded into Cisco). These folks spend a good portion of their day looking for weaknesses in systems and networks. If you subscribe to BUGTRAQ, Best of Security, NT Security, and other security mailing lists, you'll see the names of some of these folks appear regularly. They also are frequent panel members at conferences such as DEFCON and Usenix Security.

Another group of ethical hackers operates as L0pht Heavy Industries. Once described as "rock stars of computer security," the L0pht is responsible for discovering well-announced weaknesses in products such as Kerberos V4 and Microsoft NT. The most famous output from the lab is the NT password cracker developed by two of the team's members. Hacking in a private laboratory because its fun and interesting is perhaps the best motivation for finding security holes in products. That's *really* why these exploit hunting teams exist.

Early hackers broke into systems because they were curious and wanted to learn more. Many remote attacks occur for the same reason today. Not everyone is out to damage your systems, although plenty of people enjoy doing so. Staying in touch with hackers is one way that companies know the latest exploits. Don't be surprised if you find a consultant who has a history of attempted break-in attempts or even a conviction.

Security newsgroups and mailing lists are other avenues for keeping abreast of holes in systems. Most of these groups are moderated. A common rule of thumb is to notify the vendor before posting the flaw. Moderators are generally good about ensuring this happens. Unresponsive software vendors have sometimes been caught in the awkward situation of not knowing about an exploit because the mail from the discoverer was somehow lost in the corporate maze.

## General Event Monitoring or Intrusion Detection

One of the consequences of acquisitions and mergers in the security industry is the maturing of security products so that they fit better into enterprise system management solutions. General event monitoring is one of the most useful components of a distributed management framework, such as Tivoli TME, which includes the Event Manager. Site administrators are interested in all sorts of events such as when disk drives crash, when network performance begins to suffer, when the printer is jammed, or when a system halts.

Event management frameworks are designed to manage events notifications and responses across heterogeneous distributed systems. Usually, one or more event consoles can be defined as recipients for events from managed nodes. An operator can be defined to receive all events or a limited subset. Responses to events can be automated or require manual intervention. In other words, quite a bit of generality is inherent in the event management system to handle different systems management policies and event multiple unique data input sources.

Intrusion detection is really a special case of event management. The main difference is that instead of looking for a single event or a threshold of events, an IDS will look for a complex patterns of events, too. Still, building some custom event handlers for frameworks such as Tivoli's would not be too difficult for the implementation of an IDS. Tivoli's event framework even ships with a generic log file adapter that can be customized to gather events, in real time, from different data sources. One example provided is a log file adapter for syslog which gathers and parses syslog records and sends them to the event console for processing. Local filtering, to eliminate redundant or unnecessary events, is another advantage of many event management frameworks.

During the next few years, you should expect to see better integration of IDSs into systems management frameworks, especially into the event notification subsystems. IDS vendors actually benefit from this opportunity because the secure framework code, for centrally reporting events, is provided *for free* by the systems management solution. Unfortunately, "for free" usually means increased support costs for the IDS vendors because not all customers will want the same systems management framework, nor will every customer have a framework. Thus, IDS vendors will need to support their own centralized event reporting subsystems when a systems management framework is not in use at the site.

## Using Audit Logs to Find Attacks

The previous sections described two popular system-level intrusion detection products. In the next few sections, you will take a look at how using the audit logs can give you a very good picture of what is happening on your systems. Some of the types of attacks you face are described. For each of these, you will see descriptions of what a system-level IDS might need to catch the attack. No complex attack patterns are discussed because the idea is to give you a feel for the completeness of the audit logs. From these examples, you probably can see how more sophisticated patterns could be constructed by combining them.

## Two Main Reasons for Vulnerabilities

Recall from earlier discussions that systems are usually compromised for one of two reasons:

- Improper configuration by the vendor or by an administrator
- Software bugs in software you purchase and in software you develop

Even the best preventative security tool will not meet your expectations if improperly configured. Firewall scans by consultants and security organizations such as ICSA show that incorrect configurations do indeed occur. It also seems that software bugs will be with us forever. A reasonable plan for defense is to conduct periodic reviews of configurations along with source code reviews.

Modules that should especially be examined for bugs include those that provide network communications for other nodes and those modules that run with special privileges. Your code reviews should look for the following:

- Buffer overflow problems
- How resources are created, read, written, and destroyed (object reuse)
- Improper default assumptions, such as assuming the order of two events
- Handling of data input values, particularly assumptions about character content and length
- Adherence to the least privileged principle for blocks of code

If you obtained the software, such as your operating system, from someone else, chances are you do not have the source code (nor should you accept the code review as *your* problem). In the examples that follow, you will see how program flaws such as those itemized in the preceding list can open your system to intrusions. The next few paragraphs give you an overview of what can happen if software contains one of these bugs.

Buffer overflow attacks have been mentioned several times in this book already. The problem is that a program makes some incorrect assumptions about the length of a value input by the user or passed by another program. The interesting case occurs when the flawed program runs with special privileges. A buffer overflow will result in the system running an arbitrary set of instructions that the hacker supplied along with the input data. The famous Internet Worm used this as one of its techniques.

Another incorrect assumption someone can make when programming is the order of two independent events. Hacks that exploit this weakness include race condition attacks. Well-known examples include file handling. UNIX systems check only access control for the initial file open or create. Because instructions are not atomic, you can use symbolic links or world-writable permissions to substitute a file before the read or write operations occur. A common attack is to trick a privileged program into writing over the contents of a privileged file (such as /etc/passwd) when the program is writing to a world-writable file or directory.

Incorrect assumptions about a process' UMASK, UID, or GID also can lead to security violations. One common bug occurs when a privileged process creates a resource and does not explicitly set the permission bits. The resource is thus not adequately protected from other users on the system. Incorrect assumptions about the length of data can lead to buffer overflow attacks. Improper assumptions about the contents of an input field lead to hacks such as concatenating arbitrary commands on to the end of the input data. The receiving program that runs the system() command on the input string thus is tricked into executing extra commands.

Finally, violations of the least privilege principle are all too common. The programmer errs by running too much of the program with escalated privileges. The proper approach is to run only a few necessary statements with additional privileges, while setting the minimal privileges for the program as a default. The more instructions a program runs as a privileged user, the higher the probability that a hacker will find a hole to sneak through.

## Notation

For the purposes of this discussion, it will be assumed that you are using a system monitoring tool that can detect events and important attributes about those events. As noted in previous chapters, the audit logs of most systems will capture many details about system activities. Instead of giving specific listings of what the audit logs would look like for each UNIX OS you might be interested in, this chapter will give a pseudo description of what to look for in the logs. Indeed, if you have a sophisticated monitoring tool, such as Stalker or CMDS, you will not be looking at raw audit logs but will see a more meaningful interpretation of them in report form.

If during one of the following sections, you need to detect an attack by searching for a specific file delete event, you might be given a recommendation to look for audit records with the following:

- AUID = any value
- RUID or RGID = *any value*
- EUID or EGID = *any value*
- FILE_Delete audit event
- File or resource name

Other details you probably would see from Stalker or CMDS for such an event would be the file's inode value, it's creation date, last modification data and time, and other values you might need for investigating the event further.

## A Word about Sequences

A pattern-matching IDS can look at a sequence of events to detect a problem. For example, if someone is suddenly removing dozens or hundreds of files, you might be faced with a disgruntled employee about to leave a system in an irreparable state. If you wanted to detect such an attack, you could configure your monitor to look for a sequence of $N$ file deletions in a row by the same user, and ask the system to alert you when this threshold is hit. The first challenge to your thinking is the *interval problem*.

Suppose someone has 100 sensitive source files that are not backed up on any other system. This practice is bad to begin with, but it really does happen. If this intruder knows you are looking for successive file deletes, one possible way to escape detection is to delete one file each day for the next 100 days (or any number of deletions per day less than $N$). If the *scope* of your detection pattern is a login session, or a day, or a week, the pattern will not detect the problem because the threshold is not hit before a new scope boundary is hit. The pattern must reset its counter when a scope begins. Within each scope there can be any number of *intervening* events between successive file deletes. This is not a problem for the signature because it is happily counting the events as they occur, regardless of whether each delete command is followed by ls or any other command.

Most IDSs do not enable you to define a scope for resetting thresholds. Instead, the simplifying assumption is that a login session defines the scope of interest. Thus, if the user deletes $N$ files between login and logout events (in the same way that parenthesis bound a related comment), the pattern will fire. The problem with this approach is that it will not catch the trick mentioned previously.

An alternative approach would be to track *N* file deletes regardless of the number of intervening events. The problem here is still to define the scope. If the scope is defined broadly as "from the very first event for this user on this system" up until "now," the pattern will be of little use. Over a period of years, an employee is sure to delete many files. The pattern would fire every day for some user. Defining scope as a week, or as a day, or some other calendar duration is a good idea, but IDSs do not provide this capability today.

A statistical anomaly detector suffers from the same dilemma. Usually, these tools take a *per day* approach to computing the baseline, giving the number of average file deletes by each user per day. To catch a tricky hacker, per week or per month metrics also would be needed. If the perpetrator is someone who deletes hundreds of files per week as normal behavior, catching the disgruntled employee described before will be tough.

### Focusing on Local Attacks

Think about a single system for which you are responsible. One type of attack can originate from a user logged on to your system. Another possibility is that the crack is launched via a network connection to the system. For each of these two categories, different attack severities range from denial-of-service up through gaining superuser privileges.

A system with a network adapter thus faces threats from users who are logged in and running programs and from users who connect to this computer from

### An IDS Limitation

At this point, you should see a limitation of IDSs that is shared with other tools. *If you do not configure the tool properly, it will not catch intrusions or misuse by insiders.* You must specify *what* you want to monitor, unless you monitor everything. To use an IDS, you must state your monitoring policy, particularly if you want to monitor resources not predefined in the IDS, such as application binaries. As you can see, the IDS might make some assumptions that a knowledgeable hacker can use to avoid detection. This doesn't mean that IDSs do not work, it just means that catching hackers is really hard and requires tuning of the tools.

other nodes in your network. The goal of a hacker who has a login account on the system is to gain superuser privileges to have complete control. The goal of a hacker who does not have an account on the system is usually to establish an account on the system. The *usually* is added in the last sentence because it is not necessary for a hacker to have an account on a system to wreck things. Network connections to programs with security weaknesses can be exploited by crackers to do things just as if they had a login account on the system. Getting a login account just makes it easier to explore or trash a system.

In these sections, the focus is on attacks that can occur when a user eventually has login access to your system. In the next chapter, you will see how some of these same kinds of attacks can occur when someone communicates with your system over the network. *In the worst case, a remote user without an account is able to gain superuser privileges on your system.* For the moment, though, you should focus first on how local login users can exploit your system's weaknesses.

To recap the increasing severity of local problems, remember that the list goes as follows:

◆ Denial of service
◆ Local account gains read access to a resource
◆ Local account gains write access to a resource
◆ Local users gain privileges, especially of superuser

### Denial-of-Service

UNIX systems are susceptible to *denial-of-service* (DoS) attacks because, among users, many of the system's resources are shared including kernel resources, disk storage, and memory. This section describes a few DoS attacks that can occur even if the user does not have special privileges. As UNIX OSs have become more mature, they have been placing per-user restrictions on resources, such as the number of concurrently opened files, file-system quota, number of concurrently running processes, memory consumption, and network buffers. Still, it is possible to bring almost any UNIX system to a virtual stop by running a script such as the following:

```
cd /tmp
while TRUE
do
mkdir foo
cd foo
done
```

In other words, filling up the /tmp file system will affect a large number of UNIX system processes because the /tmp directory is where they often go for temporary storage. How a particular version of UNIX behaves in response to this situation varies, but some versions cannot even boot if /tmp is out of space. The attack is still possible today because /tmp might fill up before a user's file-system quota is reached.

This attack is representative of a class of attacks in which a user attempts to exhaust a resource by running the same command repeatedly. To catch this behavior, an IDS needs to set a threshold condition. You must consider two variables:

◆ At what value to set the threshold
◆ What commands or operations to monitor

A threshold of 3 for this sequence is reasonable for indicating an attack as opposed to a wandering, inexperienced user. The threshold applies to the pair of events—mkdir and cd—rather than 3 arbitrary mkdir commands in sequence. For simplicity, assume that the AUID, RUID, EUID, and corresponding GIDs have not changed across audit events. Also, recall that for each command, a separate audit record will be emitted. Because the audit trail also shows the parameters passed to the command, you could watch for a sequence of audit records with content like the following:

```
mkdir value, cd value repeated N times
```

This type of pattern would catch the specific case shown previously. If the abuser is smart, some randomness could be introduced into the attack to avoid detection. The name of the directory created each time could be randomized, but a cd still would switch to the newly created directory each time to set up the next iteration:

```
mkdir random-val1 followed by cd val1, where val1 equals random-val1,
but random-val1 changes on each iteration.
```

Certainly, dozens more possible variations exist just for this one attack. What you will *not* find in commercial IDS tools are many patterns to detect all of the combinations of ways this attack can be programmed. In pattern-matching systems, what you are likely to find is single-command thresholds. If you have a system-level IDS and you can configure in detail what the system looks for, the previous paragraphs give you an idea of what to look for in the data. Another simple, general pattern, which looks for a threshold number of operations, that consume space in /tmp is another possibility. In the audit log, the events one would look for are file create, make directory, and link. However, if you attempt to also track file writes, you could end up with too many false positives. A number of programs create and remove files in /tmp as part of their normal operations. Deciding on the threshold value is not going to be simple either. You need to set it based on observation.

A useful feature of statistical anomaly IDSs is that their general mode of operation is to count execution of user commands or audit event types. A user who runs an unusual number of mkdir commands will generate an alarm in a real-time IDS. The problem with some statistical IDSs is their granularity. For example, someone who receives a tar image that creates a few dozen subdirectories will generate a number of mkdir commands. The preceding attack is not based on generating many different mkdir commands, but on the fact that the parent directory is /tmp or one of its descendants. Merely counting the number of directory create events, even if read from the audit log, is insufficient for differentiating an attack against /tmp from a tar file extraction in another directory. Contextual information also must be examined by the statistical monitor. Therefore, if you have a statistical monitor, you'll have similar problems in choosing a threshold. You'll have the added problem of not being able to specify context information. Only pattern-matching IDSs enable you to form complex constraints with context information such as the following:

```
if the same user runs one of these three commands (link, create, mkdir)
and the user is in /tmp or in a descendent of /tmp, nuke 'em
```

### Other Denial-of-Service Attacks

If a local user wants to launch a network DoS attack remotely against your system, nothing exists to prevent this from happening. Someone can run through all of the users and purposely fail login attempts until everyone is locked out. However, if the user is already logged into your system and tries to run attacks against other systems, it is easy to detect and assign accountability for this behavior from the audit logs. You simply can look for audit records that contain the name of the program that a user is running. Most records also contain the data that the user specified as well. Many IDSs allow you to configure tagged file lists containing the names of known rogue programs. You could create a tagged file list with names of DoS programs to help watch for times when your users are carrying out these kinds of attacks against other systems.

### Tricking Other Users

A hacker prefers to gain additional access to resources on the system rather than launch DoS attacks. To get beyond the system's defined ACLs, a local user needs to trick another user into either granting this access or into operating on behalf of that user. Obviously, if you can determine someone else's password, you can impersonate them. Another approach is to trick the victim into doing something without knowing the operation is happening. The old PATH hack against inexperienced administrators is the favorite example of the latter technique. In either case, you can use this attack to gain read or write access to a resource for which you do not normally have privilege. In the end, as the "Introduction" described, all activities on a system can be reduced to read and write operations for an object.

Onc of thc oldcst tricks is to ask an unwary user to run a Trojan Horse that you have set up. The classic example is to tell the administrator that you cannot see a file that should be in your directory. To set up the attack, you create a program in your directory that has the same file name as a system utility such as ls.

```
cat >> ls
** hack code goes here, such as copying /bin/sh into one of your
    subdirectories **
/bin/ls $*
exit 0

/bin/chmod +x ls
```

Next you set your PATH environment variable so that your trick directory (perhaps your home directory) is the first directory in the search path:

```
export PATH=.:$PATH
```

You then call your friendly administrator to your desk for help. If you're smart, you will have carried out some social engineering to build up trust so that this person trusts you. The novice administrator would type the following:

```
su root
```

This command logs him in as the superuser; he then lists the files in your directory using your ls command and proceeds to show you the file in the directory listing. If the preceding script is run, you can write the hack code to create a SUID root shell in the directory of your choice.

Of course, the administrator should have typed the following:

```
su - root
```

This command loads the login profile of the root user and resets the environment. This hack is so well known that it's unlikely an administrator today would fall for it but this depends on how much training the person has received. Someone who has just been appointed lab moderator and given superuser privileges may be a total security novice and could fall victim to this attack. Even if you have trained administrators, you want to watch for this type of behavior.

To detect the path attack, you look for evidence of someone creating a Trojan Horse. In this specific case, the Trojan Horse is any well-known system command: ls, rm, who, or cat. Hopefully, the IDS you purchased already will have the list of potential Trojan Horse filenames or directory names in a configurable list that you can augment. Otherwise, you would need to compile a rather long list yourself. The monitoring program would look for the file name in the list of system directories, and if the same file name is found in one of these directories, someone is planting a Trojan Horse. In the audit trail, you will look for several events. First, you need to detect that the Trojan Horse was created by looking for audit records with the following:

◆ AUID, RUID != 0 (not the root user)
◆ FILE_Create or FILE_Rename
◆ Filename appears in one of the protected system or application directories specified in the configurable list

You need to consider rename operations because someone can create the file *foo* and then rename it to avoid detection by a monitor that looks for only file creations. Also, this particular monitor is looking for more than a normal login user trying to do this from a shell. Many SUID and SGID programs create files. If you want to consider whether someone is making the Trojan Horse via indirection, by using a SUID or SGID program, you want to look at the AUID and RUID because these do not change as a result of running SUID or SGID programs. For the moment, this audit event is labeled E1.

Next, you want to look for the event that turns this file into an executable. In AIX this would be a FILE_Mode event. For this example, the audit event for this activity will be labeled E2. The sequence of interest is E1, followed by any number of other events, followed by E2. E1 alone is probably not sufficient to warrant an alarm because the file is not really a threat until its executable bit is set. Because the sequence of events, E1 and E2, are important, you can now see the need for tracking the sequence of activity with some type of graph or state transition model. In order to avoid false positives, an alarm should be signaled if E1 and E2 have the same data values in some of their fields:

◆ Same subject (AUID and RUID)
◆ Same filename

This means that the IDS not only needs to track sequences of events, but it also must be capable of matching related data across events. This capability is a fundamental requirement implemented by pattern-matching IDSs.

When you must have the same value in fields across events and when values can vary are two conditions that greatly complicate the process of attack signature development. The core problem in signature development is to make the signature flexible enough to catch a number of problems, yet not so broad that it generates false alarms.

In the preceding example, the system should not generate an alarm if someone sets the executable bit for a *different* file from the one that was created in the first event. Also, if two different users appear in the audit records, this does not constitute an attack (at least not this attack). If two different users did appear in the audit records, you would have an attack in which two users participated—one created the file, and the other set the executable bit. Notice that these two events can be separated by any number of intervening events, so the scope problem still exists. The attacker could first create the file and then run chmod on a subsequent day, particularly if this person knew that the system was being monitored.

To simplify your task, you could just look for *either* of two separate events and request to be notified when either of these occurs:

◆ When someone sets the executable bit for a file whose name matches a system file from a configurable list of directories
◆ When someone creates or renames a file whose name matches a system file from a configurable list of directories

Using the audit trail is again advantageous here. The file chmod event in the audit log gives enough information about the parameters to the command so that you can detect that someone did indeed set the executable bit on the file.

The other part of the attack is based on getting another user, hopefully root, to run your Trojan Horse. The event you want to detect is when a privileged user runs a program whose file name matches one of the system's routines, such as *ls*. As before, an attack signature can be constructed to look for specific filenames, or it could be designed to look for the filename in a set of directories. The pattern would need to consider the following:

### The Scope Problem and Memory Requirements

A pattern-matching IDS starts with minimal data structures initialized. When an event occurs that is the first state for some patterns, data structures are allocated in memory to represent the graph for the pattern. As more events arrive, additional patterns might be set up in memory, and existing graphs may add new data structures to track the context of the events.

You can see how the scope problem affects the memory requirements of an IDS. If the scope for monitoring events begins when the system was first booted and continues until the current time, a number of partially completed graphs will be stored in memory. The total storage requirements for an IDS with a broad scope such as this would be extensive. One design dilemma that IDS vendors face is deciding when to perform garbage collection and remove *stale* or old patterns from memory. The danger is that a cracker might perform one part of an attack; the system garbage collects the pattern from memory; and then the second half of the attack is executed. The entire attack would go undetected, although a partial attack could be reported depending on how the IDS handles garbage collection.

If the scope is defined as too long of an interval, the storage requirements are too high. Should the designers choose a smaller interval, such as a single login session, attacks across login systems would be missed when they involve sequences of events. Most IDSs today rely on the a login session or a single day as the interval to use for the scope. Letting IDS customers configure the scope interval is more desirable because it enables customers to trade off storage for detectability.

---

- ◆ AUID, RUID = 0 (the root user)
- ◆ Fork or exec event
- ◆ Program name matches a program name from a reserved set of system paths

If you really are paranoid, you might prefer to be notified any time a privileged user runs a program that is not from a limited set of directories. With most commercial IDS tools, specifying a query such as this one is possible.

These simple examples have shown how you can use the audit trail to detect when local users abuse their right to use the computer and try to trick other users into doing something that grants additional privileges. Luckily, users are growing more cautious and watch for such attacks. Still, other possibilities for misuse exist when people are careless with permissions. The following are some examples.

## Writing into Another User's Special Files

Depending on the version of UNIX you are using, the system will run a login script for you during the login process just before you are given control of a shell. If this script file is world writable, other users can insert commands that run automatically when you log in. This attack is another way to trick you into running commands without knowing your password. An attack such as this is detectable in the audit trail by looking for the following:

- ◆ AUID = user-X
- ◆ File write or create event
- ◆ Object of the operation is owned by another user (not user-X)

Why not look at the EUID of the process that emits the file operation event? If the hacker manages to exploit a SUID or SGID program to change the user's files, the EUID or EGID will be set to the owner of the SUID or SGID program, not the hacker's UID. To really know the subject of the operation, you need to look at the AUID. This value is the only one that persists despite changes in the EUID or RUID.

Similar attacks can be detected by looking for other operations, such as a user reading from the directory of another user. However, watching for this type of activity may not be reasonable on your systems. If your users have a fairly open environment and constantly share data from their respective directories, you do not want to be bothered by alerts each time this happens. Looking for evidence of tampering in the special files should be enough in these cases. Should you require a tighter environment in which users should not be nosing around in directories belonging to others, you can look for events such as the following:

- ◆ AUID = user-X
- ◆ ls, fork, exec events
- ◆ Object (program executed or directory read) not owned by user-X

## Explicit Privilege Escalation

The favorite attack for a cracker is to look for SUID root programs with exploitable bugs. SUID and SGID programs owned by other users are also important. For example, if a user can crack some SGID mail program, then that person will be able to operate with the group privileges of the *mail* account. A hacker strives for three goals with SUID root programs:

- Get the program to divulge information that is readable only by the superuser
- Get the program to write to a privileged resource
- Get the program to run an arbitrary command

Depending on the internals of the SUID program being exploited, one or more of these goals could be met. If the program is interactive and run from the user's shell, the usual goal is to have it run /bin/sh; thus giving the hacker a root shell with complete control of the system. The other two goals are equally worthy of concern.

### Writing to a Privileged Resource

A number of publicized attacks against SUID root programs take advantage of a race condition that demonstrates abuse of write privileges. If the SUID program creates a world-writable file in /tmp, for example, you can replace the file with a symbolic link to a world-readable resource such as /etc/passwd. This trick can cause the SUID program to write into a resource that it had no intention of altering. The X Windows server on some systems will create temporary world-writable files in the /tmp directory. Even the sticky bit will not prevent someone from creating a link from this file to another. The sticky bit set by default on /tmp prevents someone from deleting the file.

The creation of world-writable files by privileged programs is an example of poor programming assumptions. Like the PATH problem mentioned before, the programmer made incorrect assumptions about the environment. If the SUID root program inherits its environment from the user's shell, it should not make any assumptions about PATH, UMASK, or any other environment variable. To avoid these problems, monitor your system for creation of a world-writable file by any user.

### Reading a Privileged Resource

If the SUID program consists of only read operations, the goal is to trick the program into reading another privileged file that it had no intention of accessing. For example, if you can somehow trick the program into divulging the contents of the shadow password file, you can copy this output and run *crack* against it later. Access to other privileged files can reveal credit card numbers, account balances, or other secret information that you can use for destructive purposes, such as blackmail. Low-level access to disk drives is sufficient for reading *any* of the disk's contents because the read operations bypass the file-system permissions altogether. Treat read threats with respect.

The trick to detecting when a privileged resource has been compromised is to look for audit events on these resources when the AUID is someone other than the resource's owner or root. If a normal user's AUID appears in the read of a privileged resource, you *could* have problems. Unfortunately, you cannot merely search for any occurrence of a nonroot AUID in an operation on a privileged resource. When you change your password, the passwd program is SUID root, and the event in the audit trail shows a change to the shadow password file with your AUID. You also will need to consider the program name that appears in the event. If you recall, SeOS enables you to define which program paths can be used to access particular system resources. Although not part of commercial IDSs today, this expressibility in a signature would be useful.

### Running a Command

If the program does not read any user input into buffers, the chances of executing a buffer overflow attack against it are slim. The only way to possibly sneak in a buffer overflow attack is to somehow modify the name or contents of a resource that the privileged program is accessing in the hopes that a boundary problem will be found. This attack is unlikely because many of the resources are privileged in the first place, and if the hacker could access them, another fruitful hole must exist elsewhere.

The attack that has been in vogue for quite a while is the buffer overflow attack. This is not surprising because so many privileged programs seem to be vulnerable. In principle, the buffer overflow attack is easy to detect. A SUID root program does something it should not be doing, such as forking or exec of a shell. In practice this pattern is difficult to express in general enough terms to catch *all* attacks. Privilege escalations occur many times during the day on a system, and in each event record, the user's AUID and RUID remain the same, but the EUID changes to that of the privileged user. Some individual patterns that work are as follows:

- ◆ Detect when a program is run that shows a privilege escalation (EUID becomes 0), and this program next forks or execs /bin/sh, /bin/csh, /bin/tsh, /bin/ksh, or some other shell.
- ◆ Detect when a privilege escalation occurs, followed by the copying of a program, followed by setting the program's owner to be root, followed by setting the execute bit for the file, finally followed by setting the SUID bit for the program.

Detecting a large set of buffer overflow attacks requires knowing which SUID programs legitimately fork or exec other programs and then watching for all other cases. In other words, you need to know for every SUID and SGID program what the possible valid transitions are to other programs. Yikes! It's unlikely a single person anywhere is able to specify these details for an entire operating system.

Some cases are intuitively obvious. The passwd program should not spawn a shell. SUID or SGID programs that can create a subshell are dangerous anyway. (Sendmail has been attacked this way in the past.) For the time being, you can detect the most common buffer overflow scenarios by watching for the two sequences mentioned previously. By the way, no commercial tools today detect or prevent all buffer overflow attacks. It's a nontrivial problem to solve.

Another approach is to watch for single events, such as the following:

- When *anyone* sets the SUID or SGID bit for a program
- When AUID != 0 copies a file from one of the system directories (or tries to copy a file and fails)

Creating SUID or SGID programs is something that should not happen very often on your systems, and you probably want to know about it even if it is not an attack.

### Other System-Level Attacks to Monitor

You want to monitor several other events on your system, whether the result is successful or not:

- Attempts to write, link, or delete in the system directories by a non-privileged AUID
- Attempts to modify resources such as the system time, /dev/kmem, or /dev/mem
- Attempts to modify the audit subsystem configuration
- Attempts to stop the audit subsystem
- Attempts to run known rogue programs such as zap, crack, SATAN, COPS, and others
- Attempts to enable an adapter for promiscuous mode (for sniffing the network)
- Attempts to run exploratory programs (who, rwho, finger, ps, or find)
- Attempts by unprivileged users to run privileged programs such as mount, exportfs, mknod, and so on

A simple principle to follow when defining a monitoring policy is to watch for any attempts by users to access resources that they should not be referencing. Stalker, for example, will report failed access attempts for resources when the event's AUID and the resource owner ID are not identical.

## Exceptions for Recommended Patterns

When you configure your monitoring policy, one problem will be alerts generated with an RUID=0 from the root user. If the root user logs into a system and deletes files, the RUID is 0 in the audit records. When a program is a server process that listens for input from other programs and is started automatically by the system at boot time, the RUID also will be 0. If, by sending this server program a message, the hacker can trick it into writing to another user's files, the audit event will seem to have originated from the root user. *The only way to detect this type of attack is by tracing the path of activities through interprocess communication.* Today, no commercial IDSs drill down this far into the audit stream, tracking socket or message queue transfers between processes to assign accountability.

If you want to avoid receiving notifications when the root user deletes or writes to files owned by other users, you could miss some types of attacks. On the other hand, watching every action of the root user can generate quite a bit of data that is not indicative of attacks. Unfortunately, the tradeoff is yours to make.

## Pure and Simple Bugs

Often the hacker is lucky enough to have a crack handed to them. Buffer overflow attacks require some dedicated work to create, although after the details for a particular SUID program are known, a reusable hack spreads rapidly on the net. Once in a while an exploit is so simple that it is amazing that the problem could have been missed in code reviews. One such example is the *rlogin -froot* problem in AIX. Although rlogin is a remote-connection program, a local user can run the command. By typing the following a user could gain root access to the system:

```
rlogin remotehostname -froot
```

No special programming skills were needed. The user would be delivered into a root shell with complete control over the system.

Detecting this attack on a local system is easy. When a program is run out of a shell, a fork event is followed by an exec event in the audit log. The parameters used in the program are part of the audit record. Scanning specifically for the pattern "rlogin * -froot" where * matches any characters would detect the hack.

What you would have discovered is a local user trying to launch this attack from the current system, possibly directed right back to the same system.

If your system is the target of such an attack from a remote user on another system, knowing what to look for in the audit logs is important for detecting this attack. Because the audit records emitted are different for the server that catches the rlogin request, you cannot use the same pattern as you would to catch the attack when it is launched from your system.

## Why You're Not Finished Yet

You have now taken a close look at Stalker and CMDS—two well-known system level UNIX IDSs. Both tools provide audit reduction but differ in primary focus. CMDS provides some attack pattern analysis, but its strength lies in the statistical anomaly detection techniques for which it is well known. Stalker also provides some statistical threshold notifications but boasts a wide range of attack patterns for catching intruders.

You also have seen how local users can hack a system for denial-of-service attacks and how to look for these attacks in the audit logs. An IDS will be able to detect these attacks if they are launched from your system because audit records contain detailed information about programs and their parameters. The audit system also assigns accountability in most cases when local users are the initiators of activities.

By far the greatest risk is not from denial-of-service attacks but from successful attempts by users to gain privileges. Sometimes privilege escalation can occur by tricking a user into running a command on your behalf. Other times, you can gain privilege by guessing someone's password. The most frequently occurring hack announced on the Internet today is the buffer overflow attack against privileged programs. With a little digging, a cracker can gain access to a superuser shell via one of these attacks. Luckily, the most common cases surface in the audit logs with predictable patterns. Unfortunately, a general-purpose buffer overflow pattern is very difficult to build.

Although the audit logs provide a large amount of information about what's happening on the system, they do not record all of the network activities for a system. Many of the network attacks on systems are thus not seen by system-level monitoring tools like Stalker and CMDS. Therefore, to complete your IDS solution, you need to deploy network tools as well. Turn to the next chapter to see how network sniffers catch problems that system IDSs and scanners miss.

# Chapter 9

# Sniffing for Intruders

This chapter describes how you can catch intruders by watching the network traffic at your site. From the title, you probably thought you were going to learn how to really put your nose to the trail and smell for hackers. On the other hand, perhaps you envisioned that you might pick up a good bloodhound and track down perpetrators through the electronic jungle. Luckily, no vendor is pushing either of these sniffer approaches. The IDSs described in this chapter work by monitoring network traffic as it flows across subnets at your site.

The material in this chapter is broken into two main sections. First, you'll look at how network IDSs work and examine their pros and cons. Next, some popular network IDSs are described to give you a glimpse of what to expect from leading vendors in this field. Like many of the chapters so far, as you get near the end of this chapter, you will find yourself wondering whether the use of scanners, system IDSs, and network IDSs is finally enough to solve your intrusion detection problems. You probably can guess the outcome.

## How Network IDSs Work

What makes a network IDS different from other tools about which you've read? The next few sections describe the basic approach to network intrusion detection. After this, you'll see some example attacks that can be discovered by looking at network packets.

### Networks and Subnets

Networked environments usually are divided into multiple subnets for various reasons. By separating computers into physically distinct groups, a network administrator can regulate the flow of traffic into and out of subnets. Gateways and routers control the boundaries of subnets and decide how packets are delivered to each subnet. The primary advantage of subnetting is performance.

For example, if all of the accounting computers are on the sixth floor of a building, physically configuring a separate accounting subnet will limit accounting network traffic to that floor. If other floors do not need to see these packets, why bother routing the network traffic to them? The degenerate case in which all computers are on the same subnet is undesirable because all network traffic flows on the same network. Subnets usually are set up according to departmental organizations, physical buildings, or security boundaries. Therefore, another advantage of subnetting is security.

A router can be used to block the flow of packets from one network to another. The simplest type of packet filtering firewall *is* a router. Other uses of screening routers were identified in Chapter 4, "Traditional Network Security Approaches," such as blocking IP address impersonation attempts into your perimeter network.

Naturally, some packets will cross subnets as computers communicate with each other or try to reach computers outside the company's firewall boundary. Sometimes, a subnet is completely disjointed and communicates with no other subnets. Examples include test environments in many companies. Test coordinators prefer to limit the damage of programs that are not ready for the production environment by restricting the network test environment.

As you can see, in a typical enterprise network, many different subnets are self contained. Network packets may uniquely flow within a subnet and not cross into any other subnet. If you wanted to monitor network traffic in subnets for performance, each subnet would need a separate monitor to watch its unique packets. Why? Simply put, not all subnet traffic is available from a single point on the network. If you really want to watch what everyone on the network is doing —including both insiders and outsiders—then your monitors need to pick up all of the packets. If all of your computers are on a single network, a single monitor is enough. Logically, if you have a network divided into subnets, then you need a monitor on each subnet.

## Network IDSs Sniff Network Traffic

Network adapters can be configured to run in *promiscuous mode,* which allows the adapter to grab all of the packets that it sees on the network. The default behavior of a network adapter for a computer is to grab only those packets destined for that computer (sounds like a reasonable performance enhancing choice). In promiscuous mode, the adapter grabs all packets that it senses on the subnet and passes them up to the device driver. The captured packets are passed from the device driver up to the IDS for analysis.

NetRanger developed by the WheelGroup and now owned by Cisco, has a slightly different setup. In its original form, NetRanger works with routers provided by Network Systems Corporation. The router provides network traffic information to NetRanger software running on a designated computer. Communications between the computer and the router are cryptographically secured for privacy and integrity across a socket connection. One advantage of this architecture is that the monitoring node running NetRanger and the router do not need to be on the same network. The two components of the solution need to be reachable only via some type of network, such as via a private dial-up line. A standalone version of NetRanger that uses a computer with a promiscuous mode adapter is also available now. As you might expect, NetRanger also works quite well with Cisco routers, too.

To be effective at catching intruders, network IDSs need to be positioned properly in the network. In order to catch inbound packets for a subnet, the network IDS must be positioned as the first node after the router in the subnet. Alternatively, the IDS may be placed on a gateway between two subnets to watch for attacks across the subnets. A common placement for network IDSs is immediately after the firewall in an enterprise. Because all inbound and outbound traffic must pass through the firewall, the network IDS easily can reside directly after the firewall and as the first node inside the secure network as shown in Figure 9.1.

You should be sure to understand that *the network IDS does not intercept and hold packets* before forwarding them to the intended node. Because the IDS's network adapter is capturing packets in promiscuous mode, it is merely reading the packets as they appear, not grabbing them and holding them until they are analyzed. A network IDS should not interfere with the performance of your network.

Even though the network IDS does not alter your network performance, you should have some performance concerns about the IDS itself. Because it is potentially processing packets for a large number of nodes in your network, the IDS must scale well or else it will drop packets and miss attacks. Before you plop down large amounts of money for a large-scale network IDS solution, insist on performance testing to ensure that the solution meets your needs. You may be able to get around scalability problems by deploying multiple IDSs in a chain and configuring each one to look for a disjointed set of attacks.

### Other Network IDS Features

Like any other application that you run in a distributed environment, a network IDS needs to provide useful systems management capabilities. Features needed include the following:

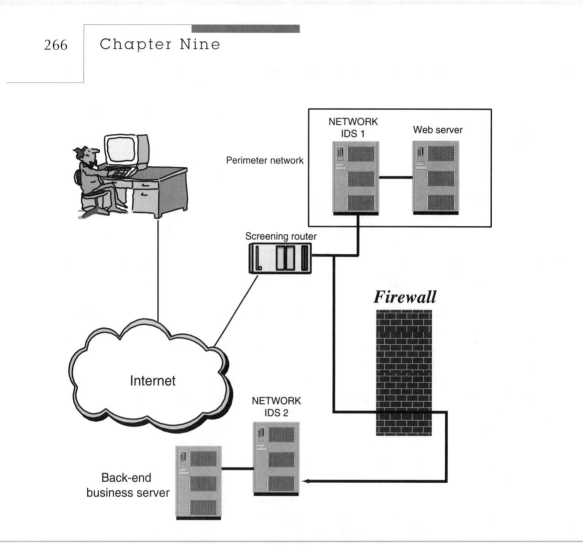

**Figure 9.1** A properly positioned IDS will see all of the inbound and outbound packets.

- ◆ Configuration of multiple network IDSs from a central console
- ◆ Centralized reporting from network IDSs to a central console
- ◆ Secure communications between distributed components
- ◆ Configurable sets of attack signatures to monitor
- ◆ Easy-to-read reports
- ◆ Real-time alerts and optional responses
- ◆ Integration with system management frameworks, such as Tivoli TME

Depending on your level of sophistication, you might also be interested in designing your own attack signatures. Not all network IDSs provide a simple way for you to create signatures.

## Network IDS Attack Recognition

What can a network IDS detect? First, because the source of information is network packets, network IDSs look for *attacks that are targeted at network protocols*. Examples include Ping of Death and SYN Flood because both of these are attacks against weaknesses in TCP/IP itself. Problems in other protocols, such as Novell IPX and Microsoft SMB, also are found.

Protocol problems result in other attacks such as the following:

- Sequence number guessing attempts
- IP address impersonation
- Session hijacking
- IP fragmentation
- Other well-known denial-of-service attacks (the "Pizza" attack mentioned earlier in the book)

Next, by analyzing packet data content (as opposed to header fields) a network IDS can look for attacks such as the AIX "rlogin -froot" bug. Other example *application attacks and vulnerabilities* detected by network IDSs are as follow:

- Various sendmail bugs (EXPN, VRFY, debug)
- phf, test.cgi, and other CGI bugs
- Buffer overflows in finger and DNS
- Various NFS, FTP, and TFTP bugs

Unlike scanners that occasionally probe your systems for these weaknesses, network IDSs look for evidence of someone mounting one of these attacks against your systems in real time. The evidence is found by inspecting the contents of packets.

Finally, scanning packet data for unauthorized strings such as "confidential", "proprietary", "secret", and other *potential leakages* is another feature found in some network IDSs. A list of keywords can be configured into the IDS. Naturally, performance concerns arise if the list is too long.

### Fragmented IP Packets

Breaking down packets into smaller chunks and reassembling them into the proper format is something that happens often in network communications. You saw how this happens between network layers on the same system, and between peer layers on different systems when you read Chapter 4, "Traditional Network Security Approaches."

A well-known attack called IP Fragmentation tries to inject or form bogus IP packets so that when they are reassembled at the target node, there is a chance for a successful hack. Various operating systems handle reassembly of fragmented packets differently. So, the attack will not always succeed.

Recall that sequence numbers are included in TCP/IP packets so that the receiving node can reassemble packets received out of order into the proper format. By messing around with sequence numbers in injected or forged packets, an attacker can trick the receiving system into overlaying already received data with something else. For example, if the target node received a packet with the sequence number for bytes 1–5 and data "smith." The hacker could send another packet with the same sequence number but data "root." Depending on how the receiving OS handles this condition, it will either overlay the first packet or discard the new (hacked) packet. The behavior of the OS determines whether the hack succeeds or not.

Chapter 7, "Vulnerability Scanners," described useful scanner tools that can be used to probe your systems for weaknesses. If a hacker is scanning your system with ISS or SATAN, a network IDS should be able to detect the activity. Of course, looking for patterns such as port scanning of TCP/IP ports is a process that also is affected by time. What if an attacker scans one port per day? Is this something that a network IDS can detect? Most network IDSs have a time-out setting that you can configure to determine the interval, which constitutes a group of related events such as sequential port scans. If you set this value too small, you could miss sequential port scans across days, for example.

## Advantages of Network IDSs

One of the main advantages of a network IDS is simple implementation. Unlike system-level intrusion detection, which requires a monitor to be running on every system, network IDSs require one monitor per subnet. Reduced cost is one consequence of this feature. Installing a single network IDS should be cheaper than installing client system level monitors on each node. In some cases, you might want to run a network IDS monitor on each of several nodes in your environment. Most network IDS architectures support this configuration today.

Now you could get really picky and claim that system-level IDSs could gather the data from each system and then forward it to a central analyzer. However, the real issue is that system-level monitoring requires you to *gather* information from each system by running some type of sensor or monitor on each system. A network IDS gathers information by actively monitoring network traffic without requiring a separate sensor on each system. Of course, network IDSs cannot detect some of the intrusions and misuses that system IDSs can, and vice versa. You'll see the limitations in the next section.

Another advantage of network IDSs is that the data which they gather comes essentially for free. Computers are emitting network traffic as part of the normal routine of communicating between each other. The network IDS needs only to attach to the network and sniff this information as it appears. A network IDS is noninvasive because it does not alter in any way the systems you want to monitor. None of the system calls in the kernel are modified or replaced on any systems in the network (with the possible exception of the network IDS node itself). Nor does a network IDS require you to introduce a new data source, such as audit logs or syslog. System-level IDSs, as noted in Chapter 6, "Detecting Intruders on Your System Is Fun and Easy," may require you to turn on auditing or syslog in order to capture activities on the system. If you already are running the audit subsystem to track system activities, this practice should not bother you. However, if auditing and syslog are not running on your systems today, a network IDS is appealing.

Perimeter security is what the network IDS is primarily designed to monitor. As more companies connect into cyberspace, increasing threats from intruders are inevitable. Network IDSs aim to simplify the task of monitoring network traffic for security violations and intrusions. Because the amount of network traffic generated by an enterprise can be tremendous, having a system that automatically looks for problems and responds to events is necessary. Note that this type of IDS is a logical extension of network performance monitoring with automated responses.

Many system-level IDSs do not have ample data to detect network intrusions or misuses. Neither the audit logs nor syslog give detailed information about network packets. To get at the content of the packets themselves, the IDS needs to do the following:

- Run as part of the OS and analyze every packet that arrives or leaves the node
- Run on a separate node that monitors network traffic for all nodes

The latter approach seems to be the most scalable today. Limitations of separate node network IDSs may force administrators to run a network IDS on each node in the future.

Network IDSs usually are equipped with some form of response or counter-measure feature. NetRanger can send commands to the router to block packets from a particular source IP address when attacks originate from that address. RealSecure and other stand-alone monitors can send *block address* commands to popular firewalls, too. One already mentioned danger of these countermeasures is that frequently the hacker is using forged addresses. You could end up blocking your biggest Web site customer if suddenly a hacker forges a SYN Flood attack from that customer's IP address.

## Limitations of Network Packet Sniffing

Although network IDSs are an essential weapon in the security officer's arsenal, it's important to understand their limitations. The following sections identify problems with network IDSs so that you can understand what to expect from them when in use at your site.

### Network Sniffers Do Not See All Packets

A network IDS works by running a network adapter in promiscuous mode to capture all of the packets coming into and going out of a particular subnet. *Notice that this is not the same as watching all of the network traffic that appears on a subnet.* Look at Figure 9.2. Here, the physical arrangement of the nodes is in a ring with node B sitting between node A and the node running the IDS. The packet "Hello B" is sent from node A to node B. However, because A and B are directly adjacent, B grabs and processes the packet sent by A. The node running the IDS never has a chance of seeing the packet.

This means that a network IDS is not designed to track all the network activities on a subnet. Instead, the IDS is positioned to look for inbound and outbound packets at the entry/exit of the subnet. Following terminology introduced earlier in the book, the network IDS catches intruders, but it does not always catch internal misuse. If the packet from A to B had been a misuse or internal hack, the IDS

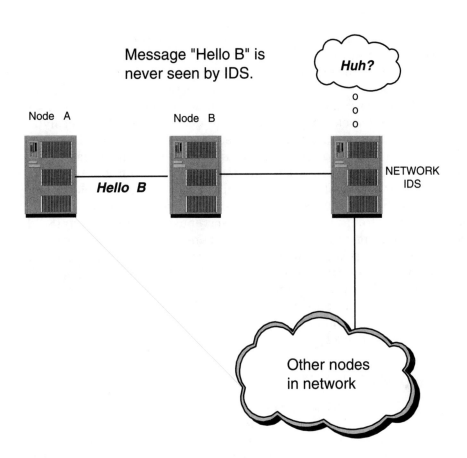

**Figure 9.2** An IDS does not see all packets on a subnet.

node would miss it. To catch attacks between nodes, an intelligent IDS sniffer would need to be run on each node.

### Network Sniffers Are Blinded by Encryption

Many sites rely on encryption for privacy of network traffic. In some cases, two corporate sites are connected by an IP tunnel. A firewall at each site implements the IP tunnel so that all traffic is encrypted as it passes across the unsecure Internet. After a firewall receives an encrypted packet from another site, the packet is decrypted and sent on to the target node in the secure network. A configuration like this *does not* hinder network intrusion detection. The packet appears in the clear as it leaves the firewall. Because the network IDS is the first node after the firewall (see Figure 9.1), the encryption does not impact the solution.

In some cases, though, an IP tunnel is established between two *arbitrary* nodes in a network. The nodes could be in the same subnet, or they could be communicating across the Internet. The IP traffic is not decrypted until the receiving node reads the packet from its network adapter. The network IDS has no way of seeing the cleartext version of the packets. Any attack signatures that require cleartext packets will not work when two nodes use an IP tunnel. Again, one possible solution to this problem is to run a sniffer on each node. Note that the sniffer must be in the OS network stack *after* the packets are decrypted.

When you connect from a browser to a Web server using *secure sockets* (SSL), the packets from your computer are not decrypted until they reach the Web server application itself. SSL packets flow through the firewall and remain encrypted. The packet arrives at the Web server node, moves up through the kernel stack, and is read by the Web server program from a socket. It is not until this last step, which only the Web server program itself controls, that the packet is decrypted. This type of application-level encryption also blinds network sniffers to many attacks such as the "phf" hack.

## Missed System-Level Attacks

As mentioned in Chapter 6, "Detecting Intruders on Your System Is Fun and Easy," system-level monitoring has access to important events such as privilege transition. A *new* attack that causes a buffer overflow and gives root privileges to a remote user will not be seen by a network IDS. If the attack signature is written properly, the system-level IDS will detect and respond to this type of situation.

Two general classes of attacks exist that a network IDS cannot detect, but a system-level IDS can. You can think of the first class as *unknown side effects*. When an activity on the system happens as the result of receiving a network packet, it's possible that a side effect will occur that violates your security policy. Examples include the following:

- ◆ Creation of a world-writable file by a privileged program as a result of processing a network packet

- ◆ Downgrading the security of an existing resource, such as making /etc/passwd world writable

- ◆ Upgrading the privilege of a user, such as changing the UID of a normal user to zero in /etc/passwd

◆ Creation of a back door, such as any program that can lead the user to a root shell

Unless the hacks that led to these breaches already are known in the security community, the network IDS will not see these events, but the system-level IDS will. If you have a scanner, some of these problems will be caught the next time it runs. In some sense this argument seems unfair because it merely states that if the attack is not known in the community, the network IDS vendor cannot build a signature to catch the attack. However, even if the initiation sequence for the attack is unknown, a system-level IDS *can detect* that a SUID root program was created. What this says to you is that you need both types of IDSs—system and network—to catch all of the attacks you face.

The other class of system-level problems that a network IDS misses *are attacks that are not based on sending or receiving network packets.* Examples include any hacks launched by directly attached terminals or TTYs. If you are connected to the computer system with a terminal, you can start a nasty brute force password guessing program, and no network sniffer will be able to detect it. Most midrange hardware vendors still sell a significant number of dumb terminals to customers. Naturally, these threats are posed mostly by insiders rather than intruders.

### The Network IDS Is Not the Destination Node

Recently, Ptacek and Newsham (1998) identified several weaknesses in intelligent network sniffers. Similar concerns about network IDSs were simultaneously identified by Paxson (1998). At the heart of the discussion is the fact that a network IDS cannot know for sure what is happening on the network nodes themselves. An inbound packet has a destination IP address for the intended recipient. The network IDS does not know for sure whether the destination node will accept a packet or discard it. To really know the behavior of the remote node, the network IDS must contain a good deal more knowledge than it does today.

For example, operating systems handle fragmented packets differently. Some OSs will discard a packet if it contains overlapping sequence numbers with previously received packets. Other OSs will accept the packet and process it; thereby overlaying existing data received earlier.

One example given by Ptacek and Newsham is the checksum on a packet. Most systems will discard a packet with a bad checksum, but some network IDSs do not currently check this as part of packet inspection. Now that the issues have been publicly indicated, you can expect future IDS releases to include this feature. Because the IDS is *not* the real recipient of the packet itself, the IDS cannot

## Getting around the Encryption Problem

The encryption issue is a particularly sticky one for network IDSs. It is highly likely that over time, you will see more encryption of application-level data. You need encryption for secure communications. There isn't much you can do to change the limitations on network IDSs when encryption hides the network packet content. IDS vendors do have a few alternatives, though.

Instead of spelling the demise of network IDSs, encryption argues for a repositioning of the technology. If a large number of applications rely on SSL, for example, the SSL libraries could be enhanced to invoke network IDS routines *after* the packets are decrypted. *The added advantage is that the IDS routines also would be running on every node that uses SSL, thus providing previously unavailable opportunities for misuse detection.*

A similar approach would be to embed the network IDS routines directly in the network stack of the operating systems. As data from a socket is read by the application, the IDS routines optionally could be called to look for attacks. A socket option that each application could set would provide granular control over when to invoke the IDS routines. A system-wide switch to enable the IDS for all socket reads is another configuration possibility. The IDS routines would be running on each node with the advantage for misuse detection again.

Repackaging network IDSs as a set of library APIs is another possibility. As applications read data from sockets, they optionally could call the IDS routines to check for problems. This is a slight variation on the socket option suggested above. One difference is that it would be easier for a vendor to market network IDS libraries than it would be to convince a number of OS providers to embed the code. Unfortunately, if the APIs are optional, it's difficult to encourage programmers to modify existing software to take advantage of the libraries. When the IDS routines are a default option in the network stack of the OS, the solution is more transparent and easier for application programmers to use.

know for sure how the destination node will really handle the packet. Many factors, such as memory limitations, determine whether a packet is dropped or processed by the intended receiver. The IDS cannot possibly know all of these variables for each node on the subnet it monitors.

This subtle point—not knowing for sure how the destination node will respond—can lead to some interesting attacks. In an *insertion* attack, an adversary will inject a packet that the IDS will accept but which the destination node will reject or drop. The IDS and the destination node are thus *in different states* because they are processing different data. A few clever hacks show how to sneak a phf (or similar) attack past current network IDSs even though they will be executed successfully on the destination machine. As a teaser to completely read the referenced papers, think about how you could send a string such as "ppppphh-hhhhhffffffff?rrrrmmmm *". You could send individual one-byte packets formed in a such a way that the destination node would drop all packets except those that combine into "phf?rm*".

You also can inject SYN packets that can trick the IDS into resetting its state, even though the target node ignores the packet. When the IDS resets its state, pattern matching that was in progress is restarted; thus, losing any attacks in progress for that TCP session.

In an *evasion* attack the destination node accepts a packet that is ignored by the IDS. For example, the attacker could send extra packets with the same sequence number as a previous packet but with different data. The IDS might drop the packet because the sequence number was already used. The destination node (depending on the OS) would accept and process the packet, replacing a previous substring with one that turns the entire message into a hack. Many other evasion attacks are possible because of protocol problems with IP, TCP, or UDP.

Another problem to watch for is denial-of-service launched against the IDS itself. While sniffing network traffic, the IDS maintains a queue for incoming packets. The amount of memory that is allocated for these queues often can be configured, but it is eventually bounded by some constraint—whether physical memory or virtual memory. If a hacker knows what the IDS is looking for, it's not difficult to inject a number of packets that must be processed. The IDS can run out of resources.

Recall that network IDSs operate in passive mode and sniff the network. They do not block packets, which is one thing that firewalls do for you. When a firewall fails, it (generally) does not let any packets through, and thus your security policy is not violated. If a network IDS fails due to resource exhaustion, your policy can be violated because the IDS does not block packets; it works by alerting you when there is a problem.

In this section, you've seen a number of problems with network IDSs. Don't let this discussion give you the impression that these IDSs are weak products. No security tool is perfect. Network IDSs are critical for improving security at your site. These IDSs also are very useful for catching a number of attacks against your network. Vendors have been responsive to concerns such as those mentioned previously and have speedily added fixes in new releases.

## Which Product Has the Best Nose?

An *Infoworld* test reported in the May 4, 1998 issue rated products as follows:

1. IBM's outsourced solution using NetRanger
2. ISS Real Secure
3. Network Flight Recorder (NFR)
4. Abirnet Session Wall

The study by the *Infoworld* team announced a suite of 16 well-known network attacks that they tried against the products. Only NFR caught all of the attacks. The team used the scripting language, with help from Anzen, to build tests that do the following:

- ◆ Probed for information, tried to gain access
- ◆ Launched denial-of-service attacks
- ◆ Attempted to overburden the IDS with a combination of the preceding

The chosen IDS were challenged with attacks such as the following:

- ◆ Ping of Death
- ◆ SATAN scanning
- ◆ ISS SAFESuite scanning
- ◆ Port scanning
- ◆ ftp cwd ~root
- ◆ phf
- ◆ SYN Flood

In all, 23 attacks were attempted individually, with two combinations of attacks completing the full suite of 25. (Some of the 16 attacks have more than one variation that is how one arrives at 23 individual attacks.)

A three-way tie for first place exists between IBM/NetRanger, RealSecure, and NFR. Abirnet fell into last place for three main reasons—it lacks systems management; it does not have specific IDS reports; and it failed to detect 7 out of 25 attacks. The reviewers nonetheless liked many of SessionWall's features. The next few sections focus on the three IDSs that tied for first place.

## IBM and NetRanger

As noted previously, NetRanger is a passive network monitor that is offered with an NSC router or as a stand-alone product on a UNIX box. Hierarchical secure remote reporting between sensor stations and a console is one of the key features of NetRanger. The WheelGroup also reports that NetRanger is more scalable than any other network IDS. NetRanger also can detect session hijacking—something that other network IDSs do not claim.

NetRanger not only detects events but also responds to them as well. Shunning IP addresses for an interval of time is one of the operations that NetRanger can send to the NSC router if you are running that combination. As you might expect, a wide range of response options are available including pager notification, e-mail, and pop-up alerts. Logging and reporting are standard features.

NetRanger allows scanning for administrator-defined strings in network packets—a feature that other network IDSs must soon provide. However, it is not a trivial task to add your own attack signatures to those already supported by NetRanger. This shortcoming is shared by many IDSs.

IBM's Emergence Response Center offers a fee-based service with NetRanger. Instead of staffing your own team of security experts, you can use IBM's strength in this area. A network operations center is staffed $7 \times 24$, and a specific expert is assigned to your account. When an event is detected, IBM's security experts notify you and help you respond to the event. Up-front planning and response policy design also are available. As hackers become more sophisticated, outsourcing your network intrusion detection seems attractive because you may not be able to staff and maintain your own center of competency.

One final note about NetRanger is worth mentioning. Some of the founders and technical leads for the WheelGroup have worked at the Air Force Warfare Information Center and at the NSA. With contacts like that, it's not surprising that a number of government sites depend on NetRanger for network intrusion detection. You know NetRanger has been tested substantially in the field.

## RealSecure

ISS is already the market leader in scanning tools with SAFESuite. RealSecure is a widely used network IDS that complements ISS's other offerings. Like NetRanger, RealSecure supports remote sensing stations, called *engines*, that

**Figure 9.3**    RealSecure's initial management panel.

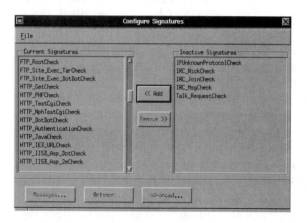

**Figure 9.4**    RealSecure attack signature configuration.

report to a central console. Naturally, communication between engines and the console are cryptographically protected using a shared pass phrase. Figure 9.3 shows the initial panel for RealSecure.

Monitoring and response options can be customized for each engine. Recall from the previous discussions that your site should have one monitoring engine per subnet (possibly more for performance gains). In Figure 9.4, you see some of the attack signatures that can be configured by node in RealSecure. As before, a comprehensive list of attacks detected is best obtained from ISS because the product is updated regularly.

RealSecure also supports a playback mode, which can be used to dig through the network traffic looking for problems. In playback mode, the product does not run attack signature recognition on the playback traffic. This feature probably will be fixed in the near future. Once activated, the console begins receiving data from the remote engines. You can choose from a number of different views on the console including by node or by event severity (high, medium, or low). Data from the engines is logged, and a variety of reports are possible.

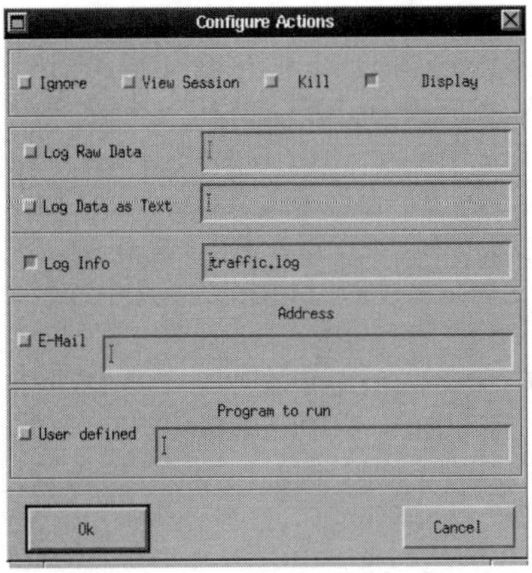

**Figure 9.5** RealSecure response configuration.

A number of different response options are available, including killing the offending network connection by sending a RST packet. Figure 9.5 gives a snapshot of how one might configure response options in RealSecure. *Templates* that declare signatures to use and how to respond to events can be applied to different engine nodes. Notifying an administrator is supported as a response along with the more aggressive socket kill option.

RealSecure runs on UNIX and NT platforms. The engines and console can run on different OS platforms, too. Regardless of the platform on which the engine is running, it can detect specific attacks against TCP/IP, NT, NETBIOS, and UNIX. For example, even if the engine is running on an NT workstation, it can detect someone trying to exploit the old AIX "rlogin -froot" bug.

ISS also relies on its X-Force team of security experts to find new attacks and create (or adjust) signatures. Discoveries can come from the X-Force's own research or from contacts that it has with the underground. ISS is well known for its NT expertise, with Microsoft often working closely with X-Force team members.

## Network Flight Recorder

The interesting feature of NFR is that it is not designed to be an IDS. Instead, NFR is a general-purpose network monitoring tool. NFR just happens to include a general-purpose scripting language that can be used to build attack signature recognition routines. Note that Checkpoint adheres to this philosophy in the firewall market by offering its INSPECT language for similar reasons. The argument, and it is a reasonable one, is that passing packets through arbitrary programs provides great flexibility in enforcing a security policy.

As a security officer, knowing that you have complete control over the attack signatures is a compelling thought. However, you must be cautious because you could make a mistake in programming. Relying on consulting services to obtain signatures for well-known attacks, and developing custom signatures for your proprietary applications is a good tradeoff. Although the general-purpose scripting language in NFR is it's most appealing feature, you probably can expect network IDS vendors to offer similar functionality soon. When NetRanger and RealSecure enables you to easily add your own signatures or adapt the ones delivered with the tools, the appeal of NFR will be challenged.

Earlier versions of NFR did not have the same level of distributed systems management provided with NetRanger and RealSecure. This level probably is supported in the version on the market today. Paging is a standard notification mechanism supported, and the summary reports are exceptional. If you invest in NFR, you'll also be able to use expertise to watch your network behavior in other ways, such as monitoring performance.

## Will Intrusion Detection Be Enough?

It would be wonderful if this chapter could close by claiming victory in the war on intruders. You know by now that perfect security is impossible. You've had a chance to see how scanners, system-level tools, and network IDSs are able to catch some hacks but miss others. Your job is to know the types of IDS tools that are available, know what they *can* do, and know what they *cannot* do in order to properly rely on them for improving your security. The bad news is that no single type of IDS today will be sufficient by itself. The good news is that you can buy several tools that *do* give you ample coverage against attacks. Today, not all of the tools will come from the same vendor, nor is it likely that they will interoperate. This situation is changing, though.

Vendors who build each type of tool make design tradeoffs when building a scanner, system, or network IDS. In the recent past, a vendor might focus on one or two of these tools types but not offer solutions covering all three categories. Alliances, acquisitions, and new product offerings by IDS vendors are becoming more inclusive. In 1998, you should see some significant improvements in this area. The final chapter of the book offers some suggestions for what you can do today, and what you can expect from IDSs in the future.

Another issue you will need to contend with is increasingly sophisticated hackers. IDS vendors try to keep abreast of new hacks and modify their tools to detect these. However, a lag always exists between a clever new way to break into a system and the products that try to find hackers.

Much of the material on intrusion detection so far has focused on UNIX systems and TCP/IP. This focus was used to keep the discussions simple. Including NT and UNIX comparisons in each section would have been too confusing. Now that you're an expert on IDSs and understand how they apply in UNIX environments, you are ready for the next chapter, which examines intrusion detection for NT.

# Chapter 10

# Intrusion Detection for NT

In this chapter, you will read about NT vulnerabilities and attacks. Each of the types of IDSs defined—vulnerability assessment scanners, system level, and network sniffers—are available for NT as well as for UNIX. Some products, such as eNTrax from Centrax are designed exclusively for NT. Before learning about the products, it is important to review some of the underlying concepts that an IDS must handle.

## NT Security Review

In Chapter 2, "The Role of Identification and Authentication in Your Environment," you had a chance to dig into the I&A process in NT. Chapter 3, "The Role of Access Control in Your Environment," described how everything in the system is treated as an object, and that all object access requests go through a single reference monitor—the *Security Reference Monitor* (SRM). Subjects in NT are processes and threads. Each process and thread is associated with an *access token* that is a complex data structure defining characteristics of the subject. One of the most important attribute lists in the access token is its *privileges*. Any time a process or thread is able to increase its privileges, that subject is able to access other resources that might normally be off limits.

Access control lists are associated with objects. Two different ACLs—object ACLs and system ACLs—were discussed in Chapter 3 as well. Object ACLs control access requests by subjects. System ACLs control activities, such as auditing for that object. Depending on the type of object, the ACL entries vary. For example, *access control entries* (ACE) for files are different than they are for registry keys.

Based on this simple review, you probably see some of the important events to monitor on NT systems. Any time a change is made to a user's privilege list in the user database you want to be notified. Changes to ACLs for important system files and directories also are potential preludes to an attack. As in UNIX systems, you should watch for attempts to install Trojan Horses. Especially serious is any attempt—successful or not—to increase the privileges associated with a thread or process.

## Sources of Data for NT IDSs

By now, it should be apparent to you that intrusion detection is a special case of monitoring. Performance monitoring tools track network traffic, system resource utilization, and application behavior. IDSs also need data from various sources to operate effectively.

In Chapter 7, "Vulnerability Scanners," you learned that vulnerability scanners that assess the state of your machines operate in one of two modes. Remote assessments are carried out from a central console and targeted at individual nodes in your network. With a remote scan, no special software is needed on the target machines. Local assessments are undertaken by software specifically installed on the node. When a scan is activated by a remote manager station or by a scheduled job, the local scanning software runs on the target node itself.

NT local vulnerability assessment tools operate much the same way as UNIX scanners. They look at configuration information on the system, inspect the contents of files, scour through registry entries, and attempt to crack passwords in the SAM. Other features, such as file-integrity checkers, are supported as well. Recall that a local scanner has the advantage of operating on the system as a login user. This means that the local scanner can read files and access other resources that a remote scanner cannot. Of course, you must install the local scanning code on each target.

Remote scanners against NT systems probe for known network configuration problems, check for back-level programs with holes, and attempt to gain access to the system by breaking in as normal users or as the administrator. The source of data for these IDSs is primarily feedback that comes from interacting with NT network services or applications, such as the *Internet Information Server* (IIS). Remote scanners benefit from the fact that they do not run client code directly on the target. For this reason, vendors can combine both NT and UNIX probing into the same product.  As in the case of UNIX remote scanners, it is possible to peer into some of the internals of an NT system even though you are not running a process on that system. For example, if the trust relationship is configured to permit remote access, some NT registry entries can be inspected. Microsoft's Server Message Block protocol also divulges information to remote scanners, including the list of currently logged in users.

Network sniffers for UNIX and NT often are combined into one product, too. The source of data is the same for UNIX and NT network sniffers. Only the attacks monitored varies between the two operating system types. Many attacks are equally applicable to the IP stacks on both, such as SYN Flood.

System-level IDSs in UNIX and NT rely on different datastreams. NT provides an event log (or audit log) that tracks many important activities on the system. Vendors, who write system-level IDSs for NT, such as Centrax and Kane, depend on the event log for the data that drives their engines.

## NT Event Log

There are really three different event logs in NT—system, application, and security. The security log is the one IDS vendors are most interested in watching. Records are stored in a log file as events occur. NT Administrators can control the behavior of the logging subsystem in a number of ways. Space is controlled by defining a limit on the size of the log file. When the threshold is hit, options include the following:

- Overwriting events that are only *N* days old
- Pushing out the oldest records as new ones come in
- Halting the system to prevent loss of an audit trail

To configure auditing, you first decide which event categories you want to monitor:

- Logins and logouts
- File and object accesses
- Changes in user rights
- Processes or thread events, such as creation and termination
- Changes to the security policy for the system, such as giving additional privileges to a user
- Restart, shutdown, and other system events

When you know which categories of events to monitor, you must enable auditing for individual users and objects. Auditing is turned on for a user through the user and group manager application. To enable auditing for an object, such as a file or directory, you use the File Manager. For a file, you can select whether to monitor success or failures for the following access types:

- Reads
- Writes

- ◆ Executes
- ◆ Deletes
- ◆ Permission changes
- ◆ Ownership changes

A final choice for directory objects is whether to audit only the current directory or to enable auditing for all of its subdirectories. This simplifies the administrators task when auditing is being configured. Caution is necessary, though. If you turn auditing on for the NT system directories and subdirectories, your event-logging activities will slow down the computer. Because all major executables are in these directories, this is unfortunate. Watching for Trojan Horses in system directories is reasonable goal for an IDS. Your only alternative is to be more granular in configuring auditing. For example, you could monitor everything *except* for read and execute events. This should catch most Trojan Horse attempts. However, if there is a file that only administrators should access, you might want to monitor *any* activity against that file. Be selective, or you quickly will notice sluggishness in your system's performance.

When you enable auditing for an object, the appropriate bits are set in that object's SACL. This activity itself generates an event that shows up in the log. Therefore, if you have turned auditing on for an object, and later you see an event that turns auditing off for that object, something unpleasant might be going on in your system.

Although not all NT IDS vendors choose to do so, a program can attach to the security event log and monitor events in real time. Today, Kane's Security Monitor and Centrax's eNTrax tools both periodically read the event log rather than process events in real time. An option to read the logs on an interval basis *or* to capture events in real time probably will be seen in future versions.

Not all events in the NT log contain sufficient data for IDSs to work. For example, remote logins do not identify the originating IP address or node name *in the event record*. An IDS vendor needs to gather this information from elsewhere in the system and correlate the information with the appropriate events—no trivial task. If the IDS is loaded as a service when the system boots, then process trees for login users can be constructed by monitoring the event log. Process and thread identifiers are associated with kernel data structures for sockets, pipes, and other communications data. Therefore, coalescing this information is possible and the IDS can use it to disconnect a remote user, who is hacking the system.

There also have been cases in which events that an IDS depended upon were no longer emitted after service packs were installed. Ripple effects of bug fixes are the leading suspects for this problem. You undoubtedly have been hit by this same type of problem when vendors of other products choose to deprecate an interface that you were relying upon for an in-house application.

## Event Records

Information provided in the NT event log record includes *header fields* followed by an event specific *description*. Header fields are listed in Table 10.1. Table 10.2 shows the fields usually found in an event description.

Not all fields are always filled in for the record. For example, if a user's privileges are modified, in the Privileges field of the event record, you will find information describing what changed. Any time you see that someone has gained an administrator privilege, it's time to investigate and determine whether the change was legitimate. Object accesses are reported in the Accesses field of the description. Both fields can contain multiple lines of information when inspected through the Event Viewer on NT or through your IDSs browser.

**Table 10.1**  Header Fields for an Event Record

| |
| --- |
| date |
| time |
| event ID |
| source of the record (security, application, system) |
| type of event |
| category (object access, system event, user event, and so on) |
| computer node name |
| user name |

**Table 10.2**  Event Description Fields

| | |
| --- | --- |
| object server name | primary domain |
| object type (file or user, for example) | client user name |
| object name | client domain |
| a handle ID | client login ID |
| operation ID | information about any object accesses |
| process ID | information about any privileges changed |
| primary User Name | |

Luckily, if you have an IDS for NT, you do not need to sit and watch events as they appear in the event log. Instead the IDS will summarize the information and display alerts when necessary. If you have the option of deciding which attacks to watch for, or if your IDS will notify you about select individual events, then you might want to think about what you should monitor to catch NT attacks. The next few sections give recommendations and describe well-known attacks against NT. The topics covered are not meant to be exhaustive. New NT hacks are posted regularly. See the NTbugtraq archives maintained by Russ Cooper at www.ntbugtraq.com. He also moderates the NTbugtraq mailing list.

## What to Monitor on NT

How do you know what to monitor on an NT system? First, you definitely want to watch for any well-known hacks. Most NT IDSs do this today. The next kind of event you want to know about is anything that might affect the security of your system. No doubt that sounds a bit broad. Unfortunately, this description is vague and does encompass a number of events. Here are some examples:

- A new user is added to your system.
- The administrator logs in or logs out.
- The administrator establishes a trust relationship.
- Someone deletes a critical system file.
- Someone changes another user's profile.
- Someone takes ownership of another user's file.

These types of activities are all single *events* that can affect the security of your system. Even a single login event is something you might want to monitor. How much to monitor depends on how tight your security must be. System monitors, such as KSM and eNTrax, have a predefined set of events or signatures they detect. If you don't know which of these events to capture, select all of them until you have a better idea of what's important. Two very important event categories to keep an eye on in NT are privilege changes and impersonation. Both are ways one can gain additional privileges.

### Increased Privileges

When a user is created on the system, a set of default privileges is granted. Privileges allow a user to perform operations such as shutting down the system, adding other users, acting as part of the operating system, creating processes, logging in remotely, and backing up files belonging to others. DAC and privileges together limit what an individual user can do on the system.

A privilege vector is stored with the user definition in the system. Privileges associated with a group also are stored with the group information in the SAM. When a user logs in, the privilege vector is constructed from privileges assigned to that user and privileges defined for groups to which the user belongs. The complete set of privileges controls what kinds of operations that user is allowed to initiate while logged in to the computer. A privilege that enables a user to act as an administrator is something to be carefully monitored. The GetAdmin hack introduced earlier in the book grants administrator rights to an arbitrary user by exploiting an NT bug. The event log contains enough evidence to spot when this happens. To distinguish the GetAdmin hack from a legitimate change in privileges, the IDS must contain a signature relating multiple events. Nonetheless, the event log *does* allow an IDS to detect GetAdmin.

NT administration somewhat simplifies the task of assigning privileges to user and groups. Sets of common privileges are grouped into *rights*. Instead of assigning individual privileges to a user, you normally assign rights through the user and group manager application. If you want, you can select privileges one at a time and grant them to specific users, too.

The NT audit log reports privilege changes for users in distinct event records. IDSs watch the log for these entries to alert you to possible security problems. The privilege vector associated with an access token also can be altered through programming interfaces provided with NT. This means that the administrative GUI is not the only way for users to increase their privileges. You saw that UNIX systems had a number of facilities for increasing privileges. SUID programs in UNIX give users temporary privileges associated with the owner or group associated with that program. NT has similar capabilities through impersonation.

## Impersonation

In earlier chapters, you learned that a critical component of computer systems is the capability for a process to act on behalf of another user. NT refers to this as impersonation. Recall that after a user logs into NT, an access token is created. In addition to containing a list of privileges and other fields, the token has a setting that defines the impersonation level for that token:

**Anonymous.**    No other process or thread is allowed to see any of the details about this token.

**Identifying.**    A process with the appropriate privileges can obtain information from the token, such as its SID, its groups, and its currently assigned privileges.

**Impersonation.**    A process with the appropriate privileges can impersonate the owner of the token on the local system (note that this does not include impersonation on a remote system).

The impersonation level for a token can be changed any time during the lifetime of the token through NT APIs. If you are writing software, you can decide whether to allow remote systems to operate with the security context of your token. If you allow impersonation, other remote services can act on your behalf. This practice is necessary for accessing remote shares, for example. However, it also could be a security hole. A hacker who plants a bogus service with impersonation privileges will be able to use your credentials to impersonate you on other remote systems.

When you are logged into a system running NT, you might interact with system services and higher privileged processes many times. These process *do* have sufficient privileges to impersonate your access token. Because the system services run with very high privileges, they are essentially downgrading their capabilities when they create a thread to handle your request and associate *your* access token with the thread.

NT does not log all of the activities associated with impersonation. This is somewhat unfortunate because many unrecorded events affect the security policy of the system. Numerous system calls are provided to create access tokens, assign privileges to tokens, associate tokens with threads or processes, impersonate access tokens, and duplicate access tokens. A process must have very high privileges in order to successfully complete an operation through one of these interfaces. For example, a process must have the right to duplicate tokens if it wants to invoke the *duplicate token* system call. When this call is requested, it is the beginning of an attempt by one process to act on behalf of another. You can understand why this is an important event to monitor.

Other than security-relevant events that you want to track, NT has been hit by a number of hack attacks. You should know that many early attacks were found in NT 3.51 and were fixed in NT 4.0. Some intrusions have been reported on NT 4.0 as well, although service packs and patches are available to correct the bugs.

## Remote Attacks

Because NT supports TCP/IP, NT is vulnerable to the protocol attacks mentioned earlier in the book—Ping of Death, SYN Flood, session hijacking, and address impersonation. Some vulnerabilities specifically are found in the IP implementation on NT. The Teardrop UDP attack is a Microsoft-specific bug found in the way NT handles UDP packets. Large datagrams can cause the receiving system to hang. Different variations on this attack have surfaced often in the last few months.

The SMB protocol begins with a challenge-response authentication phase, but like I&A servers, it is still open to impostor-in-middle packet attacks. Other attacks specific to NT itself have been publicized during the last several years. Summaries are provided in the next few paragraphs.

The *Anonymous* vulnerability was one of the first widely announced weaknesses. The problem arose from an undocumented user in the operating system known as the anonymous user. Machine-to-machine communications relied on this anonymous user for exchanging information. Because the anonymous user was still a user to the operating system, it was able to access resources available to the Everyone group. A remote user could read registry entries, list users, and obtain other data that could reduce the time it takes to crack a system. Microsoft fixed the problem with a patch.

The DNS query ID attack also gives remote users an opportunity to spoof responses from the DNS server. The query IDs were generated from a predictable sequence giving hackers a chance to forge DNS responses and to cause the victim to carry out conversations with an impostor host. This sounds much like the TCP session number guessing attack discussed in Chapter 4, "Traditional Network Security Approaches." Microsoft also fixed this bug in a patch.

Shared resources from NT are exported to other network users using NetBIOS. A share with weak permissions gives remote users access to data they should not have. Although this is not a program bug, it is an administrator configuration error that can lead to intrusions. No patch is available for this—you need to be diligent about permissions for exported and shared resources. The corollary in UNIX is the set of permissions for exported NFS file systems. Several variations of the problem exist. Any user with legitimate access to the system can *by default* have full access to a share. For this reason, it is important to explicitly set permission when a share is created. Another variation allows anyone who can access the system as Guest to also have full permissions on the share. Shares also can be protected with a password. Scanners attempt brute force attacks against share passwords to look for openings.

Microsoft's IIS was at one time vulnerable to a rather nasty problem. Arbitrary remote browsers could run any accessible command on the Web server. Two flavors of this problem were called the ".bat" and the ".cmd" bugs. A new release of IIS has since fixed the problem, but scanners look for back-level versions of the program. In the summer of 1998, a few more variations on this attack were discovered, too.

The NBSTAT command can probe remote NT systems for important information, such as the names of logged in users (similar to rwho on UNIX). A hacker now can try cracking attacks against the accounts and possibly cause denial-of-service if failed login thresholds are set.

One of the early problems encountered by NT administrators was the ntfsdos.exe attack. A normal user could run ntfsdos.exe from a floppy and bypass all of the ACLs set for the NT file system. This hack is listed here because a perpetrator did not even need an account on the system to threaten the system. A patch was released shortly after the problem was reported.

Attacks are not always directed at servers. A L0pht Security Advisory (L0pht, 1997) showed that Microsoft's Internet Explorer experienced a buffer overflow condition when processing URLs. A malicious Web server could trick your NT workstation into executing arbitrary commands. In general, browsing the Internet is difficult without risking attacks such as these. Connections are inherently anonymous, and therefore access control is minimal. Also, attacks such as the Internet Explorer URL bug point to the importance of *personal intrusion detection* products. When browsing the Web, wouldn't it be good to know if some process or thread launched by the Web browser suddenly is deleting files from your disk?

## Local Vulnerabilities

A number of security policy settings can compromise a system. A vulnerability checker, such as SAFESuite, eNTrax, or KSA, needs to plow through the system and find any weaknesses. A vulnerability is not necessarily a hack. For example, if the Administrator password is blank, this is not exactly what you would call a well-known and carefully orchestrated hack. A configuration error such as this is simply poor administration, unless you had set the password yesterday, and today you find that it has been cleared.

NT vulnerability checkers look for NT configuration problems such as the following:

- ◆ Guest account enabled, which allows remote users without an account to be able to access some of the resources on your system.
- ◆ Guest account has no password, allowing remote users access *without requiring a password* (at one time this was a default setting on NT).
- ◆ Password composition and aging rules.
- ◆ Weak passwords that can be broken with a cracker.
- ◆ Failed login thresholds.
- ◆ Permissions on registry entries (numerous hacks have occurred because registry entries were not adequately controlled with DAC, including the famous HKEY-CLASSES_ROOT key whose lack of

protection in NT 3.51 allowed arbitrary users to control which programs were launched for given file extensions).

- ◆ Remote registry access enabled, allowing remote administrators the opportunity to change critical system settings.
- ◆ Individual registry settings.
- ◆ Improper permissions on system files and directories, such as the NT perfmon utility that can be used to sniff network packets.
- ◆ Unknown services that do not ship by default with NT.
- ◆ Running services that are vulnerable to attack, such as SMB running on a Web server, which gives remote probers plenty of information useful for cracking attempts (or the Alerter, which might be used by internal hackers to display Trojan Horse screens asking other users for passwords).
- ◆ Shares with permission access control settings, giving full access to remote users.
- ◆ Whether IP forwarding is enabled, which can be used to facilitate network attacks.

For each of the problems listed, many scenarios exist. David LeBlanc of ISS identified registry key permissions for the Winlogon entry, which allowed Server Operator users to set the initial program for other users. The same flaw allowed operators to change the initial program run when the NT operating system booted. Thus, one easily could get a copy of files from another user even though under normal conditions one would not have read permission to those files. Also, Server Operator users could exploit this hole to easily gain Administrator rights. Plenty of other examples demonstrate vulnerabilities ranging from mild to severe.

This list represents only a subset of the suite of vulnerabilities a local system can face. Because tracking the security state of these items is nearly impossible with automation, you should invest in one of the NT scanners described in this chapter.

## Intrusion Detection Products for NT

In this section are descriptions of some of the leading NT IDSs. Unfortunately, it is impossible to describe all of the IDS offerings for NT today. The selections here were chosen because in many ways they are complementary rather than competitive.

## Look for These Features

As in your examination of UNIX IDSs, you need to consider both the features provided by the tools that are important for managing the IDS *and* the list of attacks detected.  You should consider the following systems management factors:

◆ Is the product client-server? If so, is it heterogeneous so that it works across UNIX and NT systems?

◆ Does the product provide distributed systems management? For example, if the event log is used, can you configure event logs on all of the target machines from the central console?

◆ How useful are the reports? Can you create your own reports from the data?

◆ What is the scalability of the tool? How many target nodes can the tool concurrently analyze?

◆ What kinds of alerts and countermeasures are possible? Can the IDS disable network connections, kill logins, disable logins, or execute administrator defined programs or scripts?

Because new product releases appear at least every quarter, you should contact the IDS vendors directly for the latest information on tools you are interested in deploying. Naturally, only by running the products in pilot projects will you be able to properly evaluate them.

## Centrax

Slightly more than a year old, Centrax (www.centraxcorp.com) is a company formed primarily by experts from the CMDS team formerly with SAIC. Many skilled IDS programmers also have joined the Centrax team. The chief product developed by Centrax is called eNTrax.

eNTrax provides key benefits to an organization including the following:

◆ Detection and response of information threats and misuse
◆ Deterrence of further misuse
◆ Damage assessment
◆ Possible prosecution support

eNTrax is comprised of two main components: a Command Console and a Target Service. The Command Console provides centralized management of the network.

Figure 10.1 shows the main eNTrax console. From the console, you can monitor, detect, and respond to security problems on remote systems. At the console an administrator is alerted to potential misuses and attacks. Responses to attacks can be configured in advance, or an administrator can choose a security alert and inter-actively respond. Today, eNTrax supports remote system shutdown, remotely killing the login session of the offending user, and disabling the login capabilities of a user. The Command Console manages configuration and collection of audit data from target computers. This feature is valuable because it consolidates log files from NT targets onto a common server. You can keep the raw audit data as NT records it or rely on the event database that eNTrax constructs from the data.

A target computer is any workstation or server on the network. Each target computer creates audit data as a user performs work such as opening files, copy-ing files, or deleting files. The Target Service, installed on each workstation and server in the network, enables a communications channel between the Command Console and the target.

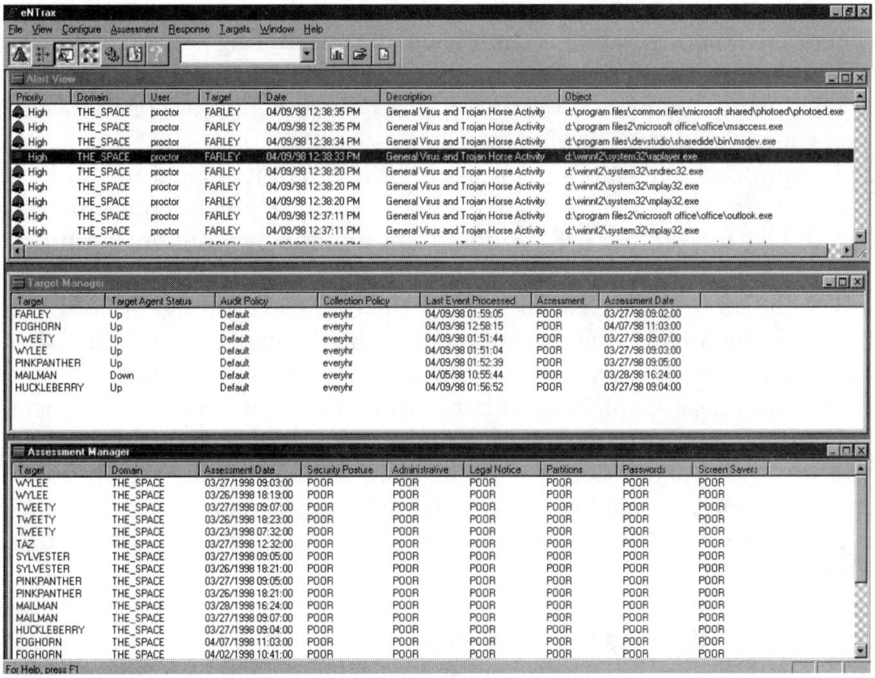

**Figure 10.1**    Command Console for eNTrax.

eNTrax provides two IDS capabilities in a single tool. Because the Target Service is running on each node, local vulnerability assessments can be carried out. You can get this same type of function with ISS SAFESuite for NT or the Kane Security Analyst (KSA). The other IDS function provided by eNTrax is attack signature recognition. Most hacker attacks recognized by eNTrax are single events today, but work to build more complex attack patterns is in progress. Remote scans against target nodes are not part of the tool today.

An administrator typically would use eNTrax as follows. First, an assessment of the targets is requested from the console to look for security weaknesses. The Assessment Manager generates reports on the strength of a computer's security. With this information, the administrator can improve the security holes that currently exist. The next step is to create an audit policy that effectively provides the capability to monitor user activities. eNTrax provides an Audit Strategy Tool component that simplifies creation of an audit policy. In addition, eNTrax ships with predefined audit policies, which can be modified as needed to suit the individual needs of an organization.

The third step is to distribute the audit policy to target computers. eNTrax provides a Target Manager that facilitates the distribution of audit policies to all target computers. After configuration is completed, the monitoring portion of eNTrax kicks into high gear. The Target Service residing on the target sends the local event log back to the Command Console for processing. Events are processed in pseudo real time with a configurable interval.

eNTrax is equipped with more than one hundred activity signatures to help identify attacks. Activity signatures are events or event sequences for which an alert is issued. Like many other IDS vendors, Centrax actively monitors the appropriate newsgroups and hacker resources to keep current with new attacks.

Analysis at the console consists of passing the event log through a detection engine that looks for attacks. Results are reported on the console and stored in a database. When an event is displayed on the console, administrators are notified of activities that appear suspicious. Other alert facilities include SNMP, pager, and e-mail notification. In a network operations center with personnel monitoring the console, the operator will look at the alerts and determine the appropriate action to take. eNTrax enables an administrator to assign priorities to events. This feature is useful because it lets the site decide which items are of high, medium, or low interest.

As noted before, responses include shutting down the user's machine, killing the login session, or disabling the login account. Automated responses to alerts can be configured in advance. The response is applicable to the entire set of targets that the console controls. An enhancement would be to permit more granular responses, such as varying countermeasures by user or by target. Figure 10.2

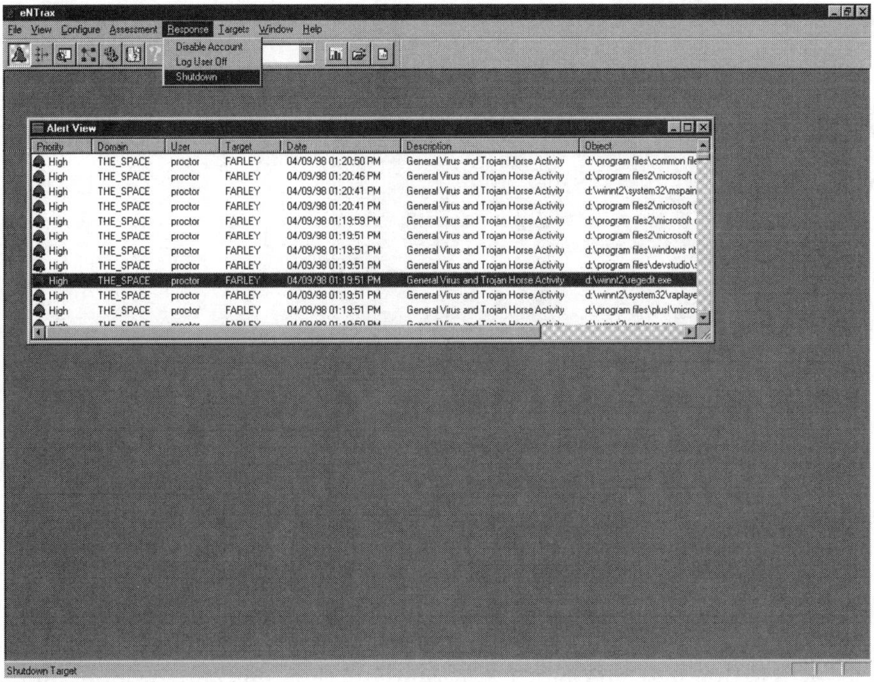

**Figure 10.2**    Event notification and responses in eNTrax.

includes a snapshot of the event notification screen and a pull-down menu for responses.

To further enhance security, eNTrax provides a Report Manager with which an administrator can generate extensive reports of user or target node activity. These investigative reports provide a look at who did what, when, and how. Information such as this helps track down potential misuse and can pinpoint damage that has occurred. A sample report is shown in Figure 10.3. Useful trend reports also can be generated from historical data.

## ISS SAFESuite and RealSecure for NT

ISS has a very concentrated team of NT security experts. Some of the developers there once worked on the implementation of NT security for Microsoft. It is even rumored that Microsoft's Web site and internal IT infrastructure are pilot test networks for new releases from ISS. In earlier chapters, you read about products from ISS. The SAFESuite family of products performs local and remote

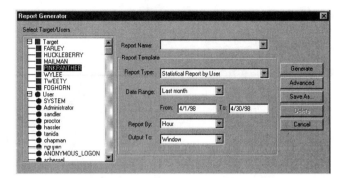

**Figure 10.3**   Sample report from eNTrax.

vulnerability assessments. RealSecure is an intelligent sniffer that looks for attacks by examining network packets. Beneficial features, such as remote management, consolidated reporting, automated responses, configurable policy templates by target, and secure communications between network console and targets, are available in SAFESuite scanners and RealSecure. These capabilities are found in the NT versions, too.

RealSecure, whether for UNIX or NT, is essentially the same core product. Both versions look for attacks against UNIX and NT systems by tracking network activities. Because network data is the source of information, a vendor does not need a separate analysis engine for UNIX and NT versions of RealSecure. ISS needed only to port the sniffer engine across different OSs. The NT RealSecure product is another flavor of the same solution that is available for a UNIX system running the same product. As you may have noticed earlier, some NT-specific network attacks must be monitored. Both UNIX and NT versions of RealSecure catch these attacks.

SAFESuite products that perform remote scans against NT systems can also be run from UNIX or NT systems because the software is not *running on* the NT system. Instead, the software is probing the NT target from another node. As in the previous paragraph, specific NT attacks must be tested, whether the console is a UNIX or an NT computer. A SAFESuite local vulnerability assessment tool also is available from ISS. The *System Security Scanner* (S3) that runs directly on the NT system inspects the system for weaknesses such as weak passwords, registry configuration problems, and other known holes. The Internet Scanner is also available for NT. For a complete list of the attacks that are checked, visit ISS at www.iss.net.

### Security Dynamics' KSA and KSM

As part of the rush of IDS vendor acquisitions, Security Dynamics picked up KSA and KSM when it acquired Intrusion Detection, Inc. KSA is a vulnerability assessment tool, and KSM is an NT event log monitor.

KSA is built upon the consulting theme of *Best Practices*. A sound security policy states guidelines such as password composition rules, login failure thresholds, password assignments, file access rights, and logging. KSA scans systems for adherence to best practices guidelines and impressively reports results. Six major areas that KSA investigates are: account restrictions, access control, password strength, system monitoring, data integrity, and data confidentiality. Some of the vulnerabilities evaluated by KSA are as follows:

- Weak password subject to cracking
- Proper registry settings
- Which NT services are enabled
- Configuration of the auditing subsystem
- Shared network drive configurations
- Trust relationships
- Known down-level versions of programs

KSA supports distributed analysis of target nodes with reporting to a central system. Another feature reads the event log and looks for violations such as failed login attempts and other security activities (administrator login events). Interesting events are counted and displayed in graphical bar charts or in printed reports.

One of the useful additions to KSA is an inverse ACL map. Knowing the resources a user or group can access, and the access rights associated with that resource are both useful reports. Operating systems easily display the object along with the subjects and access rights for that object. However, displaying the opposite view is tedious when attempted manually. KSA provides a view of ACLs from the *subject's perspective*, thus showing all resources that a subject can access. This feature, long part of RACF on mainframe computers, is not always available on other operating systems.

The KSM concentrates on event log analysis and alerts. Like eNTrax, the log is read in intervals as short as one minute. Multiple target nodes can have their event logs consolidated on a central console. Because KSM uses the event log, activities such as SYN Flood or Ping of Death are not detected. Network packets are the source of data for these attacks. Events that KSM monitors include logins, logouts, service starts, auditing configuration changes, and file accesses.

KSM ships with alerting capabilities today but does not currently support countermeasures, such as killing processes. This feature is likely to be supported in the future. Like other NT IDSs, the set of attack signatures is limited to those provided by the vendor. The capability to add signatures in the future also will be available. A number of predefined reports are provided with KSM including Most Targeted Machines, Suspicious User Activity, and a Top 10 Most Wanted Users. Data for reports can be limited to date and time ranges as well. Attack patterns analyzed include password cracking attempts, browsing, denial of service, privilege violations, ghost IDs, failed logins or file accesses, masquerading, and Administrator ID abuse.

## For Further Thought

As you've seen in this chapter, NT is a favorite target of hackers. Many of the internals for NT are not publicly available for review. At a 1997 DEFCON conference, Microsoft representatives asked a team of NT security experts what could be done to improve the security of NT. Most of the panel members remarked that documenting and publishing information would be a significant step forward.

Echoing the sentiments of other DEFCON participants, the panel members pointed out that it was difficult to securely configure NT systems for customers because the internal workings remained a mystery. Undocumented registry entries can lead to exposures because the consequences of ACL changes for those entries are not well understood by the public. Hackers, though, always find a way to *discover* the hidden secrets. In response to this request, Microsoft has sought advice from several independent security companies on the best way to document and make available this information. Hopefully, the knowledge will soon be shared.

One important message delivered over the last year or two is that a system evaluated at C2 level is not necessarily *secure*. True, Microsoft NT received its C2 evaluation with a nonnetwork attached system, but some of the attacks that have been announced against NT did not require remote access. Many weaknesses could be exploited by a user who might rely on a shared NT computer in the corner of a lab. A stamp of approval is only as good as the humans who build the system and those carrying out the evaluation. People make mistakes, and improperly protected registry entries in out-of-the-box configurations of NT show that even government-evaluated systems can still have flaws.

The popularity of NT is growing along with its install base. The market for NT IDSs is strong and also should grow during the next several years. One could predict that the marketplace for NT IDSs will be more competitive because the NT event log is easier to access and understand than UNIX audit logs. However, any of the IDS vendors currently working in the NT space will quickly point out that many mysteries lurk in the event log. Changes between service packs have caused more than one IDS vendor to rewrite code because events were no longer reported or the format of an event had changed.

Because Microsoft is planning major changes to NT security in its next major release (Microsoft 1997), you can expect the market to churn some more. Early access to NT V5.0 is a must for IDS vendors. Changes including support for Kerberos, moving registry entries into a directory service, and X.509 will push vendors to adjust their tools to incorporate and monitor new features.

# PART 3

# ROUNDING OUT YOUR ENVIRONMENT

In this final part of the book, you will first learn tips for handling intrusions. Hopefully, the previous chapters have convinced you to deploy an IDS. By doing so, you will have access to much more data when handling a security incident. After covering incident responses, we will close by reviewing the role of intrusion detection products in your environment. You will also have a chance to review shortcomings of IDSs and consider how they might be positioned in the future. By the time you finish reading this part, you will be familiar with:

- ◆ Ideas for planning for security incidents in advance
- ◆ Techniques for handling incidents when they occur
- ◆ Positioning of IDSs relative to traditional security products
- ◆ Improvements that future IDSs are likely to include

# Chapter 11

# You've Been Hit!

By now, you probably realize that no perfect solution for security exists. Given all of the possible tradeoffs you must make, and all of the potential areas in which you or a vendor can make a mistake, someone always can sneak through a hole. The attack can come from the inside, or the attack can originate from the outside and be targeted at your public Internet presence. In this chapter, you'll discover some of the options for when your buddy shouts across the room, "We've been hit!"

The three main topics to discuss about incident handling are as follows:

◆ Preparation before you're hit
◆ Detection or discovery of the incident(s)
◆ Response to the incident

## Be Prepared

The worst thing you can do is make hasty decisions when you've been attacked. Know in advance what steps to follow. Quite simply, create a plan ahead of time. You can prepare your team for a security breach by adhering to the following guidelines.

Create an incident response team and assign specific responsibilities to team members. Provide backup personnel for each member as well. If you can afford external expertise, such as that provided by IBM's Emergency Response Service or other consultants, involve them as well. Document each member's role and post contact information at key locations in your site. If you are part of a multinational corporation, ensure that any country-specific requirements are handled by allowing for national language differences, time zones, and holidays. Your team should have 24-hour coverage.

Create and publicize a site security policy. Make sure that people support the policy by soliciting input, explaining the tradeoffs you make, and emphasizing the financial consequences of lapses in security. Obtain the backing of the appropriate corporate executives in your organization. If you detect that an intruder has gained access to the payroll system, no roadblocks should hinder your ability to handle the incident. Get authorizations and exceptions worked out in advance. The last thing you want to do is sit idly by while internal bureaucracy prevents you from saving the company from disaster.

Be ready with plenty of spare tapes or other backup media. When you're hit, you'll want to get a snapshot of the environment. Make sure that the response team has easy access to product media as well, in order to restore contaminated systems. If necessary, designate victim machines in advance. You do not want to be waiting for someone to find the keys to unlock the victim's physical control device. These systems are like fire-fighting equipment—they should be ready for action at any moment.

Document your environment *in advance*. Know where all the firewalls, routers, modem pools, and other critical systems are in your network. Know the physical and logical connections for these systems. If your response team does not know the environment, they can't protect it. As before, access to these resources is mandatory. If the routers are behind a locked door, you either need ready access to that room or a good fire ax to knock the door down. Should network administration at your site be shared with other authorities or departments not under your control, develop cooperation procedures in advance.

As in any endeavor, practice makes perfect. Train response team members on the latest intrusion techniques. Knowing what to look for in advance will help you detect intrusions sooner. Many people enjoy penetration testing when it's endorsed by management. There is something exciting about sleuthing around and trying to avoid detection. Uh oh...*those statements are not intended to encourage you to hack.*

Rehearse your responses by creating sample intrusion data that the team can analyze. Think of response team training as a class in which everyone learns and in which the role of teacher can change from week to week. Decide in advance who in the team will be involved in the evaluation of the incident, and who will be busy watching for other problems. The team should not be a chaotic one in which everyone pours through source code or log files looking for evidence or data. Manage the team like any software development project and allocate specific assignments for team members. Measure and constantly evaluate your progress. You can set interim goals, such as "If we don't discover how the break-in occurred and repair the problem in one hour, we'll need to shut down the network." Practice under the same conditions that you expect to encounter. If your team is aggressive enough, a simulated midnight raid will really test their determination and skill. Just don't get too carried away. Training isn't boot camp.

Document and conduct regular reviews of the response process. Update the process, the roles and responsibilities, and the team contact information so that it is always accurate. People come and go in the organization, so the process documentation for your responses should reflect changes in the organization and changes in policy. Make the document readily available. Publish it on a Web site, keep hard copy available in easily accessed locations. Another way to get buy-in from other employees is to designate and train *incident response* deputies. You probably have seen plenty of Westerns in which a shopkeeper or farmer displays elation at being deputized by the resident sheriff. Things haven't changed that much. The security and network specialists in a company are not always viewed with admiration. Giving employees from other departments a chance to share in the responsibility for incident responses is good for a number of reasons you probably can think of on your own.

Develop an effective communication plan. Decide what types of events require you to notify local law enforcement, the FBI, other sites, and coordinating bodies like those identified in the Appendix. Decide in advance what types of events require you to notify as many people as possible and which incidents demand secrecy. If you suspect an employee is the source of trouble, privacy has legal implications. Rumors based on incorrect assumptions and inadequate data can lead to court action by those incorrectly accused. If the employee is guilty and hears through the grapevine of your suspicions, you might lose the trail of evidence. A disgruntled employee facing prosecution for computer mischief may not have much to lose, and that last hidden bomb could be detonated instead of disarmed.

Keep your users informed about potential problems. As you saw in earlier chapters, humans are the weakest link. Warn employees about giving away user names or passwords over the phone, for example. Conduct regular classes and encourage your employees to attend (perhaps by giving away prizes). The importance of user education cannot be emphasized enough because almost everyone spends some time browsing the Internet looking for competitive information, ordering from business partners, or keeping current with technology. Of course, you might want to keep some secrets. If you give detailed explanations of all of your tools and techniques, a clever insider could suddenly find new ways to go undetected.

Keep logs of important activities. Unfortunately, this area requires tradeoffs. You cannot go back and look at historical data to determine how your site was hacked if you do not keep logs. How much data to keep and how long to store the data are variables whose values you must determine. To be safe, log everything that you can without seriously degrading the performance of your systems.

Audit logs are the most comprehensive source of system activities. Network logs are equally important. Logs generated by applications also must be kept. If not already supported by the product generating the log, consider adding crypto-graphic integrity protection to your log files. Depending on your requirements, you can compute cryptographic hashes on each record or only on the log files. Ensure that you have appropriate automated mechanisms in place for log file storage. You do not want to discover that the data you need most is missing because that $500 disk drive wasn't ordered. If your systems support it, logging to write-once media is another way to protect the integrity of log files.

Keep records of system configuration changes and enforce a strict regimen for when changes are allowed. Any time the firewall packet filters are changed, a well-understood process should document who requested the change, the design for the proposed change, who implemented the change, who reviewed it, and so on. If an intrusion occurs because of one of these changes, ready access to the change log can help diagnose the problem quickly.

## Discovery and Detection

IDSs grew out of a need to search a large space of information and glean out only the important data. Many systems administrators knew that it was important to keep audit logs. They just didn't know all of the different things to look for in that mountain of data. Similarly, network packet-based IDSs filter through many megabytes of data each day looking for individual problems or attack patterns. How do you know when you've been hit? Hopefully, your IDS will tell you this. If you've deployed an IDS and configured it properly, the IDS will catch a number of common attacks intruders launch against your site.

One potential area of weakness is application logging. Most IDSs are not flex-ible enough today to read log files generated by arbitrary applications. Looking for attack patterns or statistical profiles in firewall logs is something that some IDSs are beginning to do today. However, this capability is far from perfect.

If you have installed *Tivoli's Management Environment* (TME), you can write your own log file adapter objects. These adapters will send event notifications to the central TME console. There, custom responses can be designed for each event of interest. Your adapter object can be sophisticated enough to send an *event* only when three failed logins have been detected in your custom applica-tion, for example. Thus, you should consider using something like TME's Event Console for extending your coverage of IDSs to include custom applications.

Another thing to remember is to have a site policy which actually ensures that an event will be discovered by someone. If your IDS prints reports each morning, rather than sending real-time alerts, an accountable individual should be looking for evidence of misuses or intrusions each morning. Similarly, if your system generates real-time alerts, but your paging system experiences problems the same weekend you're hit, you'll realize the importance of backup notification mechanisms such as hard copy reports. Historically, hard copy reports are often favored as *evidence* in court proceedings, although this could change as knowledge about proper use of digital signatures becomes more widespread. Thus, it's a good idea to print hard copy reports from your IDSs and assign personnel to look through these reports on a daily basis (if not more often).

## Responding to Intrusions

Garfinkel and Spafford (1996) recommend two important responses. First, remain calm and don't panic. Psychological research shows that humans do not perform well under stressful conditions, unless the task is one that the human already executes exceptionally well. Professional athletes often perform well under stressful conditions because they already are very good at running, kicking, shooting, or blocking. Chances are the same cannot be said of incident response teams. Thus, it's important to remain focused on the facts and carry out the plan you've already practiced a number of times. The next recommendation is to document *everything*. There isn't much elaboration on this point. Just do it.

A different set of suggestions is found in Chapman and Zwicky (1995):

**1st step: Evaluate the situation and decide what response is required.** You do this evaluation by accurately assessing the damage. Ask what the intruder is doing now, how far did the penetration get, what information was compromised, what changes were made to the systems, were back doors left, and other questions that describe the current state of the problem.

**2nd step: Disconnect or shut down resources if necessary.** As a rule, you do not want to let the hacker continue to work through your systems (see the next section). Responding to an incident is much like disaster recovery. If the compromised system is your public Web server, and you do not have a second site, shutdown may not be an option. At least you should be able to reset or kill the network connection. The hacker may try another network connection later, but you will have eliminated the current threat. Think of it as triage.

**3rd step: Analyze and respond to the incident.** Here, the importance of teams with designated roles becomes apparent. You cannot have the same team member digging through log files or source code and also worrying about the next weaknesses the attacker will exploit. Part of the team should be responsible for analyzing the problem, and another segment of the team should be attentive to any new incoming threats. When you are ready to repair the problem, thoroughly consider your responses. The last thing you want to do is make the situation worse. Disabling the wrong subnet addresses in your firewall could limit your ability to detect new intrusions while not affecting the hacker at all. That's why it's important to remain calm and think through your steps carefully. On most systems, you'll be working with superuser or Administrator privileges. Have someone look over your shoulder and verbally state each step before you do it to minimize errors.

**4th step: Alert other people according to your response policy.**    You can do this in parallel with the previous steps if your team is large enough. The incident response document you prepared in advance will contain the names, phone numbers, e-mail addresses, pager numbers, and other critical information for the contacts. If you diagnose a problem in a purchased product, contact the vendor's response team as soon as possible. They already may be working on the problem but have not publicized the issue yet for fear of increasing the number of attacks. Do not leak information outside the response team and those with a need to know. Most crimes involve internal collusion, so your team should not involve other internal employees unless you are sure they were not involved.

**5th step: Save the system state.**    Back up as much of the system as you can in real time. Take the backup to a victim machine on a detached network and restore the image. This machine is where you will do your debugging. Keep in mind any privacy issues with data that may appear on the backup. Medical records and credit card numbers should not be forwarded to vendors for debugging unless adequate controls are in place. Know your legal limits in advance.

**6th step: Restore hacked systems.**    If you have detected that system binaries have changed, restore them from certified original product media. To be safe, you should restore the system from scratch. Note that this restoration can be tricky because a system may have many additional products installed and configured on top of it. Getting the system back into the state before compromise may not be a simple task and could introduce other security problems. If you've kept accurate change logs, and your IDS can tell you exactly what has changed, you can get by with replacing only the programs patched by the hacker. Remove any hidden files or directories added by the hacker. Watch out for symbolic links. You don't want to remove a system file that has a symlink from a file planted by a hacker.

**7th step: Document what happened.**   Communicate the incident as necessary. Carry out a defect prevention process that will ensure that the problem does not occur again. Finally, increase monitoring if necessary. For example, if the incident went undetected for several weeks, you definitely were not monitoring the appropriate activities.

In responding to an event, you immediately will be faced with a crucial decision—how to handle the intruder. You have several options. The best advice is to disconnect or kill the network connection. If the event is an internal misuse that was flagged by an IDS, you have different legal options. Upper management will help you decide whether to allow the misuse to continue for gathering evidence (with the appropriate concern for privacy of any compromised information).

Stories of administrators contacting the intruder are plentiful. In some cases, the intruder was a *friendly hacker* who offered security advice and described the weaknesses exploited. Because you never know whether you have a curious hacker or a sociopath on the end of the connection, this type of contact can be risky. The intruder might not know what type of evidence could be left behind, and your open acknowledgment of detection could result in a hasty exit that also erases your entire system.

## Should You Pursue Your Attacker?

Perhaps as a security officer, you day dream about spending endless hours tracking down and catching intruders. You envision yourself being rewarded by company executives for heroic actions and ingenuity, which led to the recover of important intellectual property or money. And, you do all of this in a few long nights and still have time to make your tee time on Saturday morning.

Realty is far from this fantasy. Just read about how much time Cliff Stoll spent in one of the most interesting cases to date (Stoll, 1989). Going after a serious attacker is not for the faint hearted. The number of different levels of indirection a cracker will build up to hide his true identity can be mind boggling. You might *think* you're after a university student when the real hacker is actually in another country. Someone who is serious about remaining anonymous will use stolen credit card numbers, phony names, forged cellular phone access, and temporary Internet accounts. By the time you trace back to the culprit, the switch already has been made to another facade at another ISP.

This information is not intended to discourage you from pursuing criminals who attack your systems. Instead, the purpose is to ensure that you have a dose of reality to go with your zeal. After you decide to involve law enforcement agencies, consultants, and others outside the scope of your company, costs can escalate. Often phone lines are involved, which means that you need permission to trace phone calls, tap lines, or other legally daunting techniques to catch the intruder. Most hacks span multiple sites, so you'll be forced to work with other systems administrators—some who may not want to be cooperative.

In some computer crime cases, a mouse trap was set up to capture the intruder. Allowing someone to access your systems, even if you think they are in a protected subnet, can introduce greater risks. The delightful story of Berferd (Cheswick, 1992) describes how AT&T allowed a cracker to wander through some designated machines. Stoll (1989) set up similar juicy bait, such as fake memos describing topics about national security. If you decide to give hackers access to some of your systems in an effort to better track them down, make sure that you have approved the activity with senior management at your site and involve local law enforcement. Know the legal implications for your company, which certainly will be confounded if you knowingly give the intruder access.

Some commercial products boast automated responses, such as reverse SATAN scans. *Absolutely do not do this!* Intruders work from compromised systems or temporary accounts at an ISP, not from Linux boxes in their basements. When you reverse scan or reverse SYN Flood an address, you probably are trashing another innocent victim. You could end up facing a lawsuit from the other site.

Finally, if you are working for a business that has fiscal responsibility to shareholders, then you *must* consider whether pursuing someone is a greater financial risk than fixing the problem and letting the attacker go. Security is a practical matter dealing with the financial value of assets and the risk of compromise. Make sound business decisions when you consider whether to spend resources pursuing an attacker.

# Chapter 12

# Intrusion Detection: Not the Last Chapter When It Comes to Security

You need IDSs at your site in the same way you need firewalls, improved access control products, and better I&A. After reading the arguments put forward for IDSs throughout this book, you might think that intrusion detection is the last chapter in the war on computer security. It isn't. Despite its important contribution to security for systems and networks, intrusion detection also can be improved.

In this final chapter of the book, you will read about other open issues that argue for continued evolution of security solutions. The chapter begins by reviewing important topics in the book with a recap of each of the major themes in traditional security solutions. This review is followed by highlights of how you can improve upon traditional security with intrusion detection. The discussion then turns to recommended improvements for IDSs.

## Traditional Computer Security

The traditional and historically most widely adopted computer security approach is to *prevent* as many problems as possible. Monitoring always has been recognized as an important part of a total solution. However, most sites in the past did not dedicate resources for monitoring. Even the Orange Book emphasizes the importance of monitoring. For the most part, traditional security covers topics discussed in Part 1, "Before Intrusion Detection: Traditional Computer Security," of this book and includes the basic model, I&A, access control, and network security.

## The Basic Security Model

As you saw in Chapter 1, the fundamental concepts in security are subjects, objects, and access control. Most of the important security events are those in which subjects try to access objects, and a reference monitor decides whether the request is allowed. IDSs try to monitor when this process breaks down by scanning for vulnerabilities or catching attacks in progress. Because the basic model emphasizes *who accesses what*, it's not surprising that much of the security product marketplace is dominated by solutions that regulate access and try to prevent problems.

IDSs exist because people make mistakes. Intrusion detection began by looking for problems in operating systems and networks. The focus was on subjects and objects that were identified and reported on by operating systems such as UNIX. However, many applications introduce their own notions of subjects, objects, and access control. IDSs are just now beginning to look at application-level detection. Scanners, for example, often examine configuration files of Web servers. Fundamental to the proper operation of the basic model is the capability to uniquely identify the subjects and objects in the system. This is the purpose of I&A.

## I&A

When people mostly connected to large mainframes via dumb terminals, I&A consisted of logging in by specifying a userid and a password. In today's complex distributed environments, many other forms of I&A exist. Smart cards, challenge-response authentication servers, and trusted third-party servers are some of the alternatives today. X.509 is likely to be the future's leading mechanism for I&A and trust in large heterogeneous networks.

In Chapter 2, "The Role of Identification and Authentication in Your Environment," you learned about attacks against I&A and saw some steps that you could take to help stop these attacks. You need IDSs to monitor when these attacks are in progress, even if you have ways of preventing the attacks from going too far. Flaws in Kerberos and other authentication improvements were described, further emphasizing the need for monitoring. Intrusion detection not only can be used to catch attempts to circumvent I&A. It also can be used to watch the I&A tools you add to your site.

I&A and IDSs are closely bound because intrusion detection tries to track the activities of an entity, such as a person. A sequence of events executed by different users may not be a problem, but the same sequence run by a single user could be a serious hack attack. Knowing the *who* and the *what* parts of an event is a critical part of discovering attacks and assigning accountability.

One last point to remember is that I&A is not limited to people. Network nodes, software processes, and other forms of communicating entities need to identify and authenticate each other for secure message exchanges. This form of I&A impacts IDSs as well. If you think about a system which does not have any login accounts except for the administrator, you begin to see how intrusion detection is affected by other forms of I&A.

## Access Control

The second important aspect of traditional security is controlling access to resources. This is the classic notion of prevention. As you discovered throughout this book, prevention does not always work. You learned a number of attacks that circumvented the system's access control policy. For example, techniques that allowed a user to be able to gain privileges and access privileged resources were shown to be one of the arguments against relying solely on access control. Other examples included improper configuration of permissions, whether the result of a vendor error or an administrative mistake.

As in the case of I&A, individual applications might introduce their own notions of access control. Databases regulate access to records, fields, and tables by using their own techniques rather than relying on the operating system's capabilities.

IDSs rely on access control routines in the operating system to emit data about events. The IDSs need to know when a subject tries to access an object and what the outcome was for the request. This information is fed into signatures or statistical counters to determine whether a problem exists. There also is a fuzzy area between access control and IDSs because an intruder can be kicked off the system or a file's permission bits can be changed as the *response* of an IDS. In this role, the IDS is being preventative.

You read in Chapter 3, "The Role of Access Control in Your Environment," that tools such as Memco's SeOS could improve upon traditional access control mechanisms in UNIX and NT. However, even the addition of such a tool is not sufficient for all of your security needs. Although attacks against SeOS itself were not identified, some chance exists that the preventative engine will fail. If not, there is the usual risk that an administrator will incorrectly configure SeOS. Both of these reasons argue further for adding an IDS even if you have additional access control products.

## Network Security

In Chapter 4, "Traditional Network Security Approaches," you found a brief overview of firewalls, cryptographic protocols for network security, and descriptions of problems in TCP/IP. Reasons for adding an IDS even if you have these products were given. The usual suspects—software bugs and configuration errors—applied in this area of traditional security as well.

Network security includes many topics such as I&A beyond single systems, communications between processes on different systems, privacy, integrity, non-repudiation, and trust. Comments IDS vendors frequently heard about a year ago were, "Hey, why do I need intrusion detection? I have a firewall." Hopefully, this type of comment is encountered less often today. Most firewall vendors have partnerships or their own programs for intrusion detection, thus highlighting the complementary nature of the product families.

## The Rationale for IDSs

The traditional approach to security has been to shore up defenses with as much prevention as one can muster. Because numerous examples have shown that this strategy by itself is insufficient, you can improve your site security by more closely monitoring events. IDSs monitor security relevant activities by checking for specific attack patterns, individual events, configuration problems, rogue programs, buggy versions of programs, and other holes through which a hacker can sneak. If you do not monitor conformance to your security policies and inspect your configurations, you are taking unnecessary risks. Even though IDSs are not perfect and can miss some attacks, the incremental security offered by these types of products is worth the investment.

IDSs share some common characteristics. Because many are deployed in distributed environments, features such as remote configuration, secure communications, and authentication are included. Systems management capabilities such as centralized event notification, logging, templates, and automated responses to fix a reported problem are commonly seen across IDSs. Beyond these similarities, IDSs can be divided into three main types.

## Types of IDSs

The three main categories of IDS tools are scanners, system-level monitors, and network sniffers. Because each type of tool detects attacks that the others do not, these IDSs are complementary to each other. Unfortunately, no single vendor today offers all three types across multiple OS platforms in a single solution.

## Scanners

Scanners come in two flavors. *Remote scanners* run on a central node and attempt to probe remote systems from a central console for weaknesses. No component of the remote scanner runs on the probed node. *System scanners* run on the target node and thus have an advantage of being to operate as a user would. They can read files and access other resources that a remote scanner cannot. Vendors, such as ISS, offer both kinds of scanners in a single suite of products. In a different marketing twist, IBM gives away a limited version of a remote scanner with the purchase of one of its firewalls.

Because they run on an interval basis, scanners cannot detect attacks as they occur. The argument, of course, is that they were not designed to do so in the first place. You need to decide how often to run the scan if this is the only tool you use. However, if you have both a scanner and a real-time system-level IDS, the two fit together nicely. When you receive your system or when you make major changes to its contents, run the scanner to uncover configuration problems. After the system tests clean, your real-time system-level IDS can detect future unwanted changes in real time.

Some problems are encountered with this approach. For example, a real-time system monitor normally will not inspect the contents of a file that was changed. If someone changes the file httpd.conf, the system-level IDS does not scan the contents to see whether the change was unsafe. You will not detect a configuration problem resulting from this change until you run the scanner again. Obviously, the ideal choice is for the system-level IDS is to invoke the scan routine on the file when the change event is detected in the audit log. Many scanners can be invoked from the command line with an optional parameter specifying the items to scan (or a file containing the list). Note how well these two strategies fit together when combined.

## System-Level IDSs

Products that monitor the audit logs or syslog detect attacks at the system level. Instead of inspecting network packets or scanning configurations, system-level IDSs sort through the massive amounts of data provided by system logs. Any information not available through these logs determines whether an attack will be missed by a system monitor. Network packet content or low-level attacks, such as SYN Flood, are not seen in the audit logs despite the large number of network events that do appear in the logs. On the other hand, privilege transitions that occur as a result of buffer overflow attacks do *uniquely* appear in the audit logs.

Challenges for system-level IDSs include the overhead associated with gathering the data, sufficiency of the data, scalability, and the fact that each node must have a sensor. Two types of system-level tools have appeared in the marketplace. Overlap exists in the set of attacks these two types of tools can detect. In some cases, such as looking for $N$ events of some type in sequence, the approach taken by the tools is identical. Nonetheless, a definite theoretical distinction exists in the approaches.

## Pattern Matchers

Pattern-matching IDSs work by filtering data through a set of attack signatures. When a signature is recognized in the data, an event is generated. The challenge for these IDS vendors is building general and specific signatures to catch attacks. Some exception case always seems to exist which makes building signatures difficult. Much theoretical work has been done in this area, given that pattern matching is a relatively mature area of computer science and mathematics. Models, such as finite state machines, seem to have the best performance, although concerns have been expressed about the success of their detection rates. Stalker is a well-known system-level IDS in use at a number of sites.

## Statistical Anomaly Detectors

Statistical anomaly detectors establish a baseline for a number of variables for each subject of interest. The usual example given is tracking the number of times a given user runs particular commands. A threshold is set by the tool administrator. When the threshold is exceeded, an event is generated.

IDSs based on statistical anomaly have a number of proponents. CMDS is the often-quoted example that has a good-sized install base. A number of hacks and misuses can be caught by threshold monitoring. However, difficulties are encountered with this approach. Setting the baseline can be a problem. For experienced users, it's not uncommon to find noisy data and, thus, run the risk of too many false positives. The soundness of the underlying statistical assumptions also has been questioned. The difference between a legitimate and an illegal privilege escalation is not something that is detected by counting commands. CMDS contains a pattern-matching component to offset these shortcomings with the anomaly detector piece of the tool.

## NT System Level Tools

Centrax is developing some very impressive NT system-level IDS tools. The team there is very experienced at building commercial intrusion detection systems. Keep an eye on them for what is likely to be a market leader. Competition is expected from other vendors who also now offer system-level IDS for NT. The Kane Security Monitor sold by Security Dynamics is another player is this space.

Over time, NT IDS offerings will increase in the marketplace. Understanding heterogeneous UNIX audit logs is a complex process that was mastered by only a small number of vendors. NT event logs are more easily available to developers and are more easily understood. Thus, more players are sure to emerge in the NT system-level IDS space.

## Network Sniffers

Network IDSs are a critical component of your perimeter defense because they catch attacks that system-level IDSs cannot. IDSs that detect attacks by sniffing network traffic in real time watch for protocol attacks, for attempts to run well-known hacked programs, and for strings that may indicate policy violations. Most sniffers support a client-server model in which a central engine receives notifications from multiple sensors. Like most other real-time IDSs, network sniffers provide real-time alerts and options to terminate offending connections. Some risk exists in automating the *kill connection* response because often hackers forge IP addresses or launch attacks from compromised systems at legitimate sites (such as universities).

To catch attacks, the sniffer must reside where all of the packets can be seen. As shown in Chapter 9, "Sniffing For Intruders," in some configurations network packets will not be seen by the sniffer. The best placements for a network IDS sniffer are just inside the perimeter network, in the secure network immediately after the firewall, and after the router or gateway on other subnets. In these positions, the inbound and outbound network packets will be visible. However, anytime two nodes within a subnet exchange packets, and the traffic does not flow past the network IDS, there is a potential for missed attacks.

Sniffers are hampered when network traffic is encrypted between two arbitrary nodes. If the sniffer sits in the network after the firewall, and the firewall is the system that decrypts packets, then the sniffer will see cleartext packets. However, if two nodes have their own IP tunnel, only those nodes will decrypt the packets. In order to be effective in this scenario, the sniffer code must be running in the IP stack just after the packets are decrypted by the IP layer. To complicate the effectiveness of sniffers further, application-level encryption limits what a sniffer can detect to only those attacks in the network protocol itself—address spoofing, session hijacking, SYN Flood, and others. An argument put forward in this book is to allow applications to call IDS routines *after* the packets have been decrypted.

Some overlap exists between firewalls and network IDSs in that firewalls also look for attacks, such as SYN Flood, Ping of Death, and other protocol exploits. Because both firewalls and sniffers examine network traffic, it's likely that there could be convergence of these two functions. A recent *Infoworld* report rated the IBM Emergency Response Center, ISS RealSecure, and Network Flight Recorder highly in their comparison tests. However, only Network Flight Recorder caught all of the attacks in the test suite. In some respects, this result is not surprising because the evaluation team wrote custom signatures specifically to catch the attacks in the test suite.

Finally, some recent papers identify shortcomings in network IDSs. The weaknesses stem from attacks that can cause the IDS and the actual destination of the IP packet to process different datastreams. In some cases, the IDS processes packets that are ignored by the destination node. The converse also is possible. Both of these cases can lead to network-based attacks that are not detected by some sniffers. The products' owners are undoubtedly addressing these issues in upcoming releases.

## Improving upon IDSs

Because IDSs are not the last word in security, opportunities exist for improvement. Here are some important areas in which advances are needed.

### Increase Application-Level Detection

A number of network attacks are launched at Web sites almost daily. Many of these attacks can be detected by network sniffers. However, the content of much of the traffic on the Web is application specific. CGI programs, Java applets, and Java servlets are increasingly used to process mission-critical data linking customers and businesses. These scenarios are really custom applications running via the Web. As more companies deploy these solutions, there will be a greater need for application-specific IDSs.

Commonly used applications, such as Web servers, are scanned by some IDSs today. The higher level applications that run on those Web servers are not. Similarly, IDSs specifically designed for databases, Lotus Notes, and other widely used software are still missing. IDS vendors incrementally look to add application-level scan routines or attack signatures for the most popular applications. The rate at which this is occurring could be improved with a flexible attack-pattern development language, such as the language provided by Network Flight Recorder (even though it wasn't designed for intrusion detection).

The more important point is that in the future, it's likely that *only* application-level subjects and objects will have any significance. Already most Web servers have no users and groups in the standard system repositories. This makes the value of the *accountability* portion of some system-level IDSs less impressive. If all processes on the OS run as root, and the interesting activity occurs between subjects and objects uniquely meaningful only in certain applications, then IDSs must expand detection to include the application space.

## Adapt to Changing I&A

Emphasis has been given several times to the importance of the *who* in a system or network event. Not only is this important for assigning accountability, but it also is necessary for tying together related security events. You cannot recognize a sequence of events as an attack when they are coming from the same user unless you can identify the user.

A big challenge facing IDSs in the future is the changing "who" landscape. In most tools today, it is a login user ID, group ID, or audit ID that uniquely identifies the subject. When more network and system traffic is application specific, finding the *who* and the *what* requires knowledge about the applications. IDSs must be able to adapt to this evolving trend in order to continue to show value.

Another important item to watch is the use of X.509 certificates. Identification and authentication in cyberspace already is widely based on X.509 certificates. These certificates are easily thought of as application-specific credentials, even though they are widely used across multiple applications. Because it is likely that an X.509 certificate will travel through cyberspace with all of your transactions, IDSs must consider the impact of this. Attack signatures will need to consider X.509 certificates in the same way that the AUID is used today. As more applications rely on X.509 for authentication, tracking activities across systems actually will get easier. The X.509 certificate will be passed between systems because it is needed for I&A and for resolving access control requests. Assuming that the applications and OSs include the certificate in log records, a convenient way then will be available for consolidating activities of a single user across systems.

Of course, a possibility always exists that a certificate has been compromised, which means that accountability will be no more reliable than it is with UIDs and GIDs today.

## Support Common Systems Management

Intrusion detection is a subset of systems management. Events are generated by IDSs and reported to central consoles. Sometimes, an IDS requires you to create special users and passwords to protect who can run the tool. Configuring sensors and engines from a central console is often supported as well. These features are admirable, but when a customer has invested in an enterprise systems management product, all of these tasks are extra work. Systems management frameworks, such as Tivoli's TME or Cross Site, have general-purpose subsystems for event notification, remote configuration, secure communications, and administrative roles.

Today, each IDS also might include its own proprietary communications framework for secure exchanges between engines and sensors (or other distributed components). Administrative tasks to support this framework include defining administrators, configuring shared secrets, and defining relationships between cooperating nodes or software components. The problem is that an IDS introduces its own unique framework, which is just more trouble for your systems administrators. Integration with TME and similar frameworks is needed so that IDSs fit nicely with the rest of the systems management activities at a site.

The dilemma for the IDS vendor is what to do when a customer does not have one of these systems management frameworks. In these installations, you can see why it's important to have a proprietary IDS framework as a backup choice. As usual, this tradeoff is sticky. Firewall vendors face exactly the same problem and have invented frameworks as well. Unfortunately, no simple development choice is available for the vendors. They simply must support the systems management frameworks most often installed by their customers.

## Simplify Development of Attack Signatures

This is a big customer satisfier. Many people ask for easy ways to extend an IDS. Scanners are sometimes easier to augment because they can invoke custom user programs or scripts. Network sniffers and system-level IDSs have not been as lucky. Ongoing research is aimed at finding suitable languages for developing attack signatures.

A benefit of having multiple groups create attack signatures is openness. Any mistakes that an IDS vendor might have made will be quickly critiqued and corrected. Another advantage is the sheer number of signatures. Having more people work on the problems and post their results for others to use is a great way to get additional application-level attack patterns. Everyone is a winner when this is possible.

## Combine Products

The benefits of a combined product have been mentioned several times. The previous example in which a system IDS calls a scanner IDS when a file is changed is only one possibility. Some practical issues drive this requirement as well.

Buying a scanner from one vendor, a network sniffer from another, and a system-level monitor from a third is not a good solution. If IDS vendors could support a common set of standards as planned by the CIDF research project, then this would not be so bad. However, configuring different administrator passwords, using different GUIs, and trying to remember how to securely connect sensors and engines is too much extra work. ISS is headed in the right direction because they have scanners, sniffers, and one system-level tool. Today, the ISS system-level tool does not currently support UNIX. Complementary business partnerships are still possible, though.

## Support Integration into Other Products

Earlier in the book a recommendation was made for IDS vendors to support modular architectures. The idea is to provide shared libraries or object classes that other vendors could use to invoke IDS routines as part of another system. For example, if a firewall could invoke network IDS routines on incoming packets, then your site will benefit from a more comprehensive solution. These discussions already may be happening, because many IDS vendors work closely with firewall vendors. However, plenty of opportunities exist to extend this idea to operating systems, databases, and other applications. The business benefits for IDS vendors are attractive in this distribution model, too. Attack pattern languages would add to the picture, because many applications have their own notions of subjects, objects, accesses, and security problems.

## Support Research

A tremendous amount of fundamental research needs to be done in intrusion detection. This book simply does not have enough space to provide a comprehensive review of current intrusion detection research. Problems under investigation include resilience, fault tolerance, cooperating distributed analysis engines, tracking hackers across multiple systems, and attack-pattern formalisms. Pattern-matching systems have been around for quite some time in computer science and engineering. Ample opportunity is given to learn from the experiences of others in building classification systems that identify attacks against systems. Some IDS vendors already are generous in their support of basic research including IBM, ISS, and Hewlett-Packard.

## Self Reference and IDSs

The title of this chapter, which really *is* the last chapter of the book, is influenced by the delightful work of Hofstatder (*Gödel, Escher, and Bach: An Eternal Golden Braid,* 1979). Not only is the title a fun little mind teaser, it also is a slight variation on one of the most perplexing problems in mathematics and computer science, patterned after the Epiminedes Paradox, which is *a self-referencing* sentence such as, "*This sentence is false.*" which shows the difficulty with assigning meaning to statements.

Kurt Gödel used self-referential statements to rock the foundation of mathematics and logic early in this century (Gödel, 1934). At a very high level, self-referential statements are difficult to *interpret* or assign a meaning to because they present a paradox. For example, if you believe the Epiminedes sentence to be true, it expresses a falsehood. If you believe it to be false, it then expresses a truth. What fun it is. To grossly paraphrase the importance of Gödel's work, he embedded the Epiminedes Paradox into formal logic and proved inconsistencies in a universe where everything was supposed to be neatly ordered.

Computer science relies on self reference in a number of areas, such as when defining recursive subroutines. A great deal of interest has been expressed in software that can be *self-healing*, which means the software must somehow be able to examine itself. What does all of this have to do with intrusion detection? Gödel showed that self reference could twist logic all around itself. The same thing can happen in software that contains self-referential behavior. One question that is often asked of IDS vendors is what happens if the IDS fails. In other words, *who's watching the watchers?*

An IDS is software written by people. This means that it will have programming bugs and vendor configuration errors. An IDS also can suffer from configuration errors made by those who administer IDSs. The same vulnerability categories that were identified for traditional products, such as I&A tools or firewalls, apply equally to IDSs.

Knowing whether the IDS is up and running is not a hard problem to solve. This can be done with one of many solutions. One approach would be a network "ping" or checkpoint between the IDS and a process on a physically secure server. When the IDS goes down, the other node sends an alert, restarts the IDS, or takes some other corrective action. Similarly, other types of systems management tools that monitor the availability of arbitrary programs could also monitor if the IDS is up and running. However, the more interesting question is who or what monitors the IDS to make sure *it is not the source* of security problems? Can an IDS watch itself?!

Imagine that you have an IDS with countermeasures or real-time responses. One of the responses could be to kill an offending process when a hack originates from that process. What happens when the hack originates from the IDS and you have the *kill* response activated? Oops. Possibly worse, what happens if the vendor prevents you from killing the IDS itself even if the hack originated from the IDS? If a hacker finds a successful buffer overflow attack against an IDS and killing the IDS is not an option, quite a bit of damage can be done before a human responds to a visual alert. This problem is not easy to solve.

It's not hard to see how a scanner can inspect its own configuration files or even the files of other IDSs for errors. But, how do you know if the scanner itself has not been compromised? The scanner is made of one or more binaries. What are the consequences when one of these binaries is patched or hacked? If you've used the Tripwire-like function that provides cryptographic signatures for these files, the scanner could notify you when one of these changes—assuming the file-integrity checker program in the scanner has not been compromised. Defenses against tampering are available, such as running binaries off media that is read-only. (Mounting file systems read-only is not guaranteed to work because low-level device driver hacks might bypass file system checking.) One might ask the same kinds of questions about the integrity of firewalls or system-level monitors, too.

With different tool offerings by vendors, you can envision how a system-level monitor can watch for real-time changes to files that make up other IDSs, such as scanners or network sniffers. Provided that the datastream, which the system-level IDS requires, is not compromised (though it can be), this would be a useful way to know whether one of the binaries in the scanner had been hacked. In the future, you'll probably buy an IDS that has all three types—scanner, network, and system—combined into a single tool. At this point, the tool will be watching itself, which poses the same questions for automated responses and countermeasures.

## Take It Away

So many other issues are worth discussing, but it's time to move on to other things. Hopefully, you've enjoyed learning about intrusion detection tools. Following the old psychological adage about memory, "five plus or minus two," and favoring the low end of the scale, it would be good if you could at least take away three thoughts:

- Remember to think critically about security products and applications and to reduce things to simple terms. Identify the subjects and objects and make sure that you are clear about how access requests are processed. These basic ideas are at the heart of most computer security products and problems.

- Intrusion detection tools play an important role by filling gaps left by traditional security products. The preventative approach is no longer sufficient. You need to add detection and response as well.

- Intrusion detection is built from software. Therefore, IDSs are subject to the same criticisms made of other security products. Don't let this distract you too much. IDSs will evolve over time and continue to improve. The net result is better security for you.

# Hot Links for Information

To find papers on security and intrusion detection, public domain tools, and excellent hot links, visit COAST at www.cs.purdue.edu/coast. From there, you can find more security-related links than you possibly can investigate adequately.

The latest on Kerberos is found at ftp://athena-dist.mit.edu/pub/kerberos.

You can reach the International Computer Security Association at www.ncsa.com. There, you will find numerous links to vendors who build security products.

For the latest on NT security, visit www.microsoft.com/security.

Many papers are available for download from ftp.research.att.com

## Incident Response Organizations

Forum of Incident and Response Security Teams (FIRST) can be reached at www.first.org or by phone at +1-301-975-3359.

CERT can be contacted at www.cert.org or by phone at +1-412-268-7090. In addition, there are many CERT organizations available in other countries.

AUSCERT, the Australian counterpart to CERT in the United States, is found at www.auscert.org.au. The phone number is +61-7-3365-4417.

The IBM Emergency Response Team can be reached at www.ers.ibm.com.

## Intrusion Detection Research

In addition to visiting vendor sites mentioned in this book, you can learn more about intrusion detection research at the following links:

www.cs.purdue.edu/coast

www.seclab.cs.ucdavis.edu/cidf

www.seclab.cs.ucdavis.edu

www.crl.sri.com/ides
www.sri.com/emerald
www.pokey.nswc.navy.mil/Docs/intrusion.html
www.doe-is.llnl.gov/nitb/refs/bibs/bib1.html

# References

Abrams, Marshall D., Sushil Jajodia, and Harold J. Podell, eds. *Information Security: An Integrated Collection of Essays.* Los Alamitos, CA: IEEE Computer Society Press, 1995.

Ahuja, Vijay. *Network and Internet Security.* Boston, MA: Academic Press, 1996.

Albitz, P., and Cricket Liu. *DNS and BIND in a Nutshell.* Sebastopol, CA: O'Reilly and Associates, Inc., 1992.

Aleph One. "Smashing the stack for fun and profit." *Phrack*, no. 7 (1997): 49.

Anderson, J.P. "Computer security technology planning study." ESD-TR-73-51, Hanscom AFB, MA: United States Air Force Electronics Systems Division,1972.

Anonymous. *Maximum Security.* Indianapolis, IN: Sams.net, 1997.

Bell, D. E. "Lattices, policies, and implementations." In *Proceedings of the Thirteenth National Computer Security Conference* (1990): 165–171.

Bellovin, Steven M. "Security problems in the TCP/IP protocol suite." *Computer Communications Review* (1989), no. 19 (2): 32–48.

———"Packets found on an Internet." *Computer Communications Review* (1993), no. 23 (3): 26–31.

———"Problem areas for IP security protocols." In *Proceedings of the Sixth USENIX UNIX Security Symposium* (1996): San Jose, CA.

———"There be dragons." In *Third USENIX UNIX Security Symposium* (1992): Baltimore, MD.

———"Using the Domain Name System for system break-ins." In *Proceedings of the Fifth USENIX UNIX Security Symposium* (1995): 205–214. Salt Lake City.

Bellovin, Steven M., and Michael Merritt. "Limitations of the Kerberos authentication system." In *USENIX Conference Proceedings* (1991): 253–267. Dallas, TX.

———"Encrypted key exchange: Password-based protocols secure against dictionary attacks." In *Proceedings of the IEEE Computer Society Symposium on Research in Security and Privacy* (1992): 72–84. Oakland, CA.

Bishop, Matt. "Anatomy of a proactive password changer." In *Proceedings of the Third USENIX UNIX Security Symposium* (1992): 171–184. Baltimore, MD.

Brinkley, Donald L., and Roger R. Schell. "Concepts and terminology for computer security." In *Information Security: An Integrated Collection of Essays*, edited by M. Abrams, S. Jajodia, and H. Podell, 40–90. Los Alamitos, CA: IEEE Computer Society Press, 1995.

Chapman, D. Brent, and Elizabeth D. Zwicky, *Building Internet Firewalls*. Sebastopol, CA: O'Reilly & Associates, Inc., 1995.

Chapman, D. Brent. "Network (In)Security Through IP Packet Filtering." *Proceedings of the Third USENIX UNIX Security Symposium* (1992): 63–76. Baltimore, MD.

Cheswick, William R. "An evening with Berferd, in which a cracker is lured, endured, and studied." In *Proceedings of the Winter USENIX Conference* (1992). San Francisco.

Cheswick, William R. "The design of a secure Internet gateway." In *Proceedings of the Summer USENIX Conference* (1990). Anaheim, CA.

Cheswick, William R., and Steven M. Bellovin. *Firewalls and Internet Security: Repelling the Wily Hacker*. Reading, MA: Addison-Wesley, 1994.

Comer, Douglas E. *Internetworking with TCP/IP, Vol. 1, Principles, Protocols, and Architecture*. Englewood Cliffs, NJ: Prentice Hall, 1991.

Comer, Douglas E. *Internetworking with TCP/IP, Vol. 2, Design, Implementation, and Internals*. Englewood Cliffs, NJ: Prentice Hall, 1991.

Coopers & Lybrand. "Microsoft Windows NT Server: Security Features and Future Direction." Available at www.microsoft.com/security. 1997.

daemon9, route, infinity. "IP-spoofing Demystified: Trust-Relationship Exploitation." *Phrack* (1996).

Denning, Dorothy E. *Cryptography and Data Security*. Reading, MA: Addison-Wesley, 1983.

Denning, Dorothy E. "An intrusion-detection model." In *Proceedings of the 1986 IEEE Symposium on Security and Privacy* (1986).

Dole, Bryn, Steve Lodin, and Eugene Spafford. "Misplaced Trust: Kerberos 4 Session Keys." In *Proceedings of Symposium on Network and Distributed Systems Security*, IEEE (1997).

Ferbrache, David, and Gavin Shearer. *UNIX Installation Security and Integrity*. Englewood Cliffs, NJ: Prentice Hall, 1993.

Finseth, C. "An access control protocol, sometimes called TACACS." RFC 1492. 1993.

Garfinkel, Simson, and Gene Spafford. *Practical UNIX and Internet Security*. Sebastopol, CA: O'Reilly and Associates, Inc., 1996.

Harmon, Paul, Rex Amus, and William Morrissey. *Expert Systems Tools and Applications*. New York, NY: John Wiley & Sons, Inc., 1988.

Infoworld. "Test center comparison: Network intrusion-detection solutions." *Infoworld* (1998), no. 20 (18): 88–98.

ISS. "ISS Security Alert." Available at www.iss.net, October 21, 1997.

Kaufman, Charlie, Radia Perlman, and Mike Speciner. *Network Security: Private Communication in a Public World*. Englewood Cliffs, NJ: Prentice Hall, 1995.

Klander, Lars. *Hacker Proof: The Ultimate Guide to Network Security*. Houston, TX: Jamsa Press, 1997.

Klein, Daniel V. "Foiling the cracker: A survey of, and improvements to, password security." In *Proceedings of the USENIX UNIX Security Workshop* (1990): 5–14. Portland, OR.

Knightmare, The. *Secrets of a Super Hacker*. Port Townsend, WA: Loompanics, Ltd., 1994.

Koblitz, Neal. *A Course in Number Theory and Cryptography*. New York, NY: Springer-Verlag, 1994.

Landreth, Bill. *Out of the Inner Circle*. Bellevue, WA: Microsoft Press, 1985.

LaPadula, L.J. "Formal modeling in a generalized framework for access control." In *Proceedings of the IEEE Computer Security Foundations Workshop III* (1990): 100–109. Los Alamitos, CA.

Littmann, Jonathan. *The Fugitive Game*. Boston, MA: Little, Brown, and Co., 1997.

L0pht. "L0phtcrack." Available at www.l0pht.com. 1997.

Luby, Michael. *Pseudorandomness and Cryptographic Applications*. Princeton, NJ: Princeton University Press, 1996.

Macgregor, R., A. Aresi, and A. Siegert. *WWW.Security: How to build a secure World Wide Web connection*. Upper Saddle River, NJ: Prentice Hall, 1996.

Microsoft. "Microsoft Windows NT Server White Paper." Available at www.microsoft.com/security. 1997.

Miller, Barton P., et al. "Fuzz revisited: A re-examination of the reliability of UNIX utilities and services." Available from COAST at www.cs.purdue.edu/coast. 1995.

Morris, Robert T. "A weakness in the 4.2BSD UNIX TCP/IP software." Computing Science Technical Report 117 (1985). Murray Hill, NJ: AT&T Bell Laboratories.

Mudge. "Compromised buffer overflows from Intel to Sparc Version 8." Available at www.l0pht.com. 1996.

NTbugtraq. "FAQ: NT Cryptographic Password Attacks & Defenses." Available at www.ntbugtraq.com/samfaq.htm. 1997.

Okuntseff, Nik. *Windows NT Security: Programming Easy-to-Use Security Options*. Lawrence, KA: R&D Books, 1998.

PeterZ. "Weaknesses in SecurID." Available at www.secnet.com/securid.ps. 1996.

Postel, John. "Internet protocol." RFC 791 (1981).

Ptacek, Thomas H., and Newsham, Timothy N. "Insertion, evasion, and denial of service: Eluding network intrusion detection." Available at www.secnet.com. 1998.

Ramsey, R. *All About Administering NIS+*. Englewood Cliffs, NJ: Prentice Hall, 1994.

Reilly, Michael. "Finding Holes in Your NT Security." *Windows NT Magazine*, October (1996).

Rigney, C., A. Rubens, W. Simpson, and S. Willens. "Remote Authentication Dial In User Service (RADIUS)." RFC 2138 (1997).

Rivest, R. L., A. Shamir, and L. Adleman. "A method for obtaining digital signatures and public-key cryptosystems." *Communications of the ACM* (1978), no. 21 (2): 120–126.

Samalin, Samuel. *Secure UNIX*. New York, NY: McGraw-Hill, 1997.

Schneier, Bruce. *Applied Cryptography: Protocols, Algorithms, and Source Code in C.* New York, NY: John Wiley & Sons, Inc., 1996.

Sheldon, Tom. *Windows NT Security Handbook.* Berkeley, CA: Osborne McGraw-Hill, 1997.

Smaha, Stephen, and Jessica Winslow. "Software tools for detecting misuse on UNIX systems." Haystack Labs, 1994.

Snapp, Steven, et al. "DIDS (Distributed Intrusion Detection System)— Motivation, architecture, and an early prototype." In *Proceedings of the Fourteenth National Computer Security Conference* (1991), 167–176.

Stallings, William. *Network and Internetwork Security.* Englewood Cliffs, NJ: Prentice Hall, 1995.

Stern, Hal. *Managing NFS and NIS.* Sebastopol, CA: O'Reilly and Associates, Inc., 1991.

Stevens, W. Richard. *UNIX Network Programming.* Englewood Cliffs, NJ: Prentice Hall, 1990.

Stevens, W. Richard. *Advanced Programming in the UNIX Environment.* Reading, MA: Addison-Wesley, 1992.

Stevens, W. Richard. *TCP/IP Illustrated, Vols. 1 & 2.* Reading, MA: Addison-Wesley, 1994.

Stoll, Cliff. *The Cuckoo's Egg: Tracking a Spy Through the Maze of Computer Espionage.* New York, NY: Simon and Schuster, Inc., 1989.

Summers, Rita C. *Secure Computing: Threats and Safeguards.* New York: McGraw-Hill, 1997.

TIS. *Gauntlet Firewall Administrators Guide.* Trusted Information Systems, 1997.

Trott, Bob. "Microsoft hit with NT registry security flaw." *Infoworld Electric* October 14 (1997).

Vacca, John. *Internet Security Secrets.* Foster City, CA: IDG Books, 1996.

Waterman, Donald. *A Guide to Expert Systems.* Reading, MA: Addison-Wesley, 1986.

Williams, James G., and Marshall D. Abrams. "Formal methods and models." In *Information Security: An Integrated Collection of Essays*, edited by M. Abrams, S. Jajodia, and H. Podell, 170–186. Los Alamitos, CA: IEEE Computer Society Press, 1995.

Winsor, Janice. *Solaris Advanced System Administrator's Guide.* Emeryville, CA: Ziff Davis, 1993.

# Index